PELICAN BOOKS

TECHNIQUES OF PERSUASION

James A. C. Brown was born in Edinburgh in 1911.
After taking a degree in medicine at Edinburgh University, he travelled and studied in many European
countries, and during the war was a specialist in psychiatry in the Middle East. Becoming increasingly
interested in the normal individual's adjustment to
society, he joined a large industrial concern after the
war, in which he worked for seven years, subsequently writing, on the basis of his experiences, the
Pelican book, *The Social Psychology of Industry*. Later
he became Deputy Director of the Institute of Social
Psychiatry in London, doing lecturing and consultant
work in medicine and industry.

Dr Brown wrote several other books on psychology
and psychiatry, among them *The Distressed Mind* and
Freud and the Post-Freudians, which was published as
a Pelican in 1961.

He died in 1964.

J. A. C. BROWN

Techniques of Persuasion

FROM PROPAGANDA TO
BRAINWASHING

PENGUIN BOOKS

Penguin Books Ltd, Harmondsworth, Middlesex, England
Penguin Books, 625 Madison Avenue, New York, New York 10022, U.S.A.
Penguin Books Australia Ltd, Ringwood, Victoria, Australia
Penguin Books Canada Ltd, 41 Steelcase Road West,
Markham, Ontario, Canada
Penguin Books (N.Z.) Ltd, 182–190 Wairau Road,
Auckland 10, New Zealand

—

First published 1963
Reprinted 1964, 1965, 1967, 1968, 1969, 1971, 1972, 1975, 1977

—

—

Made and printed in Great Britain
by Cox & Wyman Ltd, London, Reading and Fakenham
Set in Monotype Plantin

CONTENTS

EDITORIAL FOREWORD

'MAN is a rational animal.' So, at least, does he like to believe himself to be. This book outlines and underlines some of the qualifications and reservations which this self-appraisal require. So numerous are these qualifications and reservations that they could almost support the counter-thesis that man is the most irrational of all animals. The lower animals are generally *non rational*, but few of them are so positively *irrational* as man can be. It requires considerable sophistication to be irrational. No animal could develop the systematic delusions of the insane, nor are the 'lower' animals easy prey to advertisers or political propagandists. But we must not go too far in pressing this counter-thesis. Man has the capacity to reason and to be influenced by reason in ways in which a hungry tiger, for example, has not. It is an interesting and significant fact that political and religious propagandists, and advertisers, go so far as they do in thinking up (specious) argument addressed to the reason. These arguments are an unwitting testimonial to the rationality of man. The belief that man is not only a rational but also a reasonable animal attained its greatest popularity in the late eighteenth and early nineteenth centuries. Its most charming, if rather pathetic, expression is to be found in William Godwin's *Political Justice* (1793). Godwin asserted that man is a being whose conduct is governed by his opinions. Vice is error, and errors could corrected by instruction. 'Show me,' he wrote, 'in and I shall most unambiguous manner that a certain man he carried the reasonable in itself, or most be whole species will become infallibly pursue write offenders to forsake their errors. ... It will then be continuing controversies. ... It will then be reason was so universally acknowledged the

7

offender would either readily yield to the expostulations of authority, or, if he resisted though suffering no personal molestation he would feel so weary under the unequivocal disapprobation and the observant eye of public judgement as willingly to remove to a society more congenial to his errors.' Subsequent movements of thought about the rationality of man have been movements of progressive disillusionment – to a point at which the greater danger lies in underestimating the power of rational persuasion and the power of the will-to-be-reasonable.

Godwin's error was not so much in overestimating the importance of education in fostering rationality as in underestimating the difficulties of protecting man against the forces of unreason. Through education man can become reasonable. Some indeed have done so. There are two things which schools and colleges can do and are doing, but could do more than at present. First, they could make ample provision for civilized and rational discussion and argument – argument on any, or almost any, discussible topic (excluding only topics the discussion of which might be more disquieting to anxious parents than to their children). Second, schools and colleges could give more systematic instruction on the ways in which the forces of unreason work, using as texts books covering the fields of Dr Brown's *Techniques of Persuasion*. To be forewarned is to be forearmed. Such books are essential to the armoury of all, especially the young, who wish to defend their right to think freely and to follow the argument wherever it may lead, provided only that it is supported by rational evidence. Books which deal with straight and crooked thinking and with straight and crooked methods of persuasion – together with a copy of the Holy Bible, a good dictionary, a good encyclopedia, and a volume of first aid – could well be not only on the shelves of every school library but on the bookshelves of every home.

C. A. MACE

offender would either readily yield to the expostulations of authority, or, if he resisted though suffering no personal molestation he would feel so weary under the unequivocal disapprobation and the observant eye of public judgement as willingly to remove to a society more congenial to his errors.' Subsequent movements of thought about the rationality of man have been movements of progressive disillusionment – to a point at which the greater danger lies in underestimating the power of rational persuasion and the power of the will-to-be-reasonable.

Godwin's error was not so much in overestimating the importance of education in fostering rationality as in underestimating the difficulties of protecting man against the forces of unreason. Through education man can become reasonable. Some indeed have done so. There are two things which schools and colleges can do and are doing, but could do more than at present. First, they could make ample provision for civilized and rational discussion and argument – argument on any, or almost any, discussible topic (excluding only topics the discussion of which might be more disquieting to anxious parents than to their children). Second, schools and colleges could give more systematic instruction on the ways in which the forces of unreason work, using as texts books covering the fields of Dr Brown's *Techniques of Persuasion*. To be forewarned is to be forearmed. Such books are essential to the armoury of all, especially the young, who wish to defend their right to think freely and to follow the argument wherever it may lead, provided only that it is supported by rational evidence. Books which deal with straight and crooked thinking and with straight and crooked methods of persuasion – together with a copy of the Holy Bible, a good dictionary, a good encyclopedia, and a volume of first aid – could well be not only on the shelves of every school library but on the bookshelves of every home.

C. A. MACE

EDITORIAL FOREWORD

'MAN is a rational animal.' So, at least, does he like to believe himself to be. This book outlines and underlines some of the qualifications and reservations which this self-appraisal require. So numerous are these qualifications and reservations that they could almost support the counter-thesis that man is the most irrational of all animals. The lower animals are generally *non rational*, but few of them are so positively *irrational* as man can be. It requires considerable sophistication to be irrational. No animal could develop the systematic delusions of the insane, nor are the 'lower' animals easy prey to advertisers or political propagandists. But we must not go too far in pressing this counter-thesis. Man has the capacity to reason and to be influenced by reason in ways in which a hungry tiger, for example, has not. It is an interesting and significant fact that political and religious propagandists, and advertisers, go so far as they do in thinking up (specious) argument addressed to the reason. These arguments are an unwitting testimonial to the rationality of man. The belief that man is not only a rational but also a reasonable animal attained its greatest popularity in the late eighteenth and early nineteenth centuries. Its most charming, if rather pathetic, expression is to be found in William Godwin's *Political Justice* (1793). Godwin asserted that man is a being whose conduct is governed by his opinions. Vice is error, and errors can be corrected by instruction. 'Show me,' he wrote, 'in the clearest and most unambiguous manner that a certain mode of proceeding is most reasonable in itself, or most conducive to my interest, and I shall infallibly pursue that mode, so long as the views you suggested to me continue present to my mind.' Being a rational man he carried the inferences to their logical conclusions. 'Render the plain dictates of justice level to every capacity . . . and the whole species will become reasonable and virtuous. It will then be sufficient for juries to recommend a certain mode of adjusting controversies. . . . It will then be sufficient for them to invite offenders to forsake their errors. . . . Where the empire of reason was so universally acknowledged the

7

CHAPTER I

PROPAGANDA AND COMMUNICATIONS

ATTEMPTS to change the opinions of others are older than re-corded history and originated, it must be supposed, with the development of speech. Through speech comes the power to manipulate or persuade people without necessarily resorting to physical force, and before men could speak it is unlikely that they had any opinions to change. Direct violence or the threat of violence may produce submission to the will of another individual or group, but thoughts are created and modified primarily by the spoken or written word so that, although in so-called 'brain-washing' words may be supplemented by unpleasant physical treatment, and in commercial advertising by pleasing pictures or music, it is obvious that even in these cases the essential weapons are verbal or at any rate symbolic, and the results aimed at psycho-logical. In general, and with few exceptions, psychological trans-formations require psychological techniques, and it is with such influences rather than external compliance brought about by force alone, that we shall be mainly concerned here. The whole subject of changing people's minds raises fascinating scientific and moral issues whether it takes the form of religious conver-sion, political rabble-rousing, health propaganda, the question of the impact of the mass media on popular taste, the impersonal manipulation of the masses allegedly carried out by those in the 'opinion business', or the more sinister forms of political indoc-trination practised in totalitarian states. In an age of conflicting ideologies when whole nations are being subjected to group per-suasion through new means of communication, new techniques, and the pull of mass movements led by demagogues, it is impor-tant to find out just how tough or how yielding the human mind really is; how far it is possible to produce genuine change in the individual's or group's way of thinking; and to gain some insight into the means employed to that end. Some authorities take the view that we are all virtually at the mercy of the mass media and baleful methods of group stimulation, whilst others have suggested that brainwashing and similar techniques available to the modern mind-manipulator are not only wellnigh irresistible but lead to real and permanent changes in political or religious outlook. If such beliefs are well-founded, the outlook for civilization as we know it is not pleasant to contemplate; if they are not, then critical examination must be able to show that the mind is a good deal more intractable than those who hold such views seem to suppose. On the other hand, there are sometimes circumstances in which changes of attitude are necessary and desirable, such as the sick attitudes of mental illness or the wrong ones held by many about race, issues in public health, the prevention of accidents, and so on. Most people would agree that the work of the psychiatrist is worth-while and that it is worthy of consideration how public health or safety campaigns may best be run. Whether or not, as ordinarily carried out, such campaigns have any significant effects of the type intended requires careful investigation; and this becomes all the more important if, as there is every reason to believe, well-meant but incompetently-conceived propaganda, so far from having merely negative results, can be shown to have positively undesirable ones or even to lead to effects diametrically opposed to those desired.

The Oxford Dictionary defines propaganda as 'an association or scheme for propagating a doctrine or practice', and the word takes its origin from the Latin *propagare* which means the gardener's practice of pinning the fresh shoots of a plant into the earth in order to reproduce new plants which will later take on a life of their own. Therefore one implication of the term when it was first used in the sociological sense by the Roman Catholic Church was that the spread of ideas brought about in this way is not one that would take place of itself, but rather a cultivated or artificial generation. In the year 1633, Pope Urban VIII established the Congregatio de Propaganda Fide, otherwise known as 'The Congregation of Propaganda' or simply 'The Propaganda', a committee of cardinals which had, and still has, charge of the foreign missions of the Church. Naturally this was regarded as a beneficent process which by preaching and example attempted to lead the heathen from darkness into light and it was an artificial or cultivated one only in the sense that, without outside intervention, these peoples would never have learned about Christianity. Since the missionaries were well aware of what they were doing, their propaganda was also deliberate and the modern contention that it is possible for propaganda to be unconscious, a favourite theme of Marxists and others, would have conveyed nothing to them.

Within the present century, however, the popular image of propaganda has undergone radical changes and the word has come to acquire overtones implying a process which is frequently sinister, lying, and based on the deliberate attempt on the part of an individual or group to manipulate, often by concealed or underhand means, the minds of others for their own ulterior ends. Superficially, this change can be dated from the official use of propaganda as a weapon in the total warfare of modern times, beginning with the First World War, when lies, political subterfuge, and atrocity stories were unscrupulously employed in an attempt to influence the final result. The exposure of these methods during the inter-war years led to a tremendous revulsion of popular feeling amongst the by now predominantly pacific victors, accompanied by avowals of admiration on the part of the defeated some of whom determined to make even better use of the same methods when the occasion arose. But this ambivalent feeling that propaganda is something sly, unpleasant, and frequently silly, yet also a weapon of devastating power for 'getting at' people with or without their consent, has far deeper roots than the above explanation might suggest. It arises, in fact, from certain fundamental changes in the nature of communication within technically-advanced societies, and the methods employed during the First World War and subsequently were the effect rather than the cause of wholly new developments in the structure and techniques of the modern state. What these developments are must be considered at a later stage; but it is at any rate clear that changing nuances in meaning have made 'propaganda' a difficult word to define. It is often employed in a derogatory sense, and in spite of the fact that part of the original meaning was undoubtedly the implication that it was a collective appeal to larger or smaller groups of people made either by an individual or another group, it is now frequently used as indiscriminately as the more recent 'brainwashing' to refer to the activities of any unfortunate individual who wishes to convey a piece of unwelcome or unacceptable information to another. Since the greater part of any written or spoken communication is intended to arouse some sort of response in the recipient, it is easy to see why many authorities consider that propaganda is a word which has outlived its usefulness.

If for the moment these complexities are ignored and the dictionary definition extended to apply to any scheme for propagating a doctrine or practice *or for influencing the emotional attitudes of others* we shall be in a position to glance briefly at the past history of propaganda and the conditions under which it took place. In this way it will be possible to discover some of its other characteristics, and to show how its effectiveness and the form it takes are limited by the structure and the available technical resources of the society which employs it. The obvious reason for amplifying the original definition is that the propagandist is not always doing anything so clear-cut as attempting to spread a specific doctrine or practice; for quite often, as in war propaganda, he is merely trying to arouse strong emotions of hatred or approval for or against another group from motives of expediency, strategy, or plain greed. But emotional pressure, whether it takes the form of arousing positive or negative collective feelings, or simply that of presenting emotionally biased views, is not just something added to propaganda to make it more acceptable. It is fundamental to the whole process. Rational and dispassionate argument employs a totally different technique; and when Socrates by means of questioning rather than by supplying ready-made answers to the problems raised by his pupils brought them to discover the truth for themselves, he was certainly not engaging in propaganda although his pupils' views were changed in the process. The propagandist does not engage in genuine argument because his answers are determined in advance. It follows that, if all propaganda attempts to change minds, not all mind-changing is accomplished by propaganda. In vivid contrast to the Socratic method is that found, for example, in the books of the Old Testament prophets where vehement eloquence is employed to the specific end of turning the Israelites away from the worship of false gods and evil practices towards the worship of Jehovah; for here the means include special pleading, admonition, and the threat of divine retribution. Inasmuch as he is *for* the creation of certain attitudes, the propagandist is necessarily *against* others; and the extirpation of what he regards as false beliefs and doctrines is as much his concern as the propagation of the 'right' ones. This suggests the important rule that one can only speak of propaganda when alternative views exist, and it is therefore not propaganda to teach a belief which is universal at a particular time or place. Of course, it sometimes happens that propaganda is carried on for the sole purpose of putting an end to a practice without necessarily replacing it by another, as when public health departments want to stop people from smoking, or the British stopped head-hunting in Papua and the self-immolation of Hindu widows on their husbands' funeral pyres in India. But such campaigns are carried out because the authorities concerned regarded these customs or habits as undesirable and not 'good', as those who practise them believe. The alternative view of the campaigners is implicit in their actions.

As people become more literate and, overtly at least, more civilized, the written word comes to play an increasingly important part in the spread of opinions and the creation of emotional attitudes. The existence of books raises two problems fundamental to a study of propaganda: the question of whether it is meaningful to talk of unconscious propaganda, and the issue of censorship. Neither of these problems was created by the written word (although it is easier to control what a man writes than what he says), but obviously we can only know about what went on in the distant past by way of the books which persist long after the spoken words have gone. The works of Herodotus have earned him the title of the father of history, and he has also been less sympathetically described as a hired press agent for the Athenian state. But there is really very little reason to suppose that he was any more aware of his partiality than, until recently, were the writers of our school history books aware of their own imperialist bias because the whole idea of presenting the public with objective information about the world in general is, with some outstanding exceptions, relatively new in human thought. Free expression of opinion has been rare enough and is by no means synonymous with the attempt to be objective which has seldom been regarded as particularly commendable. For centuries of European history 'truth' was Catholic truth, and we have seen that in the absence of alternative views it is meaningless to talk about propaganda whether conscious or otherwise. Significantly, the Catholic Congregation of Propaganda only came into existence when the Church began to experience the full impact of new doctrines, and new lands to convert. If by 'unconscious propaganda' is meant the sort of bias allegedly shown by Herodotus, it must be remembered that few people in the past, even when they were dimly aware that other standpoints existed, have thought it in any way unnatural to interpret events from that of their own state or religion. This is to exhibit bias, but it is not propaganda unless it is carried out with the purpose of spreading the biased view to those who do not already hold it. It may be supposed that nobody would have been more surprised than Herodotus at any suggestion that Babylonians or Egyptians should not also have held, quite justifiably, their own partial versions of history. Most societies up to the end of the Middle Ages in Europe were controlled by tradition, and such propaganda as took place had to be carried on within the permitted framework and ordinarily by the learned. This view or that might be put forward, but only against the background of a world picture which seemed to represent fixed and unalterable truth; and, for the masses, truth originated in authority rather than in the evidence of their own senses or the conclusions arrived at by independent thought. Periclean Athens stands out as a brief period when men tried deliberately to discount bias and arrive at objective truth, and Thucydides' account of the Peloponnesian War is possibly the first attempt to write impartial history; yet the Athenians executed Socrates for corrupting the youth of the city by getting them to think for themselves. Imperial Rome cared little what religious beliefs its citizens might hold, but cared a great deal for the dignity of the state; and Augustus had Ovid exiled for 'a poem and a mistake', while providing state patronage for Virgil, many of whose works are more or less barefaced propaganda against the old republican ideas and for Augustus and the Empire. These are instances of that form of censorship which is an important aspect of propaganda in so far as it selectively suppresses certain views in favour of others.

But it would probably be wrong to regard all suppression of information as being carried out from motives of propaganda. The priesthoods of ancient Egypt and Babylonia, for example, kept their pictographic scripts a closely-guarded secret from the common people. But this had nothing to do with propaganda, for whatever meaning we attach to the term can hardly comprise the limitation of religious mysteries to a priestly caste. Eventually reading became democratized with the replacement of the old clumsy scripts by the beginnings of the modern alphabet which enabled traders and scribes to record their transactions or even to write secular literature, but the spread of news was largely limited to the eyes and ears of kings. This was the case in Babylonia and Assyria, and, much later, Julius Caesar had certain items of news posted in the Forum but circulated quite a different version among members of the governing class. During the Middle Ages, much information was carried orally by special messengers, but this too was restricted to the higher clergy and the secular rulers. It must be remembered, however, that in those days news was scarce and precious. No large state of antiquity, as Bertrand Russell has pointed out, was governed from the centre to nearly the same extent as is now customary: and the chief reason for this was lack of rapid mobility and therefore of information. Thus, although both Church and state censored forbidden opinions, most limiting of news was based mainly on scarcity together with the not unjustifiable belief that such matters were no concern of the people, who would neither have understood nor wished to hear them. Again, all states from the earliest civilizations right up to the present day have had their State secrets and there have been those matters 'which it is not in the public interest to disclose'; but, although this form of censorship may often be abused, it is not ordinarily used as a propaganda weapon.

Propaganda by censorship takes two forms: the selective control of information to favour a particular viewpoint, and the deliberate doctoring of information in order to create an impression different from that originally intended. The most obvious example of the first type is ecclesiastical censorship, which dates from very early in the history of the Church but is best known in the shape of the *Index Librorum Prohibitorum*, traceable from the sixteenth century, whereby all books considered pernicious to Roman Catholics are placed on the Index by the Congregation of the Holy Office. It would be impossible here to give any idea of the great number of important works banned in this way, but an indication of the mental outlook of those responsible is demonstrated by the fact that the Copernican theory was forbidden until as late as 1822. Dante and Galen had also to be removed in the course of time, but Gibbon, Hume, John Stuart Mill, Goldsmith, Sterne, Kant, Voltaire, Croce, Stendhal, and even the works of a number of modern and specifically Catholic writers remain prohibited to the ordinary Catholic, although permission to read forbidden books may be granted to students. This is propaganda because it is selective and deliberately designed to give those towards whom it is directed a partial view of the world in which we live – a world which necessarily includes the opinions of others whether they are true or not. The philosophies of Hume and Kant may be the merest nonsense, but nobody can claim to know anything about philosophy if he has not been permitted to read their works.

A classic example of the second form of propaganda by censorship through doctored information is Bismarck's famous Ems telegram of 1870. The point at issue was whether Leopold of Hohenzollern should succeed to the Spanish throne, a candidature supported by Bismarck and opposed by the French. King William of Prussia and the French ambassador had strolled together in the pleasure garden at Ems discussing the problem, although by this time Leopold, alarmed by the fuss his candidature had aroused, had already resigned it and the threat of war seemed to have been averted. But Bismarck wanted war, and, when William sent a telegram in cipher describing the inoffensive discussion that had taken place at Ems, Bismarck and his colleagues were at first despondent at its unimportant nature. Then the chancellor suddenly saw how he could make use of it to save the situation. By cutting out a few words and sentences and then publishing the abrupt telegram as it was, he could make what had been a fairly polite interview appear as a truculent challenge and a consequent snub. The provocative alterations were made and published, and the press on both sides clamoured for war. Thus began the Franco-Prussian War in which 141,000 men were killed.

On a more humble scale is the common practice of theatres when they put up posters giving quotes from important critics which, in many cases, have been cut out of the original context in order to create a favourable impression from what may have been an extremely unfavourable review.

But the spread or control of knowledge and opinions in early times inevitably had a limited impact upon the tradition-bound majority. Only the small educated class was able to read the few available hand-written books well enough to be affected by the censorship of reading-matter, and the loudest voice of any public orator could carry only so far, making it necessary for him to employ messengers or travel about himself if he wanted his communications to get beyond the bounds of the market-place. The wider diffusion of knowledge and the freedom to develop and spread a great diversity of opinions throughout all levels of society, had to wait upon two historical phenomena: the invention of printing by moveable types in 1454, and the Reformation in the following century. The former made it technically possible to spread ideas and factual information far more quickly and widely than ever before, although it could not become fully effective until compulsory education for all had been introduced – an event which did not reach England until as late as 1870, later than in other civilized countries. The Reformation had an effect which was not entirely that foreseen by the Reformers, most of whom were as bigoted and intolerant as their predecessors, since it weakened the Church by splitting it up into so many minor sects that, at least in Protestant countries, its power to stop people thinking and saying what they pleased was greatly reduced. To be fair, it must also be added that by introducing the habit of Bible-reading the Protestants encouraged literacy, and that some of the reformers such as Luther in Germany and Knox in Scotland were largely responsible for setting up education systems along modern lines.

The first publications in England to deal with matters of contemporary public opinion and what we should now describe as news were the early fifteenth-century pamphlets which discussed various social, political, or religious issues generally from a strong partisan point of view; these were followed by the news-letters which, produced by professional London news-writers, gave the reader all the gossip and rumour of the city. The first man to print all the news of the day upon a single sheet in a regular weekly publication with a distinctive title was Nathaniel Butter, who brought out the *Weekly Newes* in 1622. All these publications were strictly censored by the state, with the exception of a brief period of freedom after the Star Chamber (which, unfettered by the law, had been used by Charles I and his party to persecute their opponents) had finally been abolished in 1641. But this resulted in such a flood of publications that the Long Parliament had to impose an even more rigid censorship on books and reading matter which, in spite of Milton's plea for freedom, was maintained by the Commonwealth. During the Restoration of the monarchy which followed, a Licensing Act in 1662 renewed the royal licensing of printing, and the freedom of the press dates from the failure to renew this act in 1695. The seventeenth and eighteenth centuries were an age of pamphlets which were produced in abundance by such writers as Defoe, Bunyan, Steele, Addison, and many lesser men, and these, like their predecessors, contained propaganda for different shades of opinion. In this respect they were no less partisan than the newspapers; for up to the end of the first quarter of the nineteenth century the English press consisted exclusively of journals of opinion which printed, or distorted, news with the single-minded purpose of converting readers to their own particular point of view. The idea of news as information played a correspondingly small part, and such important events as the Battle of

Waterloo might be dismissed in a few lines, swamped by editorial comment and scurrilous gossip. In fact, gossip and scandal often provided the editor with an additional source of income by way of bribery and blackmail, since he could threaten to publish or promise to withhold news of scandals involving prominent public figures according to the price they were willing to pay. Surprisingly, in the light of later developments, it was the growth of commercial advertising that played a major part in making newspapers honest and moderately respectable. For it soon became clear that the gaining of advertisers willing to buy space required a large circulation which could only be achieved by presenting events in a reasonably unbiased way.

From this short historical survey it has been possible to pinpoint some of the more obvious characteristics of propaganda and to show how, as a form of communication, it is influenced by the technical apparatus for spreading communications available at the time. It is now necessary to turn to the views and researches of the modern social psychologists who have made a scientific study of the subject. Kimball Young of Queens College, New York, defines propaganda as:

... the more or less deliberately planned and systematic use of symbols, chiefly through suggestion and related psychological techniques, with a view to altering and controlling opinions, ideas, and values, and ultimately to changing overt actions along predetermined lines. Propaganda may be open and its purpose avowed, or it may conceal its intention. It always has a setting within a social-cultural framework, without which neither its psychological nor its cultural features can be understood.

Leonard W. Doob of Yale, whose *Public Opinion and Propaganda* is one of the most important books on the subject, offers as one of his definitions what is virtually an abbreviated version of the above. Propaganda is, he writes:

... a systematic attempt by an interested individual (or individuals) to control the attitudes of groups of individuals through the use of suggestion, and, consequently, to control their actions.

Elsewhere, however, Doob takes into account the content of

propaganda and says that it is 'the attempt to affect the personalities and to control the behaviour of individuals towards ends considered unscientific or of doubtful value in a society at a particular time'. As it stands, this seems an inadequate definition, for who is to say what is of 'doubtful value' at any given time? Apparently the answer is that society itself must judge, since Doob continues:

... the dissemination of a viewpoint considered by a group to be 'bad', 'unjust', 'ugly', or 'unnecessary' is propaganda, in terms of that group's standards.

This is undoubtedly how many people determine what they are going to describe as 'propaganda', but it does not follow that such a subjective definition adequately describes what propaganda really is; for instance, it would exclude what we quite justifiably refer to as health propaganda. However, Doob's point that propaganda always has a setting within a particular social-cultural framework becomes clearer when he contrasts it with education. For the essence of education, he suggests, is its objectivity *in the light of scientific truths prevalent at the time*, whilst the essence of propaganda is the attempt to control people's attitudes, often in irrational directions (and always, we might add, by irrational means). Hence it was not propaganda to teach or spread the pre-Copernican picture of the solar system when it was a generally accepted theory prevalent at the time, but it certainly was propaganda when an attempt was made to censor the new theory as it arose or to conceal the fact that an alternative one existed. Somebody has said that freedom of choice presupposes a full appreciation of all the alternatives involved, and one feature common to all propaganda is that it tries to limit our choice deliberately whether by avoiding argument (the bald statement of one point of view to the exclusion of others) or by the emotional and non-objective criticism of the other side and its opinions by the use of caricature, stereotypes, and other means to be discussed later. The uneasy feeling of so many people in the face of propaganda, that an attempt is being made to manipulate them by underhand methods, is quite justified. There is nearly always something concealed by the propagandist. What he conceals may be his real aim in engaging in his campaign, the means (suggestion and other psychological techniques) employed, the fact that there are alternative views to his own, or the fact that if these are mentioned at all it is only to misrepresent them. Whether the material presented is true or untrue, the operator sincere or insincere, his aims 'good' or 'bad', is entirely irrelevant. What makes behaviour propaganda is the manner in which the material is presented, just as much as its content.

The problem of unconscious propaganda has already been mentioned, and the issues involved are again best illustrated in the field of education. Superficially it is easy to distinguish between education and propaganda, since the former aims at independence of judgement, the latter at supplying ready-made judgements for the unthinking. The educator aims at a slow process of development, the propagandist at quick results; the former tells people *how* to think, the latter tells them *what* to think; one strives to produce individual responsibility and an open mind, the other, using mass effects, strives to produce a closed one. Yet the distinction is less easy to make than might be supposed. The Soviet government, for example, like the Catholic Congregation of Propaganda, regard propaganda and education (as conducted by itself) as identical processes; according to the *Soviet Political Dictionary*, propaganda is 'the intensive elucidation of the writings of Marx, Engels, Lenin, and Stalin, and of the history of the Bolshevik Party and its tasks'. Ozhegov's *Dictionary of the Russian Language* defines 'agitation' (which has an unpleasant connotation in the West) as: 'Oral and written activity among the broad masses which aims at inculcating certain ideas and slogans for their political education and for attracting them to the solution of the more important social and political tasks.' Furthermore, Communists accept the argument of Marx that ideologies reflect the class-struggle which exists in every non-socialist system of production, and that the prevailing ideology of any period will thus be that which favours the economically dominant class; or, as a non-Communist American expressed it more crudely to Mr Justice Holmes: 'Philosophers are men hired by the well-to-do to prove that everything is all right.' In this view all non-Communist ideologies (Marx himself unlike his followers excepted the field of science as its conclusions could be verified by empirical methods) are simply unconscious, or sometimes conscious, propaganda. They are not propaganda in the 'good' Communist sense which means education, but in the 'bad' or reactionary sense which implies the intent to deceive the masses. Of course, there can be no doubt that education, as actually carried out in any country is only rarely unbiased. One social scientist went to the trouble of analysing a widely-used American text-book of arithmetic for schools and found that, in fewer than 200 pages, there were 643 problems which not only dealt with, but stressed the concepts peculiar to capitalism: rent, investments, interest, and so on. One might suppose that it is no sin to take for granted existing economic practices; yet in a socialist country this would be regarded as propaganda and, quite recently, it was reported that Russian educationists were disturbed by the frequency with which the profit motive still reared its ugly head in their own text-books and were taking steps to change them in a more progressive direction. If arithmetic can be accused of bias, how much more does this apply to the teaching of nationalist values through history, geography, and literature! These are all examples of what Doob means by unconscious propaganda, but the view taken here is that, since it is an inescapable fact that everybody is busy propagating his own point of view most of the time and there is a great deal of truth in Marx's theory about ideologies, the term virtually loses any meaning and is better dropped. None of the practices described above are propaganda unless they are part of a *deliberate* scheme for indoctrination, as happens in totalitarian countries. Doob has further complicated the issue by inferring that sincerity or lack of it on the part of the propagandist should be taken into consideration, and other writers have gone so far as to say that the propagandist is, to some extent, attempting to fool his audience. In this view, sincerity is to be defined as the state of affairs which exists when there is little or no discrepancy between the goals which an individual really seeks and the goals he publicly claims to be seeking. But any such attempt at defining sincerity underestimates the power of the human being for self-deception, and, as Doob himself admits, the propagandist is peculiarly liable to become his own first victim. In any case the issue is irrelevant since the propagandist may be calculatingly deceitful or passionately sincere; it is the method employed which is deceitful whether its operator is fully aware of the fact or not.

The first task of the propagandist is to catch his audience's attention and, in the case of minor and possibly revolutionary political parties or religious bodies attempting to propagate an unfamiliar doctrine, a considerable period of time may have to be spent in building up a receptive frame of mind. This is described by Doob as a 'sub-propaganda campaign', and most propagandists prepare the ground in this way, for example by distributing leaflets and posters or by house-to-house visits before embarking on an all-out campaign. Quite commonly, in trying to make his own message stand out against the background of many other competing stimuli, the operator will bring in another and more striking stimulus which, even if it has little or nothing to do with his actual message, is effective in catching the eye or ear in such a way as to cause it to be noted. Examples are the ballyhoo associated with American elections, the rallies of the former Nazi party at Nuremberg which created an impression of invincible power, and, of course, such everyday examples as the pretty girl or handsome male on the posters of cigarette manufacturers or the workman of fabulous strength advertising a certain brand of stout. These are not only attention-catching but by their implications of power, health, enthusiasm, beauty, and masculinity they excite the observer and serve to put him in a more receptive state of mind.

But nobody can create emotions which are not already there, and the propagandist is limited to evoking or stimulating those attitudes suited to his purpose out of the total spectrum existing in his audience, attitudes which may be innate but are more usually socially-acquired. Since all the basic motives in man are emotionally conditioned, the expert will make ample use of love, anger, fear, hope, guilt, and any other feelings, emotions, and sentiments useful to the purpose in hand. Ordinarily he will want to arouse a desire for some goal, with a view to suggesting at a later stage that he alone has the means of satisfying that desire; but he may equally trade on the propagandee's feelings of inadequacy or guilt to make him want to 'do the right thing'. Florists, for instance, in order to increase their sales devise the idea of Mother's Day so that in the long run not only will mother-love manifest itself in the sending of a bunch of flowers, but those who forget to do so will begin to feel thoroughly ashamed of themselves. It is a well-known fact that human emotions become more intense when frustrated, and people are never more prone to suggestion than when their desires for food, shelter, safety, prestige, and the rest have been thwarted – hence the frightening suggestibility of the revolutionary mob. But frustration is a relative term, and it is another common propagandist trick to create in the audience a conviction that they are thwarted no matter how well-provided-for they may actually be: 'Why should *your* garden be without its own built-in swimming-pool?'

There are two other important factors which influence suggestibility both of which will be dealt with in more detail later but should be mentioned here. Firstly, people are always more suggestible in a crowd, when their individual credulity tends to sink to the lowest common denominator, and secondly, there is good evidence that the arousal of *any* strong emotion may make the individual more suggestible even when that emotion is directed initially *against* the propagandist and his message. As Kimball Young points out, there is more than a passing truth in the old saying that people may go to a revival to scoff but remain to pray. Other lessons the would-be manipulator of people will have to learn are the value of the appeal to authority, since few if any of us ever escape the early conditioning of submission to a powerful parent or parent-substitute, which makes us peculiarly prone to listen to, or even try to emulate, later examples. So, too, the desire to keep up with the 'best people' implies the getting and holding of that authority and prestige which we have learned to admire in others. Then there is the old lesson that, although short-run propaganda may be directed towards any age-groups, that designed for complete and thorough indoctrination must be directed to children and youth since they are the most vulnerable to suggestion and persuasion techniques. Revolutionary political parties, religious bodies, and the manufacturers of cigarettes are all equally well aware of this truth. Lastly, propagandists have to learn that with few exceptions campaigns that present first one view and then the opposite – perhaps on the theory that the public should decide rationally between them – are not effective. Of course, in our definition of the term, anyone who did so would, *ipso facto*, cease to be a propagandist.

The fundamental mechanism employed by all forms of propaganda is, as we have seen, suggestion, which may be defined as the attempt to induce in others the acceptance of a specific belief without giving any self-evident or logical ground for its acceptance, whether this exists or not. Research shows that suggestibility increases from the age of four to the age of seven or eight when it reaches a maximum and thereafter declines steadily with increasing age, an observation which leads us to conclude (*a*) that it originated with the acquiring of language, the ability to communicate and be the object of communication, and (*b*) that it derives its emotional force from submission to parental authority. The unquestioning acceptance of the parents' words is at its height during these years, and gradual immunization against too easy suggestibility occurs in varying degrees when the child discovers that his parents are not omniscient or omnipotent. With increasing age, ideas and responses become more canalized and fixed, and the person builds up increasingly complex systems of belief, which he makes the basis of his actions and will defend, more or less violently, against attack. Therefore suggestion, although a powerful weapon, is likely to be effective only when the propagandist is able to give the impression that what he is advocating is in line with the propagandee's already-existing beliefs, or when the suggestion he is making is relatively superficial and offers no threat whatever to the convictions of his audience. A good example of suggestion which comes into the second category is demonstrated by an experiment carried out by the two American sociologists Sorokin and Boldyreff, who played the identical gramophone record of a portion of Brahms' First Symphony on two separate occasions to a group of 1,484 high-school and college students. On the first occasion, an introductory talk referred to the piece as superior, musically finer, and more beautiful than the other (actually the same) piece they would later play. At the second playing, the music was referred to as 'an exaggerated imitation of a well-known masterpiece, totally deficient in self-subsistence and beauty'. The suggestion that the identical record was different was accepted by no less than 96 per cent of the students; the second suggestion that the first rendering was of a more beautiful piece – i.e. a prestige suggestion coming from a supposed expert – was accepted by 59 per cent, whilst 21 per cent 'suspended their judgement' and 16 per cent disagreed. Only 4 per cent of the students, therefore, recognized that both playings were of the same record after they had authoritatively been told otherwise.

The following are some of the more specific techniques employed in propaganda and it will be noted that most of them follow the lines of well-worn channels common to the average human mind (e.g. most people *want* to feel that issues are simple rather than complex, *want* to have their prejudices confirmed, *want* to feel that they 'belong' with the implication that others do not, and *need* to pinpoint an enemy to blame for their frustrations). This being the case, the propagandist is likely to find that his suggestions have fallen on fertile soil so long as he delivers his message with an eye to the existing attitudes and intellectual level of his audience.

1. *The Use of Stereotypes*

It is a natural tendency to 'type' people, and in time this picture may become a fixed impression almost impervious to real experience. Hence the stereotypes of the Negro, the Jew, the capitalist, the trade-union leader, or the Communist, and the reactions of members of these groups come to be explained, not in terms of themselves as unique individuals, but in terms of the stereotype. In the early years of this century Sir Charles Goring of the English prison service, who was opposed to the theory of Lombroso, the Italian criminologist, that there is a specific criminal type with certain recognizable physical stigmata, had an artist draw from memory the portraits of many of the inmates of a prison. He made a composite photograph of these and found that it bore a strong resemblance to the conventional stereotype of a criminal. But when a composite picture was made from actual photographs of the same people, it bore no resemblance either to the drawings or to the popular idea of a 'criminal type'. Clearly the artist had been influenced by his stereotype.

2. *The Substitution of Names*

The propagandist frequently tries to influence his audience by substituting favourable or unfavourable terms, with an emotional connotation, for neutral ones unsuitable to his purpose. Hence 'Red' instead of 'Communist' or 'Russian', 'Union bosses' for presidents of the unions, 'Huns' or 'Boches' for Germans, 'Yids' for Jews. On the other hand, 'free enterprise' sounds better than 'capitalism' in these times, and the writer of advertising copy is often an adept at substituting long and impressive-sounding words to conceal the true identity of the relatively simple constituents of patent medicines or cosmetics.

3. *Selection*

The propagandist, out of a mass of complex facts, selects only those that are suitable for his purpose. One would not expect a Conservative politician to go out of his way to mention the Suez incident, nor a Labour one to mention unnecessarily the 'groundnut plan'. Censorship is one form of selection and therefore of propaganda.

4. *Downright Lying*

From the atrocity stories against the Saracens during the Crusades and the ridiculous tales of Belgian priests used as human bell-clappers or the human soap factories of the First World War to the Hitlerian recommendation of the big lie, falsehood has always been part of the propagandist's stock-in-trade.

5. *Repetition*

The propagandist is confident that, if he repeats a statement often enough, it will in time come to be accepted by his audience. A variation of this technique is the use of slogans and key words, e.g. 'Fair Shares for All', 'Keep the World Safe for Democracy', 'Ein Volk, ein Reich, ein Führer', 'Player's Please', 'Guinness for

Strength', and so on. Such phrases, frequently meaningless, play a large part in politics and advertising, yet what *are* 'fair shares'? What *is* 'democracy'?

6. *Assertion*

The propagandist rarely argues but makes bold assertions in favour of his thesis. We have already seen that the essence of propaganda is the presentation of one side of the picture only, the deliberate limitation of free thought and questioning.

7. *Pinpointing the Enemy*

It is helpful if the propagandist can put forth a message which is not only *for* something, but also *against* some real or imagined enemy who is supposedly frustrating the will of his audience. Hence the Nazi campaigns against the Jews and the 'pluto-democracies' which, by careful selection of targets in line with the already-existing traditions of the group, had the dual effects (*a*) of directing aggression away from the propagandist and his party, and (*b*) of strengthening in-group feelings thus improving party morale.

8. *The Appeal to Authority*

Suggestion, as mentioned above, is of its nature an appeal to authority. The authority appealed to may be religious, that adhering to a prominent political figure, or, particularly in advertising, the authority of science and the professions. For example, 'Doctors in over a thousand skin tests proved X makes your skin younger, softer, lovelier than ever!' Which doctors? And how does one test 'loveliness'? Another form taken by the appeal to authority is the appeal to the crowd, or as the Americans describe it, the 'bandwagon technique', which implies that 'everybody's doing it' and therefore that those who are not are outsiders.

Up to the point so far reached in this discussion we have come across little evidence to suggest that under ordinary conditions propaganda by means of either the written or the spoken word is a particularly powerful or sinister procedure since its efficacy is strictly limited by certain very definite social and psychological considerations. Obviously, if a totalitarian state has complete control over communications such that the ruling élite decided both what the individual citizen should hear and what, by reason of censorship, he could not hear, its power to influence his thoughts and actions would appear to be almost complete. It is never wholly complete since, even in the absence of adequate information (and censorship is more deadening than any sort of eloquence), you cannot stop people from thinking. With brief periods of freedom, this was the state of affairs throughout Europe up to the time of the Renaissance and the Reformation, and is that still existing in the modern totalitarian countries. However, there is neither subtlety nor anything of psychological interest in the purely mechanical control of information, and, as already noted, in countries which employ these methods propaganda is a 'good' word synonymous with education.

Mind-changing implies a diversity of views to which one can be changed, so the most interesting agitator or propagandist is the one faced with competition. But the more competition the more difficult the propagandist's job becomes and that is why the state of affairs during the seventeenth, and eighteenth centuries in France and Britain, when everybody was busy propagating different opinions, played a major part in creating a free society. The psychological limitations of propaganda have already been mentioned and more will be demonstrated elsewhere, but we have seen that the most fundamental one is that everybody develops a more or less rigid system of beliefs and attitudes very early in life, and, except in trivial matters, the only course open to the propagandist is to go along with already-existing trends and to attempt, possibly by lying, to show that his system is not likely to conflict with those of his audience, and is even a fulfilment of them.

Of course, these systems of belief are modified by the changing pattern of historical and technological events, but here, too, the propagandist, unless he has complete control over all information, has to move with the current. Yet today the would-be manipulator of thought is feared as never before, and in the free countries rather than the totalitarian ones. As suggested earlier, this change may date from the feelings aroused by the propaganda of the First World War, but its causes lie deeper and are rooted in the way in which social communication has developed from the free-for-all democracy of the eighteenth century to the mass society of today.

The pamphleteering of the seventeenth and eighteenth centuries played a large part in the diffusion of democratic ideas to ever larger sections of the population, both by the direct spread of such ideas and, indirectly, by the clash of many and varied points of view. This, together with the rise into power of the middle class, heralded the beginnings of democratic society in England from the revolution of 1688 on,* and brought about what has been described as 'the public of opinion', the chief feature of which was the free ebb and flow of discussion among small groups of educated citizens who met each other face to face and therefore had the possibility of answering back. Such educated groups could discuss, spread their views in publications (which in those days could be done very cheaply), organize societies to propagate their beliefs, and finally might hope to create a public opinion which the government or its legislative body would be compelled to build into the country's laws. As the American sociologist C. Wright Mills points out, this eighteenth-century idea of public opinion was paralleled by the laissez-faire economic doctrine of the time which assumed a market composed of freely-competing entrepreneurs just as the public was composed of freely-competing circles of opinions held by broadly equal individuals.

As price is the result of anonymous, equally weighted, bargaining individuals, so public opinion is the result of each man's having thought things out for himself and contributing his voice to the great chorus. To be sure, some might have more influence on the state of opinion than others, but no one group monopolizes the discussion, or by itself determines the opinions that prevail.

In short, the people are presented with problems which they discuss and decide upon; they form viewpoints which are later

* Obviously opinions differ as to when certain historical movements began: for example, some would date the beginnings of democratic society in England from the Cromwellian revolution and the freedom of the press from the removal of the newspaper Stamp Act in the nineteenth century. The authority followed here is Trevelyan's *English Social History*.

organized and compete with each other until one viewpoint wins. When this stage is reached, their representatives are ordered to carry the policy out, which they are obliged to do. Within this type of society propaganda is widespread, varied, open, and each individual effort takes place on a relatively small scale; propaganda, in the modern sense of more or less hidden manipulation of the public by powerful élites, is not a problem since formal authority rests in the public itself and its representatives. Nor has hidden manipulation been a problem to the authoritarian societies of medieval times or even of today since in these power is exercised openly and nakedly by the ruling bodies and their agents, who have no need to manipulate the public in order to gain or retain power by hiding its exercise. When only a single world-view exists, as in the Middle Ages, it is backed by tradition and enforced by temporal authority; when, as in the modern totalitarian society, an ideology is deliberately inculcated and others excluded by government control over the means of communication, the situation is for all practical purposes the same. In both cases the ideology is taught as absolute 'truth', and, as it is identified with overt power and authority, no hidden manipulation is necessary. Propaganda is uniform, open, and regarded as synonymous with education.

Eighteenth-century society was based on the beliefs that there exists a natural harmony of interests amongst men and that ultimately reason is supreme. But by the middle of the nineteenth century these views had begun to change, under the impact of new ideas, amongst the most significant of which were: (1) the assumed need for experts to decide the really important issues in political life; (2) a new conviction of the essential irrationality of man; (3) Rousseau's doctrine of the sovereignty of the whole people, i.e. the issue of mass democracy; and, finally, (4) the discovery by Marx and Engels of the class struggle. Marxian theory not only contradicted the doctrine of a natural harmony, but showed that ideologies in general were neither rational nor objective, being socially conditioned. Gradually individualism gave way to collective forms of economic and political life, natural harmony to the inharmonious struggle of classes and organized pressure groups, disinterested reason to recognition of vested interests; and, fatally, there came an increasing realization of the effectiveness of irrational appeal to the frustrated masses.

When we contrast the eighteenth-century view of a society with that of the new mass society, it will be seen that in the former there are as many people to express opinions as there are to receive them, that there exists the possibility of answering back, and that the opinions arising from discussion in small face-to-face groups are capable of leading to action even against the prevailing authority. Moreover there are no powerful institutions recognized by the government to penetrate the public, which is genuinely autonomous from instituted authority. In mass society, on the other hand, many more people receive opinions than are able effectively to express them; for the public has become a conglomeration of individuals who have to accept their beliefs and ideas through the new mass media. Communications are such that effective answering back is almost impossible, and there is a consequently reduced hope that opinion can be realized in action, since the channels of action are controlled by the authorities. Finally, there is no autonomy from government-recognized institutions; for these reach down into the masses, and in the extreme case of totalitarian governments terrorize them into uniformity by the infiltration of informers as in the former Nazi street and block system and the present-day Communist system. As Wright Mills puts it:

... there is a movement from widely scattered little powers to concentrated powers and the attempt at monopoly control from powerful centres, which, being partly hidden, are centres of manipulation as well as of authority. The small shop serving the neighbourhood is replaced by the anonymity of the national corporation: mass advertisement replaces the personal influence of opinion between merchant and customer. The political leader hooks up his speech to a national network and speaks, with appropriate personal touches, to a million people he never saw and never will see. Entire brackets of professions and industries are in the 'opinion business' impersonally manipulating the public for hire.

The numerous critics of this state of affairs have taken a gloomy view of the type of society in which nothing, it is said, lies between the mass media controlled by powerful élites and the ruling authority. Within such a society there is a decreasing feeling of 'belongingness' reflected, for example, in the publication of such books as Riesman's *The Lonely Crowd* and in the increasing emphasis laid by many psychiatrists on loneliness as an important factor in mental illness. The small professional army is replaced by the large conscript one, the small business by the mass-production industry, both of which, seeing 'morale' as a problem and equating it with conformity, employ psychiatrists and psychologists to bring this conformity about. Psychiatrists and teachers increasingly see the ideal of normality in 'social adjustment', taking care not to inquire too carefully into the questions 'Adjustment to what ? And for what purpose ?' Schools, once the place where one was taught current knowledge against a background of the traditions of the past to create the disinterested and rationally-minded gentleman, are virtually becoming centres of vocational training. Thus John Vaizey's book *Education for Tomorrow* is based on the premise that '. . . it is worth spending money on education because it assists the economy . . . because it provides a skilled and resilient body of workers at all levels, who help to keep a highly fluid economy going'. The traditions of leadership taught in our public schools, he adds, are 'extremely inappropriate in the modern world', and the ideals of personal independence and initiative, once highly prized, have become '. . . outmoded by the realities of twentieth-century economics, where detailed knowledge, research, technical flair, and a clear recognition of the toughness of the competition are of greater value'.

The new media of radio, television, and the cinema were at first welcomed by progressives, who saw in them the opportunity or, as one psychologist wrote of radio and the cinema at the beginning of this century, '. . . the possibility to enlarge indefinitely the competition of ideas' so that 'whatever has owed its persistence merely to lack of comparison is likely to go'. But this hope, say the critics, has not been realized; for even in the democracies the radio and television are controlled either directly or indirectly by the government or, worse still, by commercial companies paid by advertisers who 'give the public what it wants' – that is, according to this view, the rubbish it has been conditioned to want. In non-totalitarian countries there still exists the theoretical possibility of playing one medium off against another, but this becomes less and less realistic, firstly because most people tend to get all their information from the same newspapers, radio stations, and periodicals and are rarely seeking counter-opinions to their own; secondly, because genuine competition between media is often more apparent than real. Instead, according to Wright Mills, Vance Packard, and many others, the media and the social pressure of the masses conditioned by the media act to bring about increasing uniformity. Through them the individual is told who he is in terms of status and role, how he ought to think and behave in this role, what his aspirations ought to be and how he should strive to attain them. The manager in a large combine, William H. Whyte's 'Organization Man', has to conform to a fixed stereotype measured by the most penetrating psychological tests, his wife and family and his whole life outside the combine not being excluded as to the books they read, the kind of home they live in, and the type of car they drive. Adaptation to official policy is the ideal, the failure to do so is increasingly disapproved of, and manipulation, whether masking itself under the title of the study of 'man-management' or as courses in 'human relations', is the rule.

As for the field of advertising, all its most competent practitioners are agreed that under modern conditions of production the real function of the art is to infer differences between products that do not exist, or grossly to exaggerate the significance of small differences that do exist. Pierre Martineau's *Motivation in Advertising* expresses the issue frankly enough:

One of the difficult problems that advertising is confronted with is the increasing standardization of products and services. Any actual differences in quality, price, packaging, or service have disappeared almost to the vanishing point. Bread, milk, clothing, refrigerators, airline service, banks, or what have you: physically they are virtually indistinguishable. And yet more and more is it necessary for advertising to pre-sell the product by individualizing it – making it more desirable than anything else.

As he gradually comes to realize the extent to which he is being subjected, openly or by hidden means, to psychological pressures applied by those who hold the real power in mass society, it is not surprising that the individual citizen feels helpless and at the mercy of 'them', the power élites who increasingly control, or try to control, his attitudes. If he happens to live in one of the so-called 'democracies', the power élites will be the 'economically concentrated commercial interests who frequently express themselves as shocked at the suggestion that there is any limitation of free expression in a system in which the means of communication are owned by individuals or small groups whose main, or only, qualification may be that they can raise the necessary capital. These protestations are quite genuine, since anything (or nearly anything) *can* be said – provided that you can afford to say it and that you can say it profitably.'*

Or the individual may live in an authoritarian state, or under the control of an authoritarian Church, and under these circumstances the openly-admitted purpose of communication is to transmit the instructions, ideas, and attitudes of the ruling élite, alternative views being excluded as a matter of policy. Sometimes the means of communication will be directly controlled by the ruling group, or the control may be more indirect by means of censorship; but in either case the authoritarian state and Church, as George Orwell once pointed out, '. . . are alike in assuming that an opponent cannot be both honest and intelligent. Each of them tacitly claims that "the truth" has already been revealed, and that the heretic, if he is not simply a fool, is secretly aware of "the truth" and merely resists it out of selfish motives.' From this it follows that the heretic is either a criminal or mad, and the appropriate treatment is prison, death, or (on the assumption that he is suffering from a sort of moral imbecility) some form of 'corrective training' directed at removing 'criminal thoughts' and instilling a new code of morals. Yet (paradoxically, because the authoritarian's use of power is open and naked like that in the Middle Ages) it may be that the citizen living under these circumstances feels less manipulated than the American or Englishman whose real fear is of the

* Raymond Williams in *Britain in the Sixties: Communications* (Penguin Books, 1962).

'hidden persuaders' who attempt to manipulate him unawares. Such is the picture of the modern state as presented by its present-day critics; and, since few would care to deny that it contains some elements of truth, we are brought back to our original questions as to how far these hidden or overt pressures exist, by what techniques they are exerted, and how much the human mind is influenced by them. But the most basic question, and one which never seems to have occurred to the proponents of the manipulation theory since they regard the answer as self-evident, is whether anybody is ever in any significant degree changed at all except along the lines of his own already-existing attitudes or in adjusting to a changing environment. Is it, in fact, possible to produce *fundamental* alterations within the adult mind, *in a predetermined direction*, by any known methods whatever? Many of the attempts that have been made to do so will be discussed and evaluated in the succeeding chapters and it is hoped to show that the answer to this question is by no means self-evident. Before doing so, however, it is necessary to consider how attitudes arise, and how, in comparatively normal circumstances, they can be changed.

CHAPTER 2

THE FORMATION OF ATTITUDES

THE word 'attitude' has been defined in many ways, none of which, however, differs greatly from what the ordinary individual would understand when he heard or made use of it. An attitude has been defined by Gordon Allport as 'a mental and neural state of readiness, organized through experience, exerting a directive or dynamic influence upon the individual's response to all objects and situations with which it is related'. Bogardus defines it as a 'tendency towards or against some environmental factor which becomes thereby a positive or negative value', whilst Sherif uses the word to refer to 'the main body of what is socialized in man' which makes attitudes the main constituents of the ego or self as, indeed, they probably are. Quite simply, an attitude is a concept used by the social psychologist in order to explain without complicated references to individual psychology, with which he is not primarily concerned, what happens between stimulus and response to produce the observed effect. An American from one of the southern states is likely to respond in a markedly different way from a northerner to the same stimulus of the presence of a Negro and we explain this by saying that he has a different attitude towards coloured people. We all have such attitudes towards other persons or objects in our environment, whether friendly or unfriendly, interested or indifferent, respectful or disrespectful, assertive or submissive, so that when we say that an individual has an attitude towards his own or other countries, democracy or Communism, Negroes or Jews, Catholics or Protestants, contraception or vivisection, what we mean is that these concepts or entities act as stimuli to produce particular feelings which cause him to think and sometimes to act in a specific way. They are responses which he has learned as a result of previous rewards or punishments, satisfying or unsatisfying experiences, success or failure, predominantly with other people. Thus in those countries or parts of countries where Negroes are considered to be inferior, the general attitude towards them is determined less by actual contact with Negroes as individuals than by contact with the prevailing social attitude towards them as the result of a particular tradition. Sherif tells the story of a little girl who answered the door and then went to her mother saying that a lady wanted to see her. Her mother went to the door, and when she returned said: 'That wasn't a lady, dear; it was a Negro. You mustn't call Negroes "ladies".' It is likely that the child learned her lesson and began to acquire a new attitude through this mild expression of social disapproval. This is one of the ways in which attitudes are formed, and they are later reinforced by biased interpretations of experiences, in this case by observation of the relative lack of education of the Negroes in certain states and the poor conditions under which they live, which in turn, by what has been called the 'self-fulfilling prophecy', are in part due to the prevailing attitudes themselves.

The sociologist Robert K. Merton gives an example of this principle at work. A fair-minded unionist, with no particular bias against Negroes, nevertheless favours a policy of excluding them from his union, allegedly on a basis of rational consideration of the facts, which are that Negroes coming from the South are unused to the traditions of trade-unionism and the practice of collective bargaining. The Negro, with his low standard of living, is prepared to take jobs at less than the prevailing rates. He is, in short, a strike-breaker and, even if involuntarily, a traitor to the working class. These facts as they stand are quite true. But Merton comments, 'Our unionist fails to see that he and his kind have produced the very "facts" which he observes. For by defining the situation as one in which Negroes are held to be incorrigibly at odds with the principles of unionism and by excluding Negroes from unions, he invited a series of consequences which indeed made it impossible for many Negroes to avoid the role of scab.'

As a rule the social psychologist, although interested in where attitudes come from and their social effects, is not particularly interested in what helps to form them inside the individual human being. But from the present point of view this is one of the most important matters to be discussed, especially as some of the more recent work in psychology leads to important practical conclusions. Indeed there has never been a time when it was more necessary to find out why people hold the views they do and the methods whereby others are seeking to influence them. In order to do so, it is convenient to state straight away that all attitudes arise in one or other (or more) of the following ways and have their origin in these sources: (1) in the child-rearing experiences of the first five or six years of life from the parent-child relationship; (2) by association between individuals or the formal and informal groups met with in later life – what these are and what they include will be dealt with later; (3) from unique and isolated experiences or similar experiences repeated throughout life. By reason of the Law of Primacy, which states that the earlier an experience the more potent its effect since it influences how later experiences will be interpreted, these sources are placed in order of importance and will be treated in that order; but it must be remembered that forming a background to them all lies the society and its culture or way of life to which the individual belongs. It is this culture which the parents try to inculcate into the child in the early years by what is known as *mediated social-cultural influence*, and in later life the developing or fully-developed person learns still more by what is known as *direct social-cultural influence*, either by himself or, in however modified a form, from the social groups to which he belongs.

The question of culture has been of fundamental importance ever since during the 1930s the American anthropologists Margaret Mead and Ruth Benedict began by their studies of primitive cultures to show how very variable 'human nature' can be under different circumstances; as, indeed, the British anthropologist W. H. R. Rivers had already observed before the First World War. Such variations in social ideals of how the individual members of a society should behave are described as its basic character structure, and most of the early investigations were carried out upon small, isolated, and relatively primitive tribes, for the obvious reason that these are the most likely to be uninfluenced by external factors and free from the regional, class, and political sub-groupings which make technically advanced societies so much more complex.

It is unnecessary to go into great detail on a subject about which so much has been written already, but, as Ruth Benedict pointed out, many of those attitudes which seem to us wholly abnormal have been used by other peoples as the very basis of their social life and, on the other hand, attitudes which we regard as entirely worthy and commendable have been looked on by differently-organized cultures as quite the reverse. The Arapesh tribe of New Guinea are shocked by the slightest sign of self-assertion, boastfulness, or anger, whilst to the nearby Mundugumor the ideal is violence and aggression for both men and women; and in the same small geographical area dwell the Tchambuli where the role of the sexes seems to be reversed, the men being meek, emotionally dependent, and concerned with their personal appearance, whilst the women are dominant and managing. The Zuñi (a branch of the pueblos of New Mexico) are a people whose life is centred on religious ceremonial, being prosperous but without interest in economic advancement. They admire most those men who are friendly, make no trouble, and have no aspirations, detesting on the other hand those who wish to become leaders. Hence tribal leaders have to be compelled by threats to accept their position, and are regarded with contempt and resentment once they have achieved it. On the other hand, the former Kwakiutl of Vancouver Island demonstrate what is almost a parody of industrial civilization; the chief motive of this tribe was rivalry, which was not concerned with the usual intentions of providing for a family or owning goods but rather with the aim of outdoing and shaming neighbours and rivals by means of 'conspicuous consumption'. At their potlatch ceremonies these people would compete with each other in burning and destroying their money and valuable possessions, and accordingly their ideal was the man who would perhaps seem to us a paranoid megalomaniac or possibly an industrial magnate. The life of the Dobu of north-western Melanesia is one which encourages malignant hatred and animosity. Treacherous conduct unmitigated by any concept of mercy or kindness and directed against neighbours and friends is expected. In Bali, says Roheim, we have a wholly schizophrenic civilization.

The relevance of this for the present purpose is to show, firstly that it is a waste of time to attempt facile interpretations of behaviour in terms of a universal 'human nature' based upon fixed instincts which will respond uniformly to the same appeals, and, secondly, that complex as modern countries are, each instils, or attempts to instil, particular attitudes in its inhabitants which form what we usually describe as national character. In spite of the complexity of their social structure, Spaniards, Germans, French, Japanese, and Englishmen do tend to differ in quite significant ways which are important, and not least to the propagandist, in understanding their responses. A number of books have been written on the subject of the national character of such nations, notably Ruth Benedict's work on the Japanese and Gorer's on the Russians and Americans. It need hardly be said that these differences have nothing to do with physical factors of race or heredity; on the contrary, they are attitudes learned from childhood onwards but primarily based on child-rearing patterns which in turn are presumably related to the people's geographical situation, history, and traditions. They form the overall design which family and social groups employ when they are unconsciously moulding the individual character, that is to say, its attitudes.

Systems of child-training [writes E. H. Erikson] represent unconscious attempts at creating out of human raw material that configuration of attitudes which is (or once was) the optimum under the tribe's particular natural conditions and economic-historic necessities.

Immediately following birth, the human child is so dominated by his momentary physical needs for food, sleep, the relief obtained from emptying bowels or bladder, the need for warmth, and so on that he initially pays little attention to the people surrounding him or even to his mother who feeds him. He is not in any significant sense of the term a 'person' at all since personality only arises following interaction with other human beings. On the other hand, as anyone who has had much contact with newborn children can see, there are considerable differences in temperament between them, some being active and cheerful, others querulous, and yet others phlegmatic; such differences, together with a certain level of intelligence which may be developed or hindered by training, are innate and presumably the result of heredity acting through the nervous system, the system of endocrine glands, and even general physique since, as Sheldon and others have shown, there is good evidence that physique and temperament are closely linked. Short, stocky people tend to be liable to swings of mood and to be extroverted, tall, slender people to be relatively withdrawn and introverted.

Temperament, one supposes, is likely to have some influence upon later attitudes (e.g. one cannot easily imagine an introvert being as responsive to crowd stimuli as an extrovert), but of this we know very little. Also innate are certain drives originating in the body and formerly known as instincts, some of which have been mentioned above, although lists of human instincts are no longer in favour, since whatever innate drives we possess are so rapidly modified by the social environment that all we can do is to infer their existence from an analysis of behaviour. Thus the undoubtedly innate drive of hunger is produced by the action of certain brain mechanisms bringing about contractions of the stomach and this is the internal stimulus to seek to obtain food. But the innate drive does not function of its own, since from a very early age there is no general craving for food as such but for a special kind of food: an attitude-induced drive learned from experience must also be satisfied, and the goal is fully attained only when both innate drive and acquired attitude are appeased. An attitude comes between a drive and its goal and once personality has started to develop few drives are ever aroused without being accompanied by attitudes which have drive value of their own. Psychoanalysis is in large measure concerned with the way in which sexual – a term which includes food-seeking and elimination together with the more frankly sexual attitudes to oneself and others – or aggressive drives become modified in the process of relating the self to the surrounding social environment, notably the family. The family, acting as the potter on a comparatively undifferentiated lump of clay, the newborn child, which like clay may be hard or soft and easy or difficult to mould because of the inherent qualities which make it good or poor material, has the function of attempting to shape it into a more or less close approximation to the type of individual approved of by the society and its sub-cultures with which the child must later identify itself. This is the process we have described as *mediated* social-cultural influence and the complexity of the process is such that many attitudes other than the formal values of the society come to be incorporated in what might be described as the 'real' self or *nuclear personality* depending upon inherited differences of temperament, individual parental attitudes, and whether the child resists or cooperates with the attempts to indoctrinate it. Because of the Law of Primacy, this layer of personality consists of attitudes which are highly resistant to change and yet have important effects upon the individual's subsequent relationship to society and its generally-accepted beliefs. For this reason its origins and significance are worthy of attention.

The work of Melanie Klein with children* seems to show that from an extremely early stage of development two emotions arise which have the greatest possible relevance to our later responses to social stimuli and remain very persistent throughout life. These are anxiety and guilt, upon both of which propagandists constantly play. Like all living things the infant is exposed to external dangers, but in the first months when no distinction is made between the baby's own ego and the surrounding world the feelings aroused by external objects instead of being regarded as purely personal feelings within his own mind are attributed to the objects themselves. What gives him pleasure is a good object, what gives him pain is a bad object, and in this way the world comes to be peopled with good and bad objects which he expects to behave towards him in terms of the qualities he has attributed to them. How these are dealt with, although at an unconscious level, to a very large extent influences the individual's later social and even political attitudes. Because the baby is born with certain physical or biological wants and since he has no conception of the passage of time and indeed has no guarantee initially that his

* This work, although interesting and widely accepted, is not essential to the thesis that the basic personality structure is formed in the first five or six years of life, which is undoubtedly true. It is mentioned here as an account of how certain attitudes *may* arise even earlier than was formerly thought.

needs will be satisfied at all, he desires that they shall be satisfied at once. The failure to do so arouses crying and great anxiety, which is almost inevitable since much of his early education is involved with teaching him to accept restraints. But all anxiety resulting from temporary deprivation leads, by way of frustration, to resentment and rage which originally, according to Klein, is directed to the breast as the immediate frustrating object, for the infant as yet knows nothing of his mother as a person. When all goes well, the breast is a good object but when frustration inevitably occurs it becomes a bad one and the infant's aggression is projected upon it leading to the feeling that persecution comes from without. This stage is known as the 'persecutory position' but later in the course of development there comes the realization that the good and bad objects of earlier months are different aspects not merely of a satisfying or frustrating breast but different aspects of the same person, his mother. Occurring at a time when reality and fantasy are not yet differentiated and aggressive wishes are believed to be magically destructive, the infant comes to believe that he is in danger of destroying, or has already destroyed, the person he most needs and indeed is growing to love as the one without whom his biological needs cannot be satisfied. This stage, leading as it does to feelings of anxiety and guilt, is described as the 'depressive position', and after a period in which the child alternates between both the two phases a final stage of compromise or settling of the problem is reached when the continued presence of the mother finally makes it clear that the aggressive fantasies are less dangerous and potent than had at first been feared. Nevertheless, with many intermediate forms, the relics of these stages will persist throughout life in the form of a deep-seated sense of irrational guilt and the irrational anxieties felt by everyone whatever subsequent objects they may attach themselves to: the predominantly persecutory type projects his guilt and anxiety into the external world, the predominantly depressive tends to blame himself. In psychological terminology the persecutory type is extrapunitive, the depressive intrapunitive. Since elements of both positions are incorporated in the individual's sense of guilt, it has been suggested by Money-Kyrle, a leading follower of Klein, that two extreme types of conscience or super-ego exist, although obviously a whole range will be distributed between the two extremes: there is at the one extreme the perse-cutory type who tends to blame others for his frustrations and whose conscience is based largely upon fear of punishment, and at the other the depressive who tends to hold himself responsible and whose conscience is based predominantly upon fear of in-juring or disappointing the loved object. The former will respond to guilt feelings by propitiation, the latter by attempts at reparation. The first personality will tend towards authori-tarianism, the latter towards humanitarianism.

During the first five or six years of life the child begins to learn actively, by what the Behaviourists call 'conditioning', by trial and error, and by acquiring the habits taught by its parents. These habits are established by reward and punishment, indul-gence and deprivation; and as Freud pointed out they are learned in three stages, the first of which is the oral stage already described in the greater detail supplied by Melanie Klein when the mouth is the chief centre of sensual satisfaction and character formation. At this time, in addition to those attitudes already mentioned, the child makes a most important discovery – the discovery of his need to be loved, protected, and cared for which, although at this stage based fundamentally on self-love, becomes in the course of time the foundation upon which all the later motives and cultural imperatives are laid. It is this need for love and protection which in the adult becomes not only the basis of love between two persons, but the need for the approval of society and the desire for status within that society or the wish to possess characteristics admired in a particular community which are also among the motives to which the propagandist frequently appeals. In a competitive society the man who wants to improve his social position, to seek a status higher than that of his neighbour, to obtain power, to possess a bigger and more expensive car, is acting in a way which is based on the child's need for love and his desire to be a good little boy worthy of mummy's approval. True, the mother's approval is now the approval of his social group but the fundamental motive is the same. In a society which admired conquest, he would become, or try to become, a great warrior; in a capitalist society his success is measured in terms of wealth; and in a traditionalist society or one based on caste he would act in all ways according to tradition.

At the later stage when the infant has to learn to control his bowels and bladder, described by Freud as the anal stage, he learns other lessons: he can for the first time effectively control other people by producing or withholding his motions. Faeces are the child's first conscious possessions and productions and, according to Freud, come in later life to be associated with money or property and therefore with attitudes of generosity or meanness. (Hence the wealth of phrases connecting wealth with dirt and ultimately with faeces – 'filthy lucre', 'throwing money down the drain', 'stinking with money', and so on.) He also learns the importance of time, regularity, and cleanliness or perhaps wilfully or otherwise fails to do so, as the case may be. The anal stage, when it is associated with over-strict control on the part of the parents, comes to be related to sadistic trends, and observation suggests that nations obsessed with orderliness, cleanliness, and obedience are often found to have more than their share of sadism as a result of these frustrations. Finally, at the age of five or so, the child becomes aware of the existence of other members of the family as individuals in their own right and, from a selfishly centred absorption in the mother alone on the part of both sexes, the boy's love for his mother in a more adult way gives rise to jealousy of his rival the father (who is probably also admired and loved), whilst the girl's love for her father leads to a comparable jealousy of the mother. These are described as the Oedipus and Electra complexes respectively, and at a later stage lead to the formation of the super-ego proper when, instead of being constantly told by the parents how to behave, the boy introjects (i.e. takes into himself) his parents' standards thus forming the super-ego or primitive conscience which acts as an internalized parent to control behaviour in its more fundamental aspects. Nevertheless it is probable that when adult life is reached much of our behaviour is controlled by observing and following that of other people. The super-ego has been described as a 'psychic gyroscope' but many of our actions are 'other-directed', to use the term employed by Riesman in his book *The Lonely Crowd*, and he further suggests that in modern mass society behaviour is increasingly controlled by the expectations of others.

Following the Oedipus stage, the boy learns from his father the approved masculine traits of his society, the girl from her mother the feminine ones; hence families in which the father is dead or absent or the mother is the stronger partner sometimes lead to homosexual trends in the son. The founder of another school, Alfred Adler, showed how a sense of inferiority in childhood, perhaps in relation to brothers or sisters, an actual physical inferiority, or other real or imagined disabilities often lead to a need to compensate and, although a Freudian would not wholly accept Adler's explanation for the tendency, it is certainly striking how many power-seeking dictators have been small men (Napoleon, Mussolini, Hitler, Stalin) or belonged to what the society they ultimately ruled regarded as inferior social groups. (Of these men, only Mussolini was a native of the country he later controlled, Napoleon being a Corsican, Stalin a Georgian, and Hitler an Austrian.) It is at this stage, too, that persisting attitudes to authority arise confirming earlier attitudes of fearless and open expression of feelings towards leaders or, on the contrary, the tendency to submit to or respect power and suppress criticism. Attitudes that work and lead to the desired results in these early years become habitual in the adult: friendliness or hostility, cautiousness or impetuousness, thoughtfulness or a demanding nature, sociability or keeping to oneself, a positive attitude to health or hypochondria, and even delinquent tendencies ('Very well, if you won't give me love and attention for being good at least my naughtiness will cause you to pay some attention') – these attitudes are selected and maintained because at one time they seemed to work in the circumstances to which the child was exposed. Basically, says Dr Franz Alexander, 'whether a person will become timid or outgoing, cautious or enterprising, self-confident and optimistic or self-critical and pessimistic, aggressive or submissive, dependent or independent, generous or withholding, orderly or careless – all these personality features which make a person a well-defined individual, different from others – depends on the influence of the intimate personal environment (i.e. the early parent-child relationship) on a heredi-tary substratum'. In other words, the nuclear personality is both deep-rooted and, like all early learning, highly resistant to change partly because of its primacy in time, partly because within its limits it works and the individual knows no other safe form of adjustment, and partly because it is to a considerable extent all of a piece and cannot be dealt with by altering one item at a time. The attitudes therein are utilized and traded upon by the propa-gandist, but it is unlikely that he can alter them.

Following these childhood years, the child comes increasingly into contact with society outside the home; he is indoctrinated by a process of *direct social-cultural influence*. But society is not a homogeneous mass, since it is composed of groups of people ranging from the large more or less deliberately organized bodies with specific aims which are described as 'secondary groups' and include religious and political organizations, professional associa-tions, trades unions, the services, and so on, to the small 'primary groups' informally coming together with a dozen or fewer members who may have no other aim than enjoyment of each other's company. Society could indeed almost be said to be based on such primary groups (which include the family group) as its fundamental units rather than on a horde of unrelated individuals as was at one time believed. Elton Mayo, the Australian indus-trial psychologist who did most of his work in the United States, criticized the latter view as the 'rabble hypothesis' and showed how social life in the factory is based on the informal primary group to which management must relate itself rather than to unorganized individuals. He wrote:

In every department that continues to operate, the workers have – whether aware of it or not – formed themselves into groups with ap-propriate customs, duties, routines, even rituals; and management succeeds (or fails) in proportion as it is accepted without reservation by these as author and leader.

Such groups are of course associated with other activities than work, e.g. the group of old men who occupy the same park bench when the weather is sufficiently clement, the drinking and darts group at the local pub, the wives' meetings while out shopping, the gang of adolescents, whether their social activities be innocent or less so, the groups of friends in school, the neighbourhood group, and so on. Within these the individual, in addition to the formal status granted to him by his position in society, has an informal status which supplies him with many of his social satisfactions and he soon learns (quite apart from the laws of formal society) what things are done and not done in that particular group of which he is a member. Most people are members of several such groups, occupying a different status in each, but in some cases they will be in the group physically but not wholly of it because they take their standards from another, which is known as their reference group because it is the one to which they refer in such matters. For instance, a man may be a member of his working group in an engineering firm and, naturally, is likely to accept some of its informal standards relating to the amount of work to be done as decided informally by the group and other matters, which will be discussed elsewhere; he would not go to work in a bowler hat and carrying a rolled-up umbrella even if there are excellent facilities for changing at the factory any more than the managing director would go to work in a battered old car and wearing a cloth cap. Amongst his mates he may be an industrious and skilful worker without being regarded by the other members as of very much account (perhaps for just that reason). In addition he may spend many of his evenings studying in a small class at the local technical college, within which, because of his superior knowledge, his standing may be high, and yet other evenings may be passed at a pub where he is seen in quite a different role as a member of the darts team who is its jester and funny man, possibly to cover up for his poor ability at the actual game. Each of these groups supplies him with some of his attitudes and roles and various aspects of his status in the informal sense. But to the man himself his main reference group may be the neighbourhood group where he lives in what is considered to be one of the relatively socially superior parts of town within which he and his neighbours regard themselves as belonging, or at least aspiring to, the middle class. His family want to 'better themselves' although he would probably play down this side of his nature whilst at work. Another reference group may be the church he attends as a member of the Church of England whilst his work-mates when they go to church at all are likely to be Methodists or Baptists, especially if they live in the North of England, the Midlands, or Wales. Now all of these, but particularly his reference groups, create some of the attitudes possessed by this man and it is these groups, too, which apply the main pressures upon him to conform to the rules of society, in so far as he does so.

Society has the formal and more clumsy sanctions of the law at its command, but the main reason (apart from his super-ego) why the individual behaves himself and adjusts reasonably well to ordinary social standards is the social pressure applied by his informal groups; for example, his working group not only applies certain informal pressures regarding restrictive practices and so on – it also would be likely to disapprove strongly if he committed adultery or engaged in stealing (as stealing is interpreted in that group, which might exclude a certain amount of 'fiddling' or, in the case of a management group, claiming more expenses than one is actually entitled to). But the primary groupings do this only incidentally, being concerned basically with the values which are related to their own situation, and society and the larger secondary groups receive their loyalty only in so far as their interests coincide with those nearer home. C. A. Mace has expressed this principle very clearly in an article on 'Satisfactions in Work' (*Occupational Psychology*, January 1948):

Consider the case of a particular miner living in a particular mining village and working in a particular pit. At the present moment he is subjected to the following, among other, forms of social pressure: (1) the pressure of what England expects of him in the current crisis of production, these expectations being voiced, for example, in the leading articles of the daily press; (2) the pressure of the expectations of the National Coal Board, of the Government, and of his Union; (3) the more local pressure of the expectations of the supervisory staff of his pit; and (4) the still more local expectations of his wife and family and of his immediate associates in his daily working life. Clearly local pressures are much more potent than pressure propelled from a distance. *One might almost say that the power of an expectation at any place varies inversely with the square of the social distance of that place from the point of emission. Local pressures, moreover, may act as a kind of insulating barrier against pressures more remote in origin. This is part of the explanation of the relative ineffectiveness of long-range propaganda.** Hence the miner's response can be predicted only by those who are suitably placed to see what the more local forces are.

Anyone who has visited a mining village or read Zweig's *Men in the Pits* or Sigal's *Weekend in Dinlock* will realize the essential correctness of this judgement, and not for miners only but for such other occupational groups as shipbuilders or motor manufacturing workers, and many non-industrial formations as well. Some religious bodies insulate their members to a quite extraordinary degree from outside pressures no matter how powerful these may be, for example the Doukhobors in America and Canada and the group commonly known as the Plymouth Brethren in Britain. Clearly the propagandist or commercial advertiser would be wasting his time if he attempted to change by any ordinary methods the strongly-held attitudes of these groups in order to get the former to enlist or the latter to buy spirits.

Earlier we discussed the origins of the relatively rigid and fixed nuclear personality, the attitudes within which, arising in early life, may be said to constitute the 'real' self. But it is easy to see that in many respects people are very variable in their behaviour and these variations arise from the individual's social situation and the reference and membership groups from which he obtains this other set of attitudes which is described collectively as the peripheral personality. This is the field within which there is at least some hope of inducing change by propaganda, advertising, indoctrination, or whatever we may choose to call the particular process. A great many attitudes which are generally regarded as being indubitably part of the individual's personal organization only seem permanent because we are always observing him in the same situations, where they are part of the social role he is playing in a particular group. Ordinarily he is doing this quite unconsciously. Thus a worker may be lazy and slow in a firm where he feels victimized, and a keen and enthusiastic labourer

---

* Author's italics. It will be shown later how relevant these comments are in assessing the influence of the mass media.

in one that he likes; the girl who is shy at a dance may be pert enough in her own home or amongst people she knows well; the Italian soldier, not noted for his military prowess in an army for whose aims he cared little, might (and usually did) fight as a brave partisan. Recent experiments have shown that children who are prepared to cheat in a school examination may be entirely honest at home and elsewhere since in many schools cheating, although a heinous sin to teachers, is not regarded too seriously by pupils, just as 'fiddling' at work does not necessarily imply that the worker is generally dishonest in his other dealings. Many a doctor who appears hesitant and reserved in society dons complete confidence with his white professional coat. The fact is that such traits as bravery, honesty, shyness, and many others which we assume to be 'in' the individual are not unitary traits at all, but a part of his role in a particular group-setting. In others, of course, they may be nuclear traits, but this is much less frequent and most psychiatrists with war experience have observed how a soldier's bravery varies with the morale of his group and the tasks he is expected to fulfil. Many a man decorated for bravery in the field would lose control completely if ordered to submerge in a submarine, or even if he were trapped in a lift between floors. The peripheral or social personality, then, is the area within which changes may occur provided they are not wholly inconsistent with the nuclear personality.

Finally, it was pointed out that attitudes may arise from isolated or repeated experiences in the course of a lifetime. Thus an anti-Negro attitude may arise from a single experience of attempted sexual assault, or fear of driving a car from a single road accident. Most people who buy a particular commercial product and find it useless, harmful, or unpleasant when actually employed will refuse to buy it again. The rat which is given an unpleasant electric shock on taking a particular pathway to its goal of food will soon learn to avoid that pathway and choose another, just as the lonely individual will avoid further attendance at the church where he has gone seeking company and friendship if he finds that he is ignored by most members of the congregation. Attitudes or drives which are aroused by a particular stimulus and lead to punishment or failure in place of the promised goal soon result either in a change of attitude or alternative action towards the same goal (unless as is sometimes the case the goal happens to be punishment).

Such conditioned reflexes are fundamental to Pavlov's Behaviourist psychology, and the theory is employed in the treatment of neuroses in what has come to be known as 'Behaviour therapy'. For instance, an alcoholic who has been given the drug disulfiram ('Antabuse') instead of gaining pleasure and relaxation from his drink is made to feel extremely ill; and it is hoped that this unpleasant association will ultimately cure him of his habit. When, on the contrary, an action is rewarded the result is reinforcement and what has become a habit is perpetuated. We shall have occasion to deal with the work of Pavlov later so at this point all that need be said is that the present writer does not consider that at any essential point it conflicts with the work of Freud but feels very strongly that, in its present state of development, it is far too unsubtle a weapon to explain all the manifestations of behaviour. It may on the face of it sound logical to say that a woman adopts an anti-Negro attitude after a single attempted seduction on the part of a Negro – but would she hate all white men if the individual in question had been a white? Ordinarily she would not, and if she did one would surely want to know why, as we do in the case of the black man; what deeper attitudes in the nuclear personality were already present to lead to this result? It is a well-known fact that sexual interference in young children even of a quite drastic type only leads to harmful results afterwards in already unbalanced children and has negligible effects upon normal ones. Repeated experiences leading to punishment or lack of attainment of the goal do not always lead to changed attitudes, and many alcoholics relapse in spite of disulfiram treatment.

We may safely conclude that isolated or even repeated experiences in later life do not necessarily give rise to permanent new attitudes when these are in conflict with older and more deep-seated ones unless they are constantly reinforced, and that when permanent attitudes do arise (as in the case of the sexually-assaulted woman) it is because in fact they fit in very well with previously-existing traits. This is particularly true in the field of religion, where, in many cases, the true believer is absolutely impervious to the most objective exposure of a fake medium or faith healer in whom he or she has originally placed confidence. The will to believe is more potent than any mere experience and emotion is stronger than reason in the vast majority of people. Cases of religious conversion may appear to follow a single incident and the impression given to the observer is that of sudden change from one type of personality to another, the 'new man' in God. But, in fact, as many examples show, the conversion was preceded by a long period of mental struggle and the apparent intervention from outside really results from the eruption of unconscious material from the nuclear personality, which had been in a state of mental conflict with conscious attitudes, and finally becomes integrated, giving rise to a sense of great relief and the awareness of being 'changed'. As Jung points out:

St Paul had already been a Christian for a long time; hence his fanatical resistance to the Christians, because fanaticism exists chiefly in individuals who are compensating for secret doubts. The incident of hearing the voice of Christ on his way to Damascus marks the moment when the unconscious complex of Christianity became conscious. . . . The complex, being unconscious, was projected by St Paul on to the external world, as if it did not belong to him.

Paul did not become a wholly different person by becoming a Christian; he found a new set of beliefs which satisfied his unconscious more effectively than the old ones and for this reason the new attitudes were likely to be stable. Similarly, many atheists have been brought up in oppressively religious homes and the change from belief in, and fear of, an awe-inspiring and vindictive God to a conviction, through reading, study, and the influence of others, that there is no God provides a feeling of relief. Yet contact with many such people will lead to the conclusion that there has been little real change in the personality as such, and that the same deep-seated attitudes have only been attached to different goals. This type of atheist campaigns for his new beliefs with the same intolerance, narrow-mindedness, and obsessiveness that he manifested in his previous state; formerly he worshipped a vindictive God, now he worships 'no-God', that is all. Adherents of totalitarian political parties, if at all fervent in their beliefs, may become converted to a totalitarian religion instead, Communists may become Fascists, but convinced totalitarians do not become Quakers or liberals.

As we shall shortly see, it is useful to distinguish between opinions, attitudes proper, and character traits. Opinions are but briefly held and likely to reflect current public feeling; in many cases they reflect rather what the individual thinks he should feel than what, in fact, he does feel. They are readily changed and may be susceptible either to propaganda or to reasoned argument. Attitudes, on the other hand, are likely to be long-lived and do not necessarily reflect the feelings of the general public although they tend to reflect those of some group with which the individual has become associated. Ordinarily they are rooted in character traits which cause the individual to select from the flood of stimuli constantly impinging upon his senses only those which are consonant with his own deep-rooted beliefs. Although they are capable of changes which are quite real in the social sense, these changes are apt to be more apparent than profound. Thus the change from Communism to Fascism or, in the field of religion, to Roman Catholicism, is quite real socially in that these bodies proclaim vastly different doctrines which result in entirely divergent behaviour, but emotionally and from the standpoint of character all are on the same level on the authoritarian-democratic scale because all share the same attitude towards authority. Saul the persecutor of Christians is manifestly the same person as Paul the Christian; for, although his goals have changed, his approach to problems is still the same and the same character-traits are directed to other ends. The more he has changed (and of course from the historical and social standpoint the change was immense in its implications), the more he remains the same person.*

Character traits, arising in the early years of life, are extremely resistant to change for reasons already mentioned; they are utterly impervious to propaganda and only alterable if at all,

* As C. A. R. Crosland has pointed out, the efficiency of propaganda of all types is in inverse proportion to the importance of the issue; thus it is very ineffectual in changing moral and social attitudes, only moderately effective in influencing taste, and comparatively effective only in the marketing of commodities.

by special techniques. Belonging to the nuclear personality and rigid as they are, they nevertheless permit of a considerable variation in the manifest behaviour stemming from the individual's peripheral personality with its attitudes; for example domineering behaviour towards one's inferiors and submissive behaviour towards one's social superiors are not contradictory but complementary attitudes arising from the same trait of respect for authority; shyness and self-assertiveness are not contradictory when we realize that the individual concerned is obsessed with the need to impress others and is confident in those situations where he has special knowledge or power and shy in situations where he has not. Even such drastic influences as the deteriorative changes in the brain occurring in old age or the effects of large amounts of alcohol only serve to accentuate rather than destroy character traits, often bringing to the surface those (such as greediness, aggressiveness, or paranoid suspicion) which have for years been more or less successfully concealed. The persecutory or authoritarian type will be discussed more fully in the following chapter, but we may summarize by saying that his traits are the result of his inability as a child to live with his own impulses. He is the child who has been punished and made to feel guilty whenever he makes a mess or touches his sex organs, whenever he has a temper tantrum, or tries to strike his parent. A child who finds all his natural impulses wicked, and feels that he is disapproved of when he gives way to them, is likely to grow up hating himself and projecting this intolerable feeling upon other people or circumstances. Whenever he sees other people ignoring what he regards as the right code of morals, he wishes to punish them just as he himself was punished. Having had to fight bad impulses in himself, he cannot be permissive and tolerant towards others. His is the prejudiced personality as well as the authoritarian one; he is the moralist or upholder of conventional morals; and he has a need for definiteness which makes him tend to see every conflict in terms of black or white and causes him to be drawn towards institutionalism. Thus totalitarianism, whether in religion or in politics, appeals to this type because it leaves no question or problem open but provides certainty. Although outwardly compliant, the authoritarian is strongly ambivalent towards his parents and parent-figures, whereas the humanist, who has been brought up without fear of his fundamental impulses, expresses whatever hostility he may feel openly and does not mind uncertainty. He is mentally more flexible and seldom takes the view that 'there is only one right way of doing anything'; for him there are various shades of grey, not simply black or white.

One of the most important discoveries of psychological research in this field is the fact that prejudice in an individual is unlikely to be merely a specific attitude towards a specific group; it is more likely to be a reflection of his whole way of thinking about the world he lives in. Similarly a person's humanitarianism is not limited to certain fields but is likewise a mode of life. We have seen that these are the extreme cases at the ends of a normal curve of distribution, and experimental research seems to show that about a half of all prejudiced attitudes are based mainly on the need to conform to custom, to keep to the traditional pattern. This half, in other words, is influenced primarily by existing group attitudes rather than by child-rearing patterns alone.

CHAPTER 3

THE CHANGING OF ATTITUDES

FROM the standpoint of the experimental psychologist, four levels of attitudes have been described which vary in terms of depth and hence of modifiability. At the simplest level are mere statements of opinion made on single or comparatively rare occasions which may or may not represent the individual's true feelings about a given subject or at the best represent a purely passing interest as when we praise our hostess's brand of sherry on one of our infrequent visits. Then we may have the same statement made repeatedly over a longish period of time on all, or almost all, the occasions when it can be held to be relevant, as when we praise the same brand of sherry at all the cocktail parties to which we are invited or regularly ask our tobacconist for 'Player's please' or our wine-merchant for Guinness, of the undoubtedly health-giving properties of which we have become convinced. Both of these are opinions and, as such, are the stock-in-trade of the commercial advertiser and, although few people would be deeply disturbed if such desires were temporarily frustrated and a substitute brand had to be accepted, the modern tendency is to attempt to tie the individual's desire for a particular product to deeper motives thus making the demand more imperious and reliable. Thirdly, when it can be shown that a number of separate attitudes dealing with the same issue tend to correlate closely on one of the scales for identifying and measuring attitudes such as that devised by Thurstone we may claim to have isolated an attitude in the generally-accepted sense of the word. For example, the individual who asserts that black men should have equal rights with white may simply be expressing an opinion of the moment which is fairly remote from reality; but if he also holds strong opinions about the behaviour of the remaining colonial powers in Africa and blames much of the trouble there on their intransigence, believes that in the new governments Africans should be given equal representation with whites, and is antagonistic towards those who would limit West Indian immigration into Britain, he clearly has a strong positive attitude on the subject of Negro affairs. Lastly, attitudes may be intercorrelated to form a concept of a higher order, described by Eysenck as a 'primary social attitude' or, in terms of what has already been said here, a basic personality trait pertaining to the nuclear personality and therefore strongly resistant to any form of propaganda.

Most striking is the statistical confirmation of what Eysenck describes as a 'radical-conservative factor' corresponding to what has already been described as the authoritarian-humanitarian scale by virtue of which people are found to hold views of a radical or conservative pattern which are applied to a number of distinct fields which at first sight would appear to be logically independent. This factor must not be thought of as applying to two fundamentally opposed types but rather to a continuous and statistically 'normal' distribution in which the majority of people occupy a more or less intermediate position, with a few extreme radicals and conservatives at either end. Yet the interesting fact remains that those who incline strongly towards radicalism or conservatism in any one of the fields tested are likely to exhibit a corresponding attitude in the other fields also. For instance, the Conservative lady who is strongly patriotic and an upholder of the traditional family is also likely, as one knows from the periodic conferences she attends, to uphold strict discipline in penology, believing in capital punishment and bringing back the birch and the cat.

The 'right' or conservative attitude results from a predominance of or submission to the father-figure or its representative the super-ego, and hence to substitute father-figures met throughout life, tending therefore to respect power and authority even if the respect is often ambivalent. On the other hand, the 'left' or radical attitude results from the freedom to rebel against this figure or its substitutes in the external world; there is an adoption of the child's standpoint as opposed to that of the parent, of the standards of one's own ego as opposed to those of the super-ego. Melanie Klein, coming later in time and concerning herself almost exclusively with children, was able, as we saw in the previous chapter, to go further back than Freud to show the origin of such traits at an even earlier stage, in the depressive and persecutory characters. Of course, it is not meant to infer that these are the only sources of the attitudes in question since there are whole societies and social groups which adopt them for environmental or cultural reasons; but it is in general the case that authoritarianism in a culture reflects a similar attitude in home life and in many other spheres so that it is reasonable to suppose that the two levels, cultural and psychological, augment each other and are not alternative explanations. In Germany, for example, it is easy to see that the authoritarian family, a social system which emphasized minute social differences in terms of authority and submission like the 'pecking order' amongst hens, and the supremacy of the soldier, all formed a pattern which culminated at the top with an authoritarian government.

The more important of these correlated and contrasting right and left attitudes may be listed as follows:

	RIGHT	LEFT
1.	Loyal to a single father-figure or leader	Loyal to group
2.	Upholds family	Suspicious of family
3.	Stresses discipline in relation to education, penology, etc	Stresses freedom
4.	Anti-feminist	Feminist
5.	Stresses sexual restraint	Stresses sexual freedom
6.	Patriotic	Cosmopolitan
7.	Upholds class distinctions	Tends to 'classless' society
8.	Upholds conventions and traditions	Critical of both
9.	Upholds religion	Anti-religious
10.	Upholds private property	Socialistic
11.	Prejudiced	Unprejudiced

These political attitudes refer to fundamental emotions about the nature of society and are not to be taken as necessarily corresponding to the party programmes of specific political parties in any country – although it will be seen that in fact they correspond rather closely in many respects. Nevertheless they form the raw material of which political parties are made, influencing the individual to join one party rather than another. Again it is clear that those who possess many of these attitudes on either side are the extreme types, otherwise there would be no point in holding political elections to convert the great majority of middling cases, who for the most part get their opinions from their social milieu. Moreover, there are many left-wing politicians or trade-union leaders who possess more than their legitimate share of right-wing attitudes – who are, in fact, right-wing leaders *manqués*, possibly attached to their present party by the mere accident of having been born in a working-class home with a sense of injustice against the ruling class learned from bitter experience. After all, the union leader who is a fond family man but will have no nonsense about the equality of the sexes so far as his wife is concerned, who is a Methodist or Baptist with strong puritanical leanings, asserts the importance of union or party discipline and loyalty to the Party Leader, and is nationalistic rather than international in sympathy is by no means an uncommon figure. If, however, we introduce a further dimension, the self-explanatory tough-minded-tender-minded scale based on a concept of William James, and if this be figuratively placed at right-angles to the conservative-radical dimension, it becomes possible to pinpoint the various political parties more accurately. Thus the Fascist would fall within the tough-minded-conservative space, the Communist within the tough-minded-radical one, whilst Conservatives (in the British sense) would be tender-minded-conservative, and Liberals and Socialists tender-minded-radical respectively.

The factors mentioned have been selected as convenient for the purposes of this book out of other dimensions of the personality which are being currently studied by psychologists, and doubtless many others will be found at this deep-seated level. The main reasons why such attitudes are difficult to change have already been mentioned: (1) they have arisen at a very early age and early impressions are the most fixed being, in fact, personality traits; (2) each item of the attitude is correlated with many other items and therefore cannot be changed piecemeal. The 'rightist's' anti-femininism at this level is not a single item to be corrected on its own but part of the whole system of 'rightist' beliefs listed above so that, as Lewin has pointed out, 'the re-educative process has to fulfil a task which is essentially equivalent to a change in culture', i.e. it implies changing the individual's total attitude to life and literally making a new man of him. Such items belong to the basic self where they are all finally placed and firmly interlocked (the nuclear area of more or less fixed personality traits). Beyond this lies the more loosely organized peripheral area with gaps and possibly inconsistent beliefs where there is still possibility for change; and yet further out lie those variable ideas which may change from one day to another or merely represent polite acceptance of social conventions. This last is the area of opinions where, as old age creeps on and the picture is slowly completed, even opinions are likely to become more or less fixed. The young man's opinions are flexible so that he may change his brand of cigarettes to that smoked by his current girl-friend or he may change to tipped cigarettes because commercial propaganda has assured him that they are safer; the old man, on the other hand, is really put out if he cannot obtain his regular brand of pipe tobacco.

Since the nuclear area of deep-seated personality traits is unpromising material for the propagandist we must now turn to the areas of peripheral organization and opinions which are the social areas in which the individual's group affiliations are significant. The vast majority of people are in varying degrees sociable and those who are not, or who have difficulty in associating themselves with others, are likely to be neurotic – in one definition neurosis has been described as 'the indication and result of an inadequately realized group-effectiveness' (Henry Harris, *The Group Approach to Leadership Testing*). These groups have been classified as primary and secondary. The former (which includes the family itself) being small, with rarely more than a dozen members, and informal, with little specific purpose beyond the companionship it provides, even when it is organized around some particular activity. The secondary group, on the other hand, is a formal association of any size, but likely to be large, which has such a specific purpose and attitudes that the group would probably dissolve should these disappear; amongst these are the various religious bodies, regional bodies determined to retain their specific identity and peculiarities, the supporters of a football club, social classes, etc. But both types of group tend to possess some form of organization in that the social standing or status of each member is defined together with his function and the approved attitudes within the group which he should hold; he may conform to these completely, sometimes try to change them, or be rather passive towards them because he is in the group physically but not of it.

However, no matter how many groups we belong to, willingly or unwillingly, we take our standards from one or more reference groups. These may be synonymous with the main membership groups, and probably usually are, but this is by no means always the case. In relation to social class, for example, a family may be in the economic sense members of the working class yet take the middle class as their reference group thus creating a situation potentially full of tension both for themselves and their associates. A very persistent attitude of the British working class is the belief that any member who tries to better himself socially is a class-traitor who is disloyal to the workers, and two important results of this are the difficulty experienced by the ambitious worker who wants to become a manager or attain an even higher position in industry, and the intelligent boy or girl of working-class origin who wishes to go to a university to study for a professional career. The former is likely to experience the contempt of his mates and even to have other difficulties put in his way, the latter, apart from the deep-seated notion that anyone who is studious is in some way queer, is likely to meet the other attitude that anyone who is not earning as much money as possible after leaving school as early as possible is 'soft' and worse. Doubtless these attitudes are slowly dying out but at present they are often all too powerful, especially in certain areas. In Scotland, on the contrary, or in the United States, where the tradition of the poor boy bettering himself is a living tradition, the situation is different; in Scotland, particularly, where snobbery is attached to education rather than to class, the youth who wishes to better himself is highly regarded.

The propagandist who does not study the attitudes and way of life of those he wishes to influence stands a poor chance of succeeding. This is perhaps particularly true of industry, where a predominantly middle-class management sometimes tends to apply to the workers incentives which are based on essentially middle-class standards. Thus Elton Mayo in one part of his well-known Hawthorne researches was investigating a department of the Western Electric Company known as the 'bank-wiring' room in which fourteen men were employed in attaching wires to switches for certain parts of telephone equipment. The problem facing management in relation to this particular department was that the men's attitude towards the financial incentives of the company was one of complete indifference; in spite of the fact that the plan provided that the more work an employee did the more he was paid, neither more nor less than 6,000 units were turned out each day although it was known that 7,000 units was not an excessive expectation. Mayo soon discovered that these restrictive practices were based on a group-determined norm which represented what was considered a 'fair day's work'. The workers had their own group-determined code which put social pressure on the man who did too much (the 'rate-buster'), the man who did too little (the 'chiseller'), and the 'squealer' who told the supervisor anything to the detriment of an associate. The fact is that appeals to individual initiative so important to the middle-class worker hold much less appeal to the manual worker who has won most of his victories by cooperative effort, although this attitude, too, is slowly dying out in a more opulent and secure society. But, being a class attitude, it is highly resistant to change.

One of the most detailed studies of attitude change was carried out by T. M. Newcomb at Bennington, an American women's college with a membership of about 250 students, largely isolated (the nearest village was four miles away and the college possessed a store, post-office, and all the necessities for everyday existence), and noted for its liberal or radical attitudes because the faculty felt that part of its duty was to familiarize the students with social problems at a time (1935–6) when America was going through a period of depression and the world was approaching

war. Most of the students, however, came from highly conservative and Republican homes and the purpose of the investigation
was to observe the shift in attitude from conservatism towards
liberalism as they became members of the community and to
note whether any specific personal factors aided or interfered
with this change. The vast majority of the students did alter their
political outlook and shortly became liberals in accordance with
the norms of the group but amongst those who did so two separate categories were noted: the first, which was in the majority,
consisted of natural conformists who in another group would
have been prepared to accept other and different group norms;
the second consisted of those who were independent, usually
above average intelligence, and had based their liberal attitude
either on an intellectual basis or, as others might think, because
radicalism was a deep-seated personality trait pertaining to the
nuclear personality. This is suggested by the fact that these
students had achieved independence of their families so far as
their emotional attachments were concerned, and were by
temperament self-sufficient. The first group (the natural conformers) had achieved independence of their families too but had
then become dependent on their own age-group at the college.
Those students who did not change their attitudes also fell into
two categories: the first consisted of those who were definitely
unstable, insecure, and frustrated, the second of students who
were reasonably well adjusted but uninterested in prestige in a
college where individual prestige was associated with non-
conservatism. Although this is not suggested by Newcomb, it
may be assumed that in the latter case, too, the attitude was a
deep-seated personal trait not subject to change. The insecure
students failed to alter their views because they were unable to
enter into the group life with its associated beliefs.

This experiment shows, amongst other interesting observations, the power of group membership in changing attitudes;
what it does *not* tell us is how long these changes lasted when the
women returned to their conservative milieu. It is unlikely that
those which were merely conformist lasted long. Since the
changed attitude of the individual is in many cases a function of
the group to which he belongs it does not always, or even

frequently, survive change to another group, nor is it usually helpful to try to change the attitudes of group members individually. There have been many experiments which attempted to modify racial attitudes by giving courses of instruction on Negro life, problems, and culture yet for the most part the changes recorded have been non-existent or slight. F. T. Smith, an American anthropologist, tried a different method by taking his students, who were forty-six teachers college candidates, for two consecutive week-ends to Harlem, where they met Negro artists, writers, and business men, to demonstrate to his subjects the inadequacy of their stereotypes by introducing them to Negroes of a kind quite different from those within their previous experience. The change in attitude was not marked, but was certainly superior to that obtained by mere verbal teaching. Yet, as Lewin points out, the sentiments of the individual towards a particular racial, religious, or political group are determined less by his knowledge about that group than by the sentiments prevalent in the social atmosphere which surrounds him; even the possession of correct knowledge does not suffice to change false or dangerous attitudes. Favourable experiences with such a group, even when frequent, do not necessarily diminish prejudice towards it and may even intensify it by heightening the discrepancy between what the individual believes he *ought* to feel and what he *does* feel. 'Such a discrepancy,' adds Lewin, 'leads to a state of high emotional tension but seldom to correct conduct. It may postpone transgressions but is likely to make transgressions more violent when they occur.' These findings are summarized by Sherif, who concludes:

Attempts at changing attitudes or social prejudices experimentally by the dissemination of information or factual argument have been notably unrewarding. Some investigators have been unable to obtain any change. Others have obtained various degrees of shift in the desired direction, although there were almost always some cases showing negative or no change and (such changes as occur) are apt to be discrete and rather ephemeral. (*An Outline of Social Psychology*.)

There are, perhaps, three main reasons for this: (1) deep-seated attitudes tend to be part of an integrated pattern of associated beliefs within the individual which cannot be changed item by item, as we have already seen in the case of authoritarian-democratic or conservative-radical ones which are, in their extreme forms, more or less fixed character-traits; (2) peripheral attitudes are a function of the group rather than of the isolated individual and can only be changed by altering group attitudes collectively; (3) to try to alter an individual's attitudes by direct instruction is to imply that he is wrong and this is interpreted, consciously or unconsciously, as an attack, of which Allport says: 'It is an axiom that people cannot be taught who feel that they are at the same time being attacked.'

One of the most successful means used today to bring about attitude change is the creation of a group in which the members feel belongingness since in these circumstances the individual accepts the new system of values and beliefs by accepting belongingness to the group. Experiments during the last war showed that lecturing mothers on the importance of feeding their children orange juice yielded singularly poor results and after a few months only a small number were still following the practice. On the other hand, when they were formed into a group and invited to discuss the problem, with the doctor sitting in merely as a source of information when this was desired, the great majority accepted and continued to follow the practice indefinitely. The facts had become *their* facts and the decision theirs instead of somebody else's. Hence much advanced teaching today takes the form of a brief lecture followed by a period of discussion during which the audience identifies itself with the information, voices its criticisms, and discovers the knowledge for itself. The same is true of anti-social attitudes such as delinquency, race prejudice, and alcoholism where the feeling of group belongingness is increased when members are permitted to express openly the sentiments that the process is devised to remove. Instead of suppressing the anti-social attitudes they are brought out and discussed along with new facts in the favoured direction which are discovered by the group members themselves. But from this it also follows that those who do not find it easy to associate themselves with groups are unlikely to be changed by them, as was seen in the case of the neurotic members of the Bennington community. Similarly those who are simply asocial or introverted by nature, or who have deep-seated traits pulling them in the opposite direction, are resistant to change.

The study of crowd psychology, on the other hand, has shown that, although people do many things whilst in a crowd that they might not do otherwise, these 'new' attitudes spring nevertheless from the individual members of the crowd and not, as was formerly thought, from a mysterious entity described as the 'crowd mind'. Allport expresses this well when he says that the individual in a crowd behaves as himself, only more so. Because of this intensification of emotion it is possible to cause disorganized masses of people to behave in other than their everyday manner, to stimulate and lead them more easily than an organized public which is prepared to listen to reason and discuss a problem. But it is not possible to make them do anything. Negro-lynching crowds exist because anti-Negro feelings already exist; the crowd intensifies the feeling to the point of action but does not create it. The main distinctions between crowd and group behaviour are that the crowd is ephemeral and the individuals composing it ordinarily unknown to each other – that is to say they are not interacting as persons. The crowd is unorganized, and, apart from the leader–led dichotomy, has no structure. Its effect upon the individual member is temporary, and always in the direction of primitive and often destructive behaviour. The primary, and in some respects the secondary groups are exactly the opposite in their characteristics: their influence on the individual is prolonged and often permanent, they have a very definite structure, their members are usually known to each other and are more likely to be led in the direction of creative and rational action. In short, the crowd *draws out* primitive attitudes, the group *creates* new and ordinarily more realistic ones.

Another way in which attitudes of groups or individuals may develop is through the mental mechanisms described by Freud, which, however, work unconsciously rather than consciously. They are a response to frustration, which leads to a desire to make life less uncomfortable by changing our attitudes towards the situation. In fact, a great deal of what goes by the name of public opinion can be understood as a series of reactions to adversity. Amongst the commonest of these is the one known as *rationalization* in which we pretend to ourselves that whatever is, is best, that things might be worse, or give foolish reasons for what has really been done upon impulse. Thus lower-middle or working-class people who actually envy the upper class and its wealth may tell themselves that wealth does not bring happiness (neither, of course, does poverty) and that, in any case, they are more respectable, moral, and altogether better citizens than the group they envy. Or, since most people are taught the importance of being kind and thoughtful to others and of hating cruelty, they must bring in rationalizations when their behaviour does not conform with their ideal so that their self-respect may be salvaged, if not retained wholly intact. Race prejudice, for example, is always accompanied by theories introduced in order to justify current practice: thus Negroes are lazy, just like children, biologically inferior, or simply love to be bossed. Southerners in America rarely admit to hating Negroes and will often say that, on the contrary, they 'feel for them deeply' and recall with affection a Negro servant or the black 'mammy' who brought them up – but, they will add, Negroes need a firm hand, otherwise they will get into trouble on account of their naturally primitive impulses. Those who think that the Negroes are being unfairly treated or grossly discriminated against will be told that they do not understand the problem because they do not live in the area and that their accusations are unfair or lying. Such rationalizations arise in one of three ways: (1) they may, as in the case of the Negro problem, be part of the ready-made traditions of the group handed down from one generation to another in order to make an increasingly intolerable situation seem reasonable and to remove guilt from the group itself; (2) they may be created by leaders and propagandists and receive the willing acceptance of the group in order to make a new and unpleasant situation more tolerable, as, for example, the German thesis that in the First World War their army was never defeated in the field but was traitorously let down by the actions of Communists and Jews on the home front; (3) commonly, as in the case of the class attitudes mentioned above and many other national troubles, they arise from the natural tendency of people to rationalize an accepted fact which cannot in the meantime be altered.

Secondly, there is the mechanism of *displacement* in which the thwarted goal is replaced by a substitute one upon which the original emotion of hate, and sometimes love, is displaced. Hence the phenomenon of the scapegoat or of love on the rebound. Frustration always leads to aggression which may be turned against the frustrating object, against the individual himself, thus leading to depression and self-hatred, or more readily (when battering against the frustrating object is likely to lead only to more pain and further frustration) against a substitute object. This object is likely to be selected, amongst other reasons, because it is a weaker one which cannot hit back. Hens, for example, have a regular 'pecking order' such that, when a weaker hen is attacked by a stronger one, the former when unable to fight back attacks a still weaker one than herself and so on right down the line of order to the weakest bird. The anti-Semitism of the Nazis was such a displacement of aggression in the face of frustration, and it was noted during the Second World War that the German Propaganda Ministry was particularly likely to intensify its efforts in this direction following military defeats or further cuts in the food ration. Of course, the Jews were not selected indiscriminately but because they represented a traditional and culturally acceptable scapegoat in central and eastern Europe generally.

A mechanism which often seems to be confused with displacement is *projection*, in which the impulses people do not wish to recognize in themselves are attributed to others, the classic example being the old maid who fears sexual assault whenever she is alone with a man or who has an irrational fear of finding a man under her bed. As is widely recognized, the true reason for her behaviour is that her own thwarted sexual impulses, being forbidden conscious recognition, are projected upon some external object in the environment. This is such a common mechanism that very often if one asks someone to describe the sort of person he dislikes most he will give (unconsciously) a very good description of himself; for it is the sins of which he himself is most guilty that he seeks for in others. Accusations of aggressiveness against other countries are often a very clear indication of aggressive intentions on the part of the accuser and, as Freud and others have pointed out, the solidarity of the group is promoted by projecting all wickedness against some out-group. Freud, indeed, believed that wars were almost inevitable because, unless such projection could occur, a country would soon be divided against itself in civil feuds.* Projection does not always have this sinister meaning, however, for the world as seen by most people is largely a projection of what lies within themselves, and other people's behaviour, otherwise a mystery, is explained in terms of one's own probable reactions in a similar situation. In fact, the less we know, the more we are likely to project and therefore political or metaphysical systems are frequently a projection of situations which actually exist or are about to come into existence within the individual or country concerned: Nietzsche's Superman was not unrelated to his own sense of inferiority, nor was the concept of the 'survival of the fittest' unrelated to the economic set-up in England during the mid nineteenth century. Leaders frequently encourage projection during political campaigns, when their audience is encouraged to believe that those who have already joined a particular party are 'ordinary people, just like yourselves'. By causing the audience to associate itself with ordinary people in general, it is hoped to get them to vote accordingly.

Identification, although to all appearances the opposite of projection, may occur in the same situations, and each serves to complement the other. Here, instead of love or hatred being projected upon another in order to deny them in oneself, the individual identifies himself with the person concerned and believes himself to feel likewise. It will be remembered that the child identifies himself with his father and introjects his father's super-ego so that certain aspects of the parent become his own, and in just such a way does the individual react to later figures of authority (assuming that his basic feelings are not anti-authoritarian). Thus social psychologists in general are in agreement that the success of a group-leader is partly related to his ability to act as a substitute for the person, usually the parent, with

---

* cf. Jung's dictum that the bitterness of Swiss politics was due to the fact that, for longer than almost any other European country, they had escaped being involved in war. 'The Swiss,' he said, 'have introverted war.'

whom the individual first learned to identify; Freud, going further, believed that the leader took his authority from the members' substitution of himself as their ego-ideal: '[the group] is a number of individuals who have substituted one and the same object for their ego-ideal and have consequently identified themselves with one another in their ego.' He pointed out too the frequency with which leaders in fact refer to their followers in such terms as 'my children' or individual members as 'my son' whilst the leader is often spoken of as 'father' (Stalin, for example, was often described as 'the father of his people'). Hence identification of members one with the other and all with their leader is at the root of morale; but identification is of even greater relevance as the process at the root of all sympathy and pity, which makes it one of the most important factors in the maintenance of society.

In *compensation* the original drive is frustrated and another goal is sought through a drive which has not been involved in the original frustration. Anna Freud describes this mechanism as *restriction of the ego* and gives as an example the small girl of ten who, finding herself incapable of being sufficiently attractive to interest the boys she admires by reason of her beauty, compensates by giving up feminine interests and setting out to excel intellectually. Adler, as already mentioned, thought of this as being one of the most important mental mechanisms whereby people compensated for a feeling of inferiority, and it was pointed out how frequently those who subsequently become powerful figures in society have begun with some social or physical handicap. One finds the same process at work in small or new countries, the small country claiming that in spite of her smallness her history is honourable and her milk and water always germ-free, whilst the large country with a short history may claim to have invented practically everything from the steam engine to antibiotics and radar. In a wider connotation, leaders of countries in time of war or in that state of permanent 'cold war' which characterizes the totalitarian state when many drives must remain unsatisfied take care to provide bread and circuses as substitute goals for the masses to make them forget their frustrations. Hence such governments turn a blind eye to drunkenness and sexual promiscuity in time of war or in periods of relative peace initiate such movements as the German 'Kraft durch Freude' (Strength through Joy) and the Italian 'Dopo Lavoro' (After Work) of Fascist times. But each society has its own kind of circus and hopes that after the performance is ended the participants will return less reluctantly to their dull round of daily life.

Conformity, the desire to be like other people, is described as a mental mechanism by some American social psychologists who point out that from earliest childhood the child is taught that conformity brings safety and security, and it may already have been noticed how frequently this process is brought in to explain why people adopt certain attitudes. One may feel from this side of the Atlantic that undue emphasis is placed on the mechanism; for although the Americans of today are doubtless in many respects a nation of conformers and there is a natural desire to conform within certain limits in all nations without which social life would be impossible, all peoples are not at all equal in this respect and without non-conformity social progress would be impossible. Renaissance Italy, eighteenth-century England, and for the matter of that America herself up to about the mid-1930s were all nations which valued non-conformity and individualism, and these were periods of great social and technical progress. Although it will be agreed that the majority of people must always tend to conform in most things if a nation is to remain stable, there is some danger in accepting without question the results of experiments in social psychology most of which have been carried out in the United States, and applying them to situations in other areas where they may not apply. This danger is exemplified in a well-known experiment carried out by Kurt Lewin which, on the other hand, does show that attitudes may be changed by changing the type of social structure within which the individual is functioning.

In this experiment, equated clubs of ten-year-old boys were placed under three types of adult leadership: authoritarian, democratic, and laissez-faire. In the authoritarian group the leader dictated all policies and activities; under democratic leadership the boys decided their own programme, aided and encouraged by the leader; and the laissez-faire leader remained completely aloof unless asked questions directly. The tasks assigned to the groups were various handicrafts such as model-making, designing toy aeroplanes, carving, and so on. It was found that the autocratically ruled groups were either apathetic or over-aggressive. In the former case they were tense, dull, and submissive but when the leader left the room they ran about, shouted, and showed all the signs of released tension, whilst in the latter they were resentful of their leader because he restrained them, but being also afraid of him, they showed their aggressiveness indirectly: they would pretend that they had not heard when spoken to, break rules 'by mistake', leave before time was up, and damage materials. Significantly, they were not only aggressive towards their leader but also amongst themselves, disparaging each other's work, refusing to cooperate, and picking on weaker individuals as scapegoats. When at the end of the course members were told they could keep the models they had made, many boys in this group proceeded to destroy the models on which they had been working for many weeks. The laissez-faire groups were chaotic and aggressive although without the tension of the previous one; practically no work was done and the behaviour was completely uncontrolled whether or not the leader was present. In contrast, the democratic group thought highly of their leader, looked forward to the meetings, and worked well together, proving more constructive than either of the others. Their projects were described as 'our models', the group as 'our group', and they always spoke of what 'we' would do. The work of the more skilful members was looked on with admiration in place of the jealousy shown by the other groups, these being looked on as an asset to the group. When the leader left the room work went on as before. In fact the democratic group was shown, on many counts, to be superior.

What, in fact, we learn from this experiment is (a) that attitudes are influenced by the social structure itself; and (b) the superiority of the democratic type of arrangement in the small primary group under the conditions prevailing at the time of the experiment in the United States. It does *not* prove (a) the superiority of the democratic form of government in modern mass society where conditions are totally different from those obtaining in a small face-to-face group; nor does it prove (*b*) that the results would be the same in a country where the tradition is autocratic as in Germany – experience, indeed, suggests the contrary.

The importance of suggestibility in altering attitudes has already been mentioned and clearly *suggestion* is one of the main weapons of the propagandist or commercial advertiser. The extreme form of this process is in hypnotism (which will be discussed later), where the individual carries out the suggestion made by the hypnotist; but in many circumstances of normal life we almost automatically carry out actions suggested by others by what is, in effect, a conditioned response to a stimulus such as a word or tone of voice. It is generally agreed that this type of behaviour is acquired in childhood, when we learn to follow the leadership of adults for whom we have affection or who have prestige in our eyes. On the other hand, when resentment is felt towards authority, as in the 'radical' type of personality, there exists the contrary tendency of negative suggestion: here there is a tendency to go to the opposite extreme and thwart every suggestion from the detested source. In line with what we have already found in relation to groups, hypnotists have in general found that the person most susceptible to hypnosis is not the neurotic or socially isolated person but the thoroughly normal and socialized one. Suggestion is frequently the release of an already-existing pattern within the individual rather than the creation of something new. Nor need the response be immediate; for memory makes possible a great variety of conditioned responses and a tendency to respond long after the exposure to the original stimulus. Since the original stimulus first arose in relation to the parents, prestige is a potent factor in affecting the response to suggestion and we tend to believe statements from people whom we either love and respect or who are in a high position – hence the use of celebrities by advertisers who get them to endorse their products. In an American college a group of students was given a set of statements connected with their holding conservative or liberal opinions and asked to tick off those with which they were in agreement. A month later the same test was again given, but this time the remark was made that a number of eminent educators had accepted certain of the liberal views on the paper. The result was a shift towards the liberal end of the scale obviously brought about by this prestige suggestion.

However, without doubt the most potent influence in bringing about opinion change is the gradual alteration in the social climate arising from unconscious adjustments to technical change, and many results which are claimed as successes by propagandists have in fact been brought about in this way. A deep and universal truth is expressed in Hegel's statement that 'man in so far as he acts on nature to change it, changes his own nature'; for an important aspect of human adjustment is the ability to change with changing circumstances and technical innovations form part of the environment to which we must adjust. In India, for example, efforts have been made by government propagandists to get rid of caste distinctions and in China the Communist government has attempted to break up the deep-rooted loyalties of the long-established family system with its reverence for the old and attachment to parents and ancestors. These changes are, in fact, rapidly occurring, but more in response to the industrialization of these countries than to government propaganda. In all lands industrialization has initially weakened family ties and resulted in a fall in the birthrate because, whereas children are an asset to the agriculturist, they are a handicap for the industrial worker, who has to support them until they leave school; nor is it possible to maintain caste distinctions indefinitely when what the factory manager wants is 'hands' regardless of religious or caste ties. Similarly in Britain the Industrial Revolution brought about new attitudes towards the poor who, from being regarded as the special objects of God's care in the Middle Ages, soon came to be seen as the lazy and feckless failures of the industrial system, which also brought about new attitudes in relation to competition by causing a change from the old static society to one in which social mobility was the ideal. It was industry, too, which effectively put an end to slavery in the United States because as an institution it was ill-adapted to the newly-evolved industrial society and there is no doubt that the change would have occurred even had William Lloyd Garrison never lived nor *Uncle Tom's Cabin* been written.

One of the most intensive propaganda campaigns ever carried out was that of the Anti-Saloon League in America (founded in 1895) which in 1909 established a printing plant of its own which from the time it began printing up to the beginning of 1923 produced more than 157 million copies of temperance papers, two million books, five million pamphlets, 114 million leaflets, two million window placards, and eighteen million small cards. The League caused a tremendous body of legislation to be passed, leading up to the Prohibition Amendment of 1920, which was finally abolished in 1933, although not to any significant degree by the propaganda efforts of the Committee Against the Eighteenth Amendment. Prohibition was abolished because it brought in bootlegging and organized racketeering, its administration was expensive and ineffectual, and it resulted in widespread disrespect for the law. In fact it failed because it ran counter to modern trends. Propaganda is limited by prevailing interests, social trends, and prejudices; it is encouraged by ignorance of the facts and is more likely to succeed when it flows with the social current than when it flows against it. In fact, as Edward R. Murrow has said of television propaganda, the propagandist can retard or accelerate a trend in public opinion, but he cannot reverse it.

Apart from the merely negative result, many other traps await the unwary campaigner. All propaganda messages tend to occur in three stages: the stage of drawing attention and arousing interest, the stage of emotional stimulation, and the stage of showing how the tension thus created can be relieved (i.e. by accepting the speaker's advice). Sometimes it may prove impossible to attract public attention, or, because the message runs counter to existing trends or the personalities of the audience, to stimulate emotion. But, as shown in the case of race prejudice quoted by Lewin, it may be still more dangerous to arouse emotions without supplying an acceptable way of releasing them even though the message has been, in part, accepted. The man with racial prejudice may become convinced that he *ought* not to feel that way, yet the way he *really* feels remains unchanged, thus setting up a severe conflict between his official values and his basic ones which give rise to guilt feelings and tension. The discrepancy between the two arouses even more hostility than before which may be discharged either against the original objects of prejudice or, by what is known as the 'boomerang effect', against the campaigner himself. Nobody likes to have been proved wrong over some deeply-felt issue, and the result is increased aggression rather than the resolution of a social conflict. Tensions, in short, have been raised without the possibility of release in the desired direction; for in the deepest levels of their being the crowd reject the solution of becoming 'nigger-lover'. Thus it is possible to alter attitudes without changing behaviour and this may happen even when the propagandist has fully succeeded in putting over his message. For example a politician may convince his audience that the Liberal party has the best programme, yet they may vote Conservative because they do not believe that the Liberals in their particular constituency stand a chance and fear that splitting the vote may benefit the Labour party, which they dislike even more than they do the Conservatives. There is a good deal of evidence that the publication of opinion polls during an election may influence results in this way in spite of apparently successful propaganda, although often in unforeseeable directions. Some, as in the case just quoted, may be moved to support another party because it appears that their own is unlikely to succeed; others, as probably happened in the Dewey campaigns for the American presidency of 1944 and 1948 when the bulk of the propaganda was on the side of this candidate, may vote against a party precisely because the opinion polls appear to predict its inevitable success. Examples of the opposite state of affairs in which behaviour is changed without any corresponding change in attitude are common; when in Rome, most of us behave as the Romans. So an American from a segregationist part of the South who would ordinarily never dream of sitting next to a Negro in a bus is unlikely to make a fuss when he finds himself in that situation in New York, and it is obvious that many of those who help to create the usual 99·9 per cent poll in favour of an existing totalitarian government are acting against their real convictions out of fear or a sense of helplessness. In spite of the propagandist, people tend to select out of the environment only those items which happen to fit in with their way of life at a given time. But not only do they select, they may actually distort the message, and many lecturers must have had the experience of being congratulated after a lecture for expressing a viewpoint which is actually the opposite of the one he was trying to put forward. Unacceptable information is either distorted to make it fit the existing structure of the mind and current trends, or is totally ignored by the mechanism described by psychologists as *denial*.

Failure on the part of the propagandist to understand a particular audience may lead to other unforeseen results. During the initial 'phony' period of the Second World War, French soldiers from the south of France manning the Maginot line were told over the German loudspeaker system that British soldiers had landed in the north and were already making love to and seducing French women. The soldiers only laughed heartily at this information, since their wives and girl-friends were, of course, safe in the south: the Germans had underestimated the regional bias of the Frenchman, the strictly local patriotism which does not always see beyond its own narrow boundaries. Replying to the opposition's criticisms and accusations whether in war or politics is also not without its risks; for there are many circumstances in which the only effect of such an action is to spread the adverse criticisms over a wider field and lead people who would otherwise never have heard of them to suppose that 'there is no smoke without fire'.

Nor is knowledge of a particular audience always enough and, especially in propaganda directed to beneficent ends such as health or safety campaigns, it is necessary to know a good deal more about psychology than can be discovered by intuition alone. 'Common sense' is often a dangerous guide and certainly an unreliable one. For example, the debate in the House of Lords on the effects of cigarette smoking which took place early in 1962 demonstrated clearly that the majority of those who spoke were convinced that the best way to stop young people from smoking was to instil them with a sense of fear or even terror as to the possibility of developing lung cancer. Indeed it is probable that most people would agree that fear of consequences when presented in the most dramatic way possible is a potent deterrent in putting a stop to undesirable behaviour. Now this is simply not true in many instances; psychologists have long been aware that, by reason of what is known as the Law of Reversed Effort, the more frightened people become of the consequences of an action, the more they may be impelled to continue or even increase committing it. Striking confirmation of this fact was obtained in an experiment carried out by Janis and Feshbach, who on a random basis divided an entire freshman class in a large Connecticut high school into four equivalent groups. A fifteen-minute illustrated lecture was prepared in three different forms, all of which contained the same information about the causes of tooth decay and the same series of recommendations as to how to avoid it by the use of appropriate dental hygiene. However, the three lectures – one of which was given to each group (the fourth group acted as a control and was given a talk on a quite unrelated subject) – differed, not in subject-matter, but in the mode of presentation. The first contained a strong emotional appeal to create anxiety by emphasizing the serious consequences of tooth decay, diseased gums, and other dangers that can result from inadequate hygiene. The second presented a 'moderate' appeal in which the dangers were described in a milder and more factual manner, whilst the third presented a 'minimal' appeal which did not dramatize the consequences of tooth neglect but gave advice about hygiene. Subsequent results showed that, although immediately after the lecture anxiety about their teeth was felt by 42 per cent of the 'strong' group, 26 per cent of the 'moderate' group, and 24 per cent of the 'minimal' one, the practical effects of the various appeals were very different. Those who followed the advice given, which included going to a dentist for a check-up, included only 8 per cent of the 'strong' group, but 22 per cent of the 'moderate' and 36 per cent of the 'minimal' one. The frightening appeal was therefore markedly less effective in producing conformity to its message than the purely factual one. Fear is extremely potent in drawing attention to a message, but, at any rate in health propaganda, it is more likely to lead to unsatisfactory results than material which is relatively neutral in presentation. There are other circumstances, e.g. in religious conversion, where this is not always true, but, generally speaking, fear is a double-edged weapon in most forms of propaganda.

CHAPTER 4

PSYCHOLOGICAL WARFARE

IN spite of earlier examples there can be little doubt that the First World War represents the earliest occasion when, towards its close at any rate, propaganda became a fully-fledged instrument making use of a scientific approach which attempted some sort of objective technique. However this stage was not reached in Britain until the summer of 1918, when at Crewe House a Department for Enemy Propaganda was set up under Lord Northcliffe and an International Committee was established, also in London, for the same purpose and containing representatives of Britain, the United States, France, and Italy. In America itself President Woodrow Wilson set up the Committee on Public Information under George Creel in 1917 which employed the experience gained from commercial publicity and advertising to disseminate its propaganda to both home and foreign audiences. At that time radio was not available for mass communication, and accordingly the chief media were pamphlets, bulletins, leaflets, newspapers, posters, and, especially in America, films and public speeches. The chief aims of such propaganda, in this as in any other war, were (1) to mobilize and direct hatred against the enemy and undermine his morale; (2) to convince the home public of the rightness of the Allied cause and increase and maintain its fighting spirit; (3) to develop the friendship of neutrals and strengthen in their minds the belief that not only were the Allies in the right but that they would in the end be victorious, and, if possible, to enlist their active support and cooperation; (4) to develop and strengthen the friendship of the nations fighting with us.

Whatever techniques were used on either side the basic idea was to build up strong in-group attitudes and feelings on our own side accompanied by opposed attitudes of hatred towards the enemy as a dangerous out-group, a mechanism which appears to be almost innate in man when faced by frustrations and anxieties. The infant experiences the satisfying breast as a 'good' object, the frustrating one as a 'bad' object, until at a later stage the good and bad aspects of the parents lead to an ambivalence where feelings of love and hate co-exist. Hence the black-white, good-bad theory, which not only leads to exaggerated hatred of the enemy but alleviates our own sense of guilt when we too behave brutally and by projection of our evil impulses on to the enemy build up our own morale and increase the sense of unity. There is nothing like a war for breaking down class and other barriers and creating feelings of friendship and cooperation within a country because all its previously inwardly-directed aggression and resentment comes to be directed against an external enemy, and it is only in the last stages of a losing effort or after a war has been won that disunity begins to show itself once more. So in the First World War the forces of patriotism prevailed even against the sentiments of international Marxism which up till then had united the proletariats of France and Germany; they prevailed too against the not inconsiderable pro-German feelings in Britain and later in the United States. The British public was unaware of its Government's commitment to come to the help of France if she were attacked, and for many years and in spite of the provocations of the Kaiser's aggressive policy since the beginning of the century many people, if not violently pro-German, were at any rate more favourably inclined to Germany than to France. There were many important British statesmen, mostly Liberals, who both loved and admired Germany and so far as the man in the street was concerned there were probably influences at work dating from the Napoleonic Wars, together with the persistent and partly racial conviction that the Germans were 'more like us' which was still being expressed by many British soldiers when the War was over. Possibly also the feelings and sentiments aroused by Queen Victoria and Albert the Prince Consort during the previous century – although these were not shared by her son Edward VII, who was a convinced Francophile – played their part. However, as it happened, the issue was solved, so far as Britain was concerned, by Germany when she invaded Belgium, thus not only breaking a long-established treaty guaranteeing Belgian neutrality but permitting herself to be presented in the light of a bullying Great Power attacking a small and relatively helpless neighbour. *Punch* expressed the opinion of the nation in general in a cartoon representing a large and threatening bully pushing aside a gate into a field defended only by a small but defiant boy, and the nation's patriotic sentiments were increased by the declaration of war and the arrival in France of the British Expeditionary Force. From this point the nations on both sides began to consolidate their internal forces – an action which was less deliberate than the coming into play of the same psychological mechanism which had already destroyed the former solidarity of the German and French proletariats; in Germany the Kaiser stated publicly that he knew no political party, and the Union Sacrée announced by the French Chamber of Deputies and Senate expressed the solidarity of all political parties and classes. In Britain too sentiments of pro-Germanism, pacifism, and the long-standing convictions of the importance of individual liberty went by the board. Everything became black or white, good or evil, with the bad out-group and the good in-group, and soon stereotypes, slogans, and atrocity stories began to make their appearance. The Germans had their stereotypes of the British as 'perfidious Albion', whose demand for the 'freedom of the seas' was merely another name for 'Britannia rule the waves', of the French as deliberately seeking revenge for their defeat in the Franco-Prussian War of 1870, and of the Russians as seeking to put into effect their doctrine of Pan-Slavism. On the other hand, the Allied stereotypes were of Germany's 'insane nationalism' and 'German militarism', the Kaiser being described as 'the mad dog of Europe'. In the early period of the war posters bore the slogan 'Your King and Country Need You' beneath the picture of a stern Kitchener pointing a finger at the observer, and at a later stage there were the demands for 'A War to End War', a war to 'Make the World Safe for Democracy', and the 'Self-Determination of Peoples'.

While there can be no doubt that the Germans in Belgium treated Belgian nationals harshly and specifically contravened the rules of international law on at least two points – the refusal to recognize the existence of a 'resistance army' and the treatment of those who did resist as free-shooters – and in addition executed large numbers of hostages, there can be little doubt in the light of subsequent knowledge that they were not guilty of the frightful atrocities attributed to them by the Allies. Tales of Germans cutting off the hands of children, boiling corpses to make soap, crucifying prisoners of war, and using priests as clappers in cathedral bells were nauseating yarns widely believed among both Allies and friendly neutrals. On the German side there were accounts of the use of dum-dum bullets, the use of guerrillas and 'savages' from Africa and Asia to fight civilized peoples, the imprisonment of civilians, and mutilations and brutality on the part of the Allied troops. Where all of these stories took their origin is not certain; some, such as that of the children's chopped-off hands, were admitted to by a British journalist after the war, the legend of the 'Angels of Mons' (not, of course, an atrocity story) came from a story by the author Arthur Machen, and some even came from attempted satires on the part of the Germans themselves. Thus the account of the priests and the bells was taken from an article in a German paper which asked in effect: 'What next will they believe of us?' But probably most arose from garbled accounts of some event with a grain of truth in it which gained in sensationalism what it lost in veracity as it passed from one individual to another. Naturally, not everyone believed these stories until the Bryce Commission, an official body, seemed to back them up when for many people they came to be accepted as indubitable truth. There are, however, deeper psychological reasons why such rumours are often accepted in wartime: (1) they are in part a projection of our own sadistic impulses, our own 'bad' selves, which serve the function of making us feel 'good' and bolstering public morale; (2) since civilized man has been brought up to feel that many of the acts associated with war, and even war itself, are evil, atrocity stories act by justifying to some extent the unpleasant things we ourselves must do; (3) the mind, as we have seen, possesses a sort of pattern so that when gaps due to lack of knowledge make their appearance the natural tendency is to fill them up (this is one of the causes of gossip and rumour quite apart from warfare), but how they are filled up will depend upon our general attitudes at the time, e.g. when our general impression of a person is unfavourable the rumours we spread about the aspects of his affairs of which we are ignorant will be unfavourable too; (4) lastly, war itself is a regression to more primitive patterns of behaviour, a revival of primitive fantasies, which soon become apparent in the behaviour of combatants and non-combatants in both the aggressive and sexual fields – in fact the civilians, who have less opportunity for an outlet in action, are usually worse than the military, and many accounts by soldiers after the First World War (e.g. Siegfried Sassoon's *Memoirs of an Infantry Officer*) express disgust at the much more overtly expressed sadism of the civilians whom they met when they came home on leave.

This propaganda was mainly intended for the consumption of the Allies and neutrals, and was spread, in the absence of radio, by the relatively primitive methods already mentioned: the press, leaflets, posters, speeches, and occasionally films. The problem remained of how suitable material could be transmitted to Germany and the other enemy countries; for although propaganda had been directed by the Allied army headquarters against enemy troops in the front line it was not until the establishment of Crewe House early in 1918 that serious attempts were made to spread it to German civilians and throughout the Austro-Hungarian Empire. These depended largely on leaflets and pamphlets carried by balloon, shells, or aircraft, in addition to the device of sending news-sheets to those in neutral countries who could be relied upon to forward them to someone in Germany. The news thus disseminated at this late stage in the war was factual, in the main truthful, and served (or so it was claimed) to create a reputation for reliability both in supplying information and refuting German accounts which were said to be untruthful. Stories, too, were supplied to the Allied or neutral press which, appearing to present an unfavourable impression of conditions in Britain, in fact revealed a state of affairs considerably better than in Germany although, as Lindley Fraser points out in his valuable book on propaganda, such a technique assumed that enemy sub-editors of newspapers were appreciably less intelligent than their readers: it would require a rather foolish sub-editor to let pass the information that British housewives were indignant at the introduction of a second meatless day if in Germany there were three or four. Lastly, as in the Second World War, secret agents actually within the enemy countries were called upon to help by distributing leaflets (often purporting to come from within Germany itself or from a neutral country), by writing slogans or attaching posters or slips of a revolutionary nature to buildings, and by spreading those demoralizing rumours to which people are much more susceptible when frustrated, perplexed, or kept in ignorance of what is actually going on.

The problem of what to say about our war aims and plans for the post-war world was initially a serious one for Crewe House since clearly milder aims are likely to be more effective than harsh ones and either than none at all. Yet the Government, pre-occupied with carrying on the war and sometimes not very clear itself in view of the conflicting aims of the Allies, was not always in a position to help. Germany, it was generally agreed, would have to return Alsace and Lorraine to France, return the annexed areas in the East to help form a new Polish state, and in addition pay severe reparations for the damage it had caused. Turkey, too, would have to give up the Arab States formerly under its domination. The Austro-Hungarian Empire was a more difficult issue since it was possible either to try to drive a wedge between Germany and Austria by placating the latter country or, on the other hand, to encourage the break-up of the Empire. This problem was finally settled by President Wilson's principle of self-determination for all nationalities which meant the Czechs, Slovaks, Poles, Rumanians, and the rest under Austrian rule.

From the point of view of the psychology of propaganda what we should like to know is whether all or any of these efforts could be described as successful. Professor Kimball Young, as an American psychologist, seems to have no doubt that they had some effect, and writes 'What George Creel called "paper bullets" may not have won the First World War, but they certainly had an important part in supporting the morale of the Allies and in breaking that of Germany.' Lindesmith and Strauss, also American social psychologists, claim as an 'outstanding example' the success of the English and American governmental propaganda campaigns in getting the United States into the First World War and indeed many Americans are still convinced that this is what really happened, although some would assert less charitably that the effort was accomplished by Britain alone with the implication that both her methods and intentions were sinister. Historians in general think otherwise, and Nye and Morpurgo (*A History of the United States*) express the commonly accepted view when they write:

> The United States entered World War I on the Allied side for a variety of reasons, but one is clear: America could not afford to do otherwise. It is true that American loans to the wartime trade with the Allies gave the nation a heavy financial interest in an Allied victory. . . . It was also true that British propaganda was singularly good and German bad, British diplomacy excellent and German inept. Yet neither loans nor propaganda nor diplomacy put the United States into war. The plain fact is that the United States realized that it could not afford to take the risk of allowing Germany to supplant Britain as the dominant force in Europe.

The British authorities did indeed carry out a systematic and intensive campaign in America initially because much American opinion was hostile, partly for traditional reasons connected with the war of Independence and partly because the British blockade of German ports caused resentment as violating the principle of the Freedom of the Seas; it would also be absurd to pretend that Britain did not want America to enter the war. But America entered the war for her own good reasons and, although both British and American propaganda may have helped to convince the isolationists and possibly to unite the nation behind the government, it certainly did not bring about American belligerence for that is not how international affairs are decided.

The atrocity stories possibly increased hatred for the Germans; but this was already being done by the Germans themselves much more effectively by their own inept behaviour in carrying on actions which, whatever immediate advantage they may have brought, antagonized the feelings of other nations and made the truth seem almost as bad as the fictions. The shelling of Louvain

Cathedral (allegedly, and quite probably, being used as a look-out post by the Allies), and the initial invasion of neutral Belgium, may have been tactically justifiable but were serious psychological blunders which made the world see Germany as a bully and a vandal; the sinking of the *Lusitania* with the loss of 12,000 men, women, and children (one hundred and fourteen of whom were Americans) and the execution of Edith Cavell were regarded almost everywhere as atrocities even if it were true that the *Lusitania* was carrying arms for the Allies and Miss Cavell could be described as an enemy agent. Further examples were the declaration of unrestricted submarine warfare and the use of poison gas, the sabotage of American war plants and espionage in the United States, together with the attempts to incite trouble in Mexico and elsewhere. These actions in America and Mexico were not, of course, atrocities but they inflamed American public opinion as much as if they had been. The German insensitivity to the psychological reactions of other nations, including the neutrals, almost certainly did more harm to her cause than any amount of Allied propaganda, although the Germans after the War continued to insist on its effectiveness in causing them to lose the struggle. It was used as a scapegoat to maintain in effect that their army had not been beaten in the field but had been let down by those behind the lines who had allowed their minds to be poisoned by British propaganda. Historically this is wholly untrue; for towards the end of the war civilian morale in Germany was almost certainly higher than that of the army, lulled as the people were by their home propaganda with its constant promises of early victory and its increasingly unjustified optimism. German propaganda as a whole was indeed ineffectual, being carried out largely by army officers of the old school who did not really believe in its value. It, too, in spite of later denials, had its atrocity stories, but its worst failing was that it allowed itself to be constantly on the defensive, expending most of its energies in announcing that Allied propaganda was both untrue and unfair and making laboured attempts to correct what were regarded as false impressions. This broke one of the first rules of the propagandist, which is that his message must always be positive, never negative. The attempt to correct 'unfair' propaganda merely has the effect of bringing the original statements back to the minds of the recipients and spreading them amongst those who might otherwise never have heard them. The worse a country's situation the stronger reason for presenting a positive suggestion of confidence and indifference to danger. Lastly, there was an important technical factor that largely nullified the effect of German propaganda to the outside world; for at an early stage in the War the British had cut the submarine cables which were Germany's only really effective means to send information overseas. Hence the main German news agency, Wolf's, was unable to communicate whereas the Allied Reuter's and Havas could do so all over the world.

In spite of all these efforts on either side to influence the result of the First World War we find it difficult to disagree with the conclusion of Lindley Fraser, a leading British authority:

Our verdict on British propaganda to Germany during the first world war must be that though it was doubtless skilfully carried out within its limits yet it did not and could not decisively affect the course of events.

The First World War with its relentless mobilization of national resources and competition over new methods of destruction was the first total war. It is possible to quote the example of the American Civil War in which the conditions were somewhat similar, but public opinion played hardly any part in the limited warfare of earlier times, fought by professional soldiers who felt little need to know why they were fighting. Modern propaganda became necessary, as Raymond Aron (*The Century of Total War*) points out, because the soldier and citizen had become the same person and the general public, believing itself to be naturally peaceable, demanded reasons from its leaders for turning soldier. To prove the enemy wholly responsible has become a sort of governmental duty and a considerable part of internal propaganda is preoccupied not with maintaining the morale of the fighting forces so much as with clearing the conscience of the whole nation. Initially the explosion of patriotic fervour in all the combatant countries created a national unity in which lesser divisions were forgotten and, for Germany, the early successes redoubled their fighting spirit whilst increasing the resolution of the British and French. But at a later stage, when the Western Front became almost stationary, resolution gave way to resignation and fervour to reluctant acceptance. In Aron's words, 'ideology usurped the place of genuine feeling'. Initially ideologies were adapted to the country behind the lines and to the enemy and neutral civilians, whilst the combatants were killing one another without contempt or hatred and even at times feeling a certain community of feeling vis-à-vis the civilians; but as the war dragged on it became necessary to stimulate the soldier's will to fight too, by the use of such grandiose and vague principles as the right of peoples to self-determination, the 'war to end war', and so on. Both sides knew (or claimed to know) what they were fighting *about* but neither said what it was fighting *for*. Nobody in 1914 had cared a whit about oppressed nationalities, ending secret diplomacy or spreading democracy, but to obtain the sympathy of the world or to keep up the morale of their own countries governments resorted to ideologies from the stage of the American intervention and the Russian Revolution onwards; the age of ideologies had begun. Furthermore, as the cost of operations mounted it was felt essential to inflate the prospective fruits of victory. Total war demanded total victory, and this, in turn, led to the Treaty of Versailles.

There were other psychological phenomena of warfare, and particularly modern total war, which marked the years of 1914–18. People, both at the commencement of the war and on the occasion of military victories, had numerous opportunities to experience the situation of being one of a crowd which (although in a more disciplined form) was the usual situation of the soldier. It was Le Bon who, in 1896, first pointed out the fact that:

Whoever be the individuals that compose it, however like or unlike be their mode of life, their occupations, their character, or their intelligence, the fact that they have been transformed into a crowd puts them into possession of a sort of collective mind which makes them think, feel, and act in a manner quite different from that in which each individual of them would think, feel, and act were he in a state of isolation.

This he explained in terms of (1) the feeling of invincible power which makes the crowd more primitive and less subject to control by conscience or fear of punishment; (2) the fact of contagion or imitation; and (3) the crowd's heightened suggestibility. Today nobody would think in terms of a 'collective mind' but rather of the anonymity of the individual when he loses himself in a crowd and the feeling of permissiveness he develops when the observed behaviour of others makes him believe that he can safely express emotions and behaviour he would ordinarily repress, but otherwise Le Bon's description still stands. The usually isolated individual enjoys the sensation of freedom from conventional restraints and the awareness of power which participation in a crowd gives him and he may express views or commit acts of which he would otherwise be ashamed. Then there is the freedom from a normal sense of guilt (or even one developed to an abnormal degree) which occurs when a nation's total guilt has been projected upon an external enemy and hate and resentments ordinarily disruptive of social unity have been similarly dealt with. Within the national boundaries everyone becomes more helpful, more tolerant, more kindly to others; conventional sexual morals crumble and the birth rate goes up as the suicide and neurosis rate goes down. The suicide is enabled to turn his would-be aggression against himself outwards and the neurotic to fit in more easily to a morally permissive society within which he is led to feel that he is doing a useful job of work. The many ordinary men and women in frustrating jobs, with no job at all, or with frustrating home situations, find a new purpose in life and possibly other work, other friends, and freedom from home ties unwillingly borne. In so far as the real facts of what is going on remain unknown or censored, rumour spreads, but to make up for that there are military bands, patriotic songs to sing, heady speeches to make one feel good, and both politicians and the clergy to assure us that we are on the right side. Although these emotions and psychological advantages wax and wane with the changing fortunes of each side it is probably true to say that they form some of the reasons why (up to the present, at any rate) many men and women unconsciously want war. There were many after the First World War who were prepared to admit that they had never found life so full and meaningful as when they were fighting against the Germans. Inhibitions and doubts were removed and the primitive passions of hate for one group and love for the other were given full expression, whilst in addition unreserved concentration on the pursuit of a single activity became possible. Identification with one great purpose swept away the everyday smallness of purpose and selfishness and enabled them to achieve a feeling of personal integration and meaningfulness unknown before. It was these phenomena which caused Freud after 1918 to postulate an instinct of innate destructiveness which he described as the 'death instinct'; in this theory he described two equally powerful instincts or drives, the one a drive towards life or Eros, the other towards irrational destructiveness and death which he described as Thanatos. If the drive to death were turned to outside objects it manifested itself as an urge to destroy whilst if it remained within the individual its aim was self-destruction. In short the theory of the death instinct asserts that we have to destroy others in order to avoid destroying ourselves. The theory, it is true, did not postulate the inevitability of war since there are many other ways of psychologically or physically destroying ourselves or others, either wholly or partially (e.g. group hatreds and prejudice, drug addictions, drink, or accident proneness), but it made Freud very doubtful of the possibility of stopping the occurrence of wars save by the use of superior force such as an armed League of Nations, in the terms employed in those days. This is a depressing theory which has not been generally accepted, yet the fact of outward aggression being turned back against the group itself when active warfare ceases or when enthusiasm turns to boredom as our own side appears to be losing explains many of the negative psychological phenomena of war: the breaking-up of national unity and the reappearance of the class-struggle, the splitting up of former groups of allies, and the return of the sense of guilt in relation to the conduct of the war, are all post-war results which we have observed twice in a generation.

The conclusions drawn from the experience of the First World War were that, although in 1918 more than 2,000 propaganda balloons each carrying 1,000 leaflets were released every week and throughout October of the same year no less than 5,360,000 leaflets were dropped on Germany, their combined effect was relatively slight and civilian morale corresponded a good deal more closely to military successes and failures or the stress of the food shortage than to any effort of the propagandists. It was demonstrated too that lying propaganda in the long run defeats its own end for, even if the majority of the public are temporarily taken in, the minority who are not will from then on be hostile and mistrustful, and the more lies are told the greater will this minority become. Thus, with the advent of radio, the policy of the BBC during the Second World War was based on the fundamental principles of truth and consistency; in other words, as Lindley Fraser puts it:

Do not say anything which you do not believe to correspond with the facts as known to you; and secondly, do not say anything to one country, or audience, which is or looks inconsistent with what you are saying to any other country or audience.

These principles, as he points out, were not smug or hypocritical but had been forced upon us by past experience in the First World War. The BBC, in face of the immense barrage of propaganda put out by the Fascist countries, had come late into the struggle so far as the period between the wars was concerned and its first effort was a service in Arabic for defeating the anti-British propaganda sent out by the Fascists to the Middle East and North Africa. Later in the same year, services in Spanish and Portuguese for Latin American listeners were followed by French, German, and Italian ones for Europe. Only by 1941 or 1942 did the British foreign radio services become a real force for the enemy to combat. It was potentially all the more formidable in that, unlike the conditions in the First World War, the enemy had been shut off almost entirely from truthful information for years before the war began and propaganda was therefore likely to make a correspondingly powerful impact. The information was not, of course, spread in an entirely unbiased way; for example although no attempt was made to belittle disasters, it was pointed out what losses the enemy had sustained in bringing them about and emphasized that, no matter how long it took, the war would go on until victory was achieved, with consequent losses which would be the greater on both sides. This ran counter to German home propaganda which had committed itself, not only to victory, but to one which would come in a short time and with every year that went by the hollowness of this promise became more evident. Finally, as in the First World War, only much more so, the Germans had engaged in actions which horrified the whole free world and caused it to feel 'that profound and icy mistrust which the German arouses whenever he gets power in his hands', which Nietzsche had described as 'the aftermath of that vast and horrible fear with which for long centuries Europe dreaded the wrath of the Teutonic blond beast'.

The Overseas News Department of the BBC in its attempt to ensure consistency even avoided so far as possible those two tricks of the propagandist which, although not necessarily involving the telling of downright lies, are capable of implying them: selection of news and the increasing or decreasing the apparent significance of events in accordance with one's own bias. All news bulletins were centrally prepared and checked, so that without necessarily being the same (the Italians for example would naturally be given more news about what was happening in North Africa than in occupied Norway) propaganda bias was avoided. Mistakes, of course, sometimes arose when misleading information came in from the Service Departments, but when they were discovered they were corrected as soon as possible. Within these boundaries it was hoped to depress the enemy, divide the enemy powers against each other, and cheer friends. During the early months of the war the tendency existed to make a distinction between the Nazis and the military on the one hand and the German people on the other under the slogan 'Peace with the German people, certainly; peace with the Nazis, never', but it was soon realized that the opposition in Germany was a small and powerless minority, and from then on a more aggressive policy was adopted. Not that the news bulletins were exciting or amusing – quite the contrary; but this general soberness of tone was found to be more impressive in its impassivity to those already deafened and distrustful from their own propaganda.

On the other hand, the BBC counter-propaganda activities were of a quite different nature from its news bulletins. In this the Nazi and Fascist leaders were satirized and jokes were made about their eccentricities, exaggerations, and broken promises. Records of their speeches showing up inconsistencies were re-broadcast from records in the BBC record library, and so on. Care was taken that, whilst broadcasts to occupied France were made by Frenchmen, political comment in the German service was as far as possible delivered by British subjects in order to avoid the accusation (as happened in the German use of such men as 'Lord Haw-Haw') that the information was untrustworthy as being presented by a traitor and possibly a Jew. In dealing with the other enemy countries such as Italy, Bulgaria, Hungary, and Rumania the assumption was made that the people had no great liking for the war and were only being led into unnecessary sacrifice by the Fascist ruling cliques; they were encouraged to believe (as was indeed the case) that the Germans despised them and were using them for their own purposes. How effective British radio propaganda was it is impossible to say; it is however known that many millions in occupied Europe and Germany listened to it, and that the Germans attempted to jam its transmissions. Lindley Fraser sums up thus: (1) the Reich Propaganda Ministry exaggerated its efficiency partly because of Hitler's declared belief in propaganda and partly because of the apparent success of Nazi propaganda for home consumption; (2) BBC propaganda in the long run doubtless did much to alter the feelings of the average German listener but nothing whatever to alter his behaviour; (3) once again, as in the First World War, British counter-propaganda was successful in showing up German propaganda – but less because of its own virtues than by the mistakes of its opponents. The two cardinal mistakes made by the Germans were the same as in 1914–18 – first, they antagonized the rest of the world by the brutality of their actual behaviour, and secondly they allowed their own propaganda to be constantly on the defensive. Thus the BBC commentators were frequently attacked by name showing that attention was being paid to what they said and this goes against the fundamental principle that propaganda should be constantly on the attack and present its own side of the question exclusively. As we have seen, attacking statements made by the enemy, unless one is in a position of great strength, only serves to draw attention to these statements, and creates the impression that 'there is no smoke without fire'. The only other occasion when one is justified in assuming the defensive position is when the enemy's attack is so crushing that on the whole an answer may do more good than harm, because the battle is as good as lost. The Propaganda Ministry under Goebbels only learned these lessons when it was too late. Once again, it is evident that the effect of propaganda on the enemy was less important than the influence of military successes or failures and other circumstances on the home front. Nor did British propaganda succeed in causing uprisings amongst Germany's unwilling allies, although it undoubtedly played an important part in correlating the efforts of the resistance movements in occupied countries and in bolstering up their morale.

By 1942, the BBC was joined by the American propaganda machine which initially worked from New York and San Francisco. But in 1944 the new A.B.S.I.E. (American Broadcasting Station in Europe) was set up in London which relayed the 'Voice of America' programmes from the States and contributed some material of its own. Later, with the invasions first of North Africa and then in Normandy, a joint Psychological Warfare Board manned by civilians, but directly responsible to Supreme Allied Headquarters under General Eisenhower, was set up and the use of leaflets began once again, with more effective results (after the establishment of a front line) than hitherto. It will be remembered that, especially during the early months of the war, leaflets or pamphlets were scattered over enemy territory by aircraft and balloons but it is more than doubtful whether these had any useful effect, their obvious defects being that few can have reached their targets and, being printed, they were sometimes out of date by the time they were ready to distribute. The front-line distribution of leaflets was quite another matter and these were dropped by aircraft or fired by shells, the messages they bore being less careful about the general principles of consistency and frankness and only truthful about matters on which the enemy had contradictory information. It was suggested that the war was being lost by the Germans and their allies, that in any case the present campaign could only result in either death or surrender, that local commanders were incompetent and cowardly, that it was not dishonourable to surrender under hopeless conditions, and finally that those giving themselves up would be well-treated according to the rights of the Geneva Conventions. The latter statement was to counter enemy threats to would-be deserters that the British and Americans treated their prisoners badly. A type of leaflet in common use took the form of a 'free pass through the Allied lines', which, although it can have made little difference to the way a prisoner-of-war was received, was nevertheless frequently used by deserters. Loud-speakers and public-address systems were also employed, telling how the enemy could surrender himself with least risk, and captured German soldiers would often add to their message by telling why they did not regret having surrendered. There is, of course, no means whereby one can assess accurately how many men were induced to desert by these means since there was no method of telling exactly why any given individual deserted, but it would appear that in the Italian and North African campaigns the numbers must have mounted into many thousands, especially when the enemy had his back to the wall and his morale was already shaken. For this reason the Germans made little use of leaflets and printed material, because in the early months of the war their blitzkrieg methods were so successful as to make them unnecessary whilst, after the invasions of North Africa and Europe, the Allies were continually on the offensive and there is little to be gained by distributing surrender leaflets to an advancing army with high morale. The ineptitude of the German approach to the problem is shown in an example quoted by Fraser, in which a German officer in command of a sector of the front in Italy who had been attacked with personal allegations in leaflets dropped to his men written, of course, in German, replied by dropping leaflets in English on the Allied lines denying the allegations. It does not seem to have occurred to him that the only people to whom the allegations could have mattered were his own men and that, in replying to them in leaflets designed for the British forces, he was only spreading a rumour about which they could not possibly have known anything until he chose to inform them.

Finally, both the Germans and the Allies made use of 'black' propaganda during the Second World War – that is to say, propaganda which tried to conceal its own source. During the early months of the war the Nazis possessed at least three radio stations which sought to give the impression that they were situated somewhere in Britain. None of these stations reached large audiences and they could be on the air only for a few hours a day so it cannot be supposed that they had much effect. One, entitled Radio Caledonia, was allegedly the voice of Scottish Nationalism speaking against England, another known as the Workers' Challenge Station put forward unorthodox left-wing views, and a third, the New British Broadcasting station, gave news bulletins and comments in the style of the BBC but with a concealed pro-German bias. During the first nine months of the war there were also secret stations directed at France which may have been more successful. The Allies do not seem to have employed 'black' radio until the later part of the war when Soldatsender Calais (later Soldatsender West) made its appearance, purporting to be run by German soldiers for those on the Western Front. At the same time leaflets in the form of newspapers were dropped over the German lines similarly purporting to be by Germans for Germans. These broadcasts and leaflets were not bound by the usual rules of honesty and consistency kept to by the news transmissions of the European Services of the BBC, and had, in addition to this advantage, the fact that those Germans caught listening to them could readily plead ignorance of their source. Of course, as Sefton Delmer, who was given the assignment of forming the 'black' radio section, notes in his book *Black Boomerang*, the assumption upon which this kind of activity was based was that in a totalitarian society subversion is best spread through a simulated official source, so to that extent it is not propaganda in the ordinary sense at all. If the Germans accepted opinions and orders in the belief that they came from official sources, they were merely carrying on their former behaviour of obeying those they believed to be their leaders.

Thus 'official' stations sent out confusing messages to U-boat crews and the Wehrmacht forces in Western Europe and, towards the end of the war, Delmer was able to take over with a powerful medium-wave transmitter whole sections of the Nazi official radio and issue fake orders which resulted in thousands of refugees jamming the roads of Germany. In addition to the leaflets, faked ration cards were dropped by the R A F and many other ingenious devices were employed. Apart from the 'official' stations, there was a professed 'underground' station which, in line with the tactics of the more conventional propagandist, played on the average German's right-wing patriotism by in effect claiming to show that, although there was nothing wrong with Germany's goals, the Nazis were not the right people to achieve them. This, as we have seen, is the old technique of playing along with existing attitudes whilst subtly re-directing them, and the station featured *der Chef*, an ultra-patriotic, ranting, foul-mouthed militarist of the old school who denounced the Nazis as opportunist Bolshevik scum. Middle-level Nazi officials were covered with abuse and invented defamatory detail, notably sexual perversion, while neutral businessmen believed to be trading with the enemy had the real or imaginary details of their private and commercial lives 'revealed' over the radio. Latterly these methods brought chaos to large areas of the country and millions no longer knew whether the orders they obeyed came from Goebbels or British propaganda. But, in spite of these successes, Delmer makes no extreme claims and always took the view that his activities were purely ancillary to military operations.

Many of the enemy broadcasts to the soldiers of the Allied forces made use of the attractions of sex or musical entertainment as bait to draw attention to their propaganda message. Thus the Japanese attempted to gain the interest of American soldiers by printing pornographic pictures on one side of the leaflets they distributed and confining the propaganda appeal to the other side. The Germans made a similar use of sex which was sometimes tied directly to the theme of the message, one leaflet showing a semi-undressed woman being caressed by an American soldier with a warning to the British soldier fighting on the Continent that the Americans stationed in England were seducing wives and sweethearts while the British were being killed in France. Similarly, 'Tokyo Rose' on the Japanese fronts tried to produce some effect by making jokes and *double-entendres* about sex and giving quite good imitations of American forms of entertainment. At one time or another all the Axis powers attempted to copy radio practice in the United States, inserting their propaganda into musical programmes like a commercial plug. Another attempt to attract attention used by both sides was the broadcasting of the names of captured prisoners, soldiers found dead on the battlefield, or sailors whose bodies had been washed ashore; these were often inserted into news broadcasts or propaganda talks and proved, it is hardly necessary to say, highly effective in drawing listeners. During 1942, for instance, when the Americans were eager for any piece of news, Radio Tokyo was employing this device with the result that listeners on the West coast of America whose hobby was short-wave radio reception were turning their hobby to gain by offering to supply families with news after payment of a fee. Finally the government authorities were compelled to put a stop to this practice and instead telegraphed excerpts from the broadcasts to the families concerned with the warning that the source was the enemy radio. According to Doob, the American and British operators of Radio Luxembourg after that station had fallen into Allied hands began a programme entitled 'Letters Which You Do Not Receive' in which a sentimental female voice, giving names, read out excerpts from love letters found on the bodies of German soldiers killed in battle. Apparently, however, this programme was rather rapidly abandoned in the interests of good taste.

The main difference between propaganda during the Second World War and that of 1914–18 was, of course, the ability to make use of radio. But, even so, the technical difficulties were considerable because, although theoretically radio waves show no respect for national boundaries or fortifications, reception from particular areas even under ideal weather and atmospheric conditions was often difficult and sometimes unintelligible. Particularly was this the case with the Americans, whose broadcasts to the Orient had to be made on one wave-length during one half of the year and on another during the remainder. Even when the waves reached their target the audience might be prevented in various ways from listening to their message; listening to enemy broadcasts was a capital offence in Germany and many German and Japanese sets were only capable of receiving local broadcasts; the waves might be jammed; and in the Soviet Union sets were confiscated at the outbreak of the war and replaced by instruments capable of receiving only 'wired broadcasts' transmitted over telephone lines by the official Soviet stations. Leaflets too, except when directed against front-line troops, are a very uncertain mode of delivery. The main point of the present chapter, however, must be that, by and large, propaganda is successful only when directed at those who are willing to listen, absorb the information, and if possible act on it, and this happens only when the other side is in a condition of lowered morale and is already losing the campaign. So far as the soldier is concerned, political propaganda is a waste of time since, as Edward Shils and Morris Janowitz have shown of the German Army, soldiers are held together less by any political dogma than by the tightly knit arrangement of loyalty to their own primary groups. Under ordinary conditions, few could be persuaded to surrender because each man was integrated into a primary group whose members depended upon each other for friendship and the other sentiments that maintain morale. Those who deserted under such conditions were socially isolated men who had not achieved integration within the group. Allied front-line propaganda became more effective when it later abandoned the political emphasis and began to stress such themes as individual or group survival and the hopeless position of some of the troops. Pressure was put upon the primary group in such propaganda, and the message of the leaflets was such as to cause the men to begin talking to each other about their poor military position, their desire to stay alive for their families' sakes, and the reasonableness of honourable surrender. It is the primary group which cements opinions and attitudes and it is therefore this centre which can most effectively be attacked; hence all revolutionary movements have been anti-family. But, by and large, our conclusion must be that actions speak louder than words, the actual strategic position of the enemy being more important in determining his attitudes than any amount of propaganda; for the mind itself is a filter which permits passage only to those messages for which it is prepared unless reality is so pressing as to overwhelm it completely. In addition, it is a coloured filter, which not only subtracts but, especially when ignorance exists about the real state of affairs, adds to and colours with its own particular spectrum whatever scraps of information are available. War propaganda can often change attitudes but, unless the real situation is catastrophic, it rarely changes behaviour; and propaganda which does not lead to action has very largely failed.

CHAPTER 5

POLITICAL PROPAGANDA

POLITICS is clearly one of the fields in which propaganda plays a large part and if we want to see it at work the obvious place to look is in parts of the world where political change has been revolutionary. Of course the term 'revolutionary' is rather a vague one which has been used in at least three different ways all of which, however, imply that change has been rapid and, if not necessarily violent, at any rate accompanied by a considerable disruption of the previously existing form of society. There is the type of revolution in which there is a sudden political shift in the locus of sovereignty, such as the French and Russian revolutions; the type in which an abrupt cultural change takes place as in the Protestant Reformation; and the type where there is a change in the whole social order in its fundamental institutions, classes, and the entire set of attitudes and habits of a people caused largely by technical innovations as in the so-called Industrial Revolution. Marxists assume that all revolutions, and indeed all social change, are brought about by alterations in the economic relationships within a society, and to them revolution always comes from below, anything else being by definition 'counter-revolution'. Thus in their eyes the Russian revolution is properly so described since it was a revolution of the downtrodden proletariat whereas the Nazi and Fascist ones were counter-revolutions staged against the rising proletariat by a dying capitalism.

Here we are concerned with the sudden uprising, whether it be counter-revolutionary or not, since obviously there can be revolutions by the privileged as well as by the under-privileged. Both the Industrial Revolution and the land enclosures in six-teenth and seventeenth-century England were brought about by the rich. In the latter the woollen industry became prosperous and grazing more valuable than growing crops with the result that the landowners drove off their tenants and enclosed their common land thus bringing about profound changes in the social and economic structure of the country. These, however, were not in the narrower sense political movements, and so we shall not be concerned with them although it is often difficult (as in the case of Zionism) to know where to draw the line; Zionism had all the three characteristics of political revolutions: leaders (who are often not professional politicians), discontented masses of people, and a propaganda machine which, or so it seems, helped to tip the balance in one direction or the other. Propaganda seems to exert more influence in the political uprising than in any other field; hence the need to study this type of revolution further.

Contrary to the beliefs of Marxist determinism it would seem to be the case that, when people are ready for a mass movement, they are often ready for any movement which seems likely to prove effective and not solely for one which adheres to a particular doctrine or programme. Thus in Germany before Hitler it was often in the balance whether the restless youth of the nation would join the Communists or the Nazis; and in the conditions of Tsarist Russia Jewish youth was ripe either for Communist revolution or for Zionism. Dr Chaim Weizmann in his autobiography *Trial and Error* quotes a saying of his mother in those days: 'Whatever happens, I shall be well off. If Shemuel [the revolutionary son] is right, we shall all be happy in Russia; and if Chaim [the Zionist] is right, then I shall go to live in Palestine.' Communism and Fascism or Nazism although poles apart in their intellectual content are similar in this, that both have emotional appeal to the type of personality that takes pleasure in being submerged in a mass movement and submitting to superior authority. Hence Hitler could say: 'The *petit bourgeois* Social Democrat and the trade-union boss will never make a National Socialist, but the Communist always will.' And Roehm, one of his henchmen, could boast that he was able to turn the reddest Communist into a Nazi within four weeks. At the same time, F. A. Voigt notes that the Communist Karl Radek regarded the Nazi Brown Shirts of the S.A. as a reserve for future Communist recruits. It has often been pointed out that the evangelical campaigns of the Wesleys saved Britain from the revolutionary movements which affected almost every other country in Europe at that time, and in fact the early organization of the Methodist Church had many of the characteristics of a revolutionary movement. It would seem to follow (a) that all mass movements draw their adherents from the same types of humanity and appeal to the same types of mind; (b) that such movements are often competitive so that a gain of adherents in one is a loss to all the others; and (c) that all mass movements are interchangeable and one readily transforms itself into any other. A religious movement may develop into a social revolution or a nationalist movement; a social revolution into militant nationalism or a religious movement; a nationalist movement into a social revolution or a religious movement. Thus Islam, beginning as a religious movement, becomes a social and ultimately a nationalist one, Kemal's social revolution becomes a nationalist movement in Turkey, and England's would-be social revolution becomes transformed by Wesley's Methodism. Since a political mass movement has to compete with other demands for loyalty, it is initially against both religion and the family, as the two social bodies which attract the most deep-rooted emotions. Therefore the Nazis, the Turkish Nationalists, the revolutionaries in France, and the Russian and Chinese Communists are or were anti-religious or attempted to substitute for the original religion one of their own. The Nazis and the Communists created their own saints, their own rituals, their categories of official books and censored ones, their own code of conduct, their hymns and songs, and the French Revolution initiated a whole new religion which had its altars set up throughout the country with the inscription: 'The citizen is born, lives, and dies for the Fatherland.' The Russian Communists are concerned to reinterpret their canonical books as circumstances change, and even to re-write history every few years; but of this more will be said later. In the early years of the revolution, the family is attacked and informing against relations is encouraged until the loyalty of all citizens can be counted upon: at this point the attack diminishes – a sure sign that the revolution is past its peak.

Revolutionary fervour which brings about mass movements is an interesting phenomenon and to suppose that it is brought about by miserable conditions alone is far too simple a view, since, if this were the case, we should have social revolutions over the greater part of the earth. Misery does not automatically create discontent, nor is the degree of discontent proportionate to the degree of misery – on the contrary, discontent is the greater when conditions have improved for the originally rejected members of the population or when they have worsened for the better-off. Paradoxically, the more attainable the goal, the greater the dissatisfaction at not having reached it or at having fallen away from it. Alexis de Tocqueville in his study of France before the Revolution noted that the condition of the common people had never improved more rapidly than in the twenty years before the cataclysm and yet 'the French found their position the more intolerable the better it became'. It is not the very poor who have become inured to their condition or even the respectable poor of long standing who complain, but rather the 'new poor' who have bettered their condition or suddenly worsened it who make revolutions. Hence it was the rising middle class who made the French Revolution, and the depressed gentry with the formerly well-to-do peasants who had been dispossessed of their lands by the enclosures in England and transformed into city wage-workers who furnished the recruits for Cromwell's new army. Abject poverty, therefore, or a completely crushed spirit, brings about no revolutions. Again, in a society with the institution of slavery the trouble-makers are the newly-enslaved and the freed slaves. Nor is the contented person a revolutionary. The religious man satisfied in his beliefs, the skilled craftsman with creative work, the average member of the middle groups of the population at the present day, or even the physically and mentally healthy individual does not begin the trouble.

Revolutionary leaders belong to the categories of the rejected, the minority group, the social misfits, the mentally unbalanced, the power-seeking (to compensate for feelings of inadequacy), the jealous lower middle class, the discontented ex-serviceman, and the self-centred who have lost faith in themselves. For these, a rising mass movement has attractions, not by reason of its doctrine alone, but because it can cure their frustrations by freeing them from their ineffectual selves and submerging them in a closely knit and confident corporate whole. Such people may speak in the name of liberty but what really motivates them is their 'fear of freedom' as Erich Fromm describes it. Poor physical health often acts in the same way, and Emerson (or was it Carlyle?) has written to the general effect that the man who has some ailment to irk his bowels sets out to change the world. Hitler, Napoleon, and Stalin (who always described himself as 'an Asiatic') were all citizens of countries other than the one which they finally came to lead, most of them were small in stature, and most of them came from moderately poor 'fringe' families. Above all, none of them were professional politicians; for to the revolutionary political experience is a handicap. He must have an extravagant belief in the possibilities of the future and it is better that he should be totally ignorant of the great difficulties he will have to face. The experienced politician, like Von Papen in Germany, comes in when the movement is already a going concern and when a revolution begins to attract people of this type it has become conservative and seeks to preserve what has been achieved rather than to create something new. According to the expert Hitler:

The more posts and offices a movement has to hand out, the more inferior stuff it will attract, and in the end these political hangers-on overwhelm a successful party in such number that the honest fighter of former days no longer recognizes the old movement. When this happens, the mission of such a movement is done for.

In his imperious demand for self-expression, the leader, like the populace, may be polymorphous in his search for a cause; Mussolini tries Socialism before he becomes a Fascist, and the pathetic traitor William Joyce turns to the Nazis because, as Rebecca West points out, 'it was his love of England, slanting across time, which made him a Fascist'. Applying for entry into the London University O.T.C., Joyce once wrote (and there is no reason to doubt his sincerity): 'As a young man of pure British descent, some of whose forefathers have held high position in the British army, I have always been desirous of devoting what little capability and energy I may possess to the country which I love so dearly.' The conversion of Paul, so far from being unusual, is a common pattern amongst would-be revolutionaries.

It is not only revolutionaries but politicians in general whose personalities and motives are worthy of further study; as Harold Lasswell remarks in his *Psychopathology and Politics*, the only book known to the writer which actually documents the concealed motives of (anonymous) American politicians: 'Our conventional schemes of "political motivation" seem curiously aloof from the manifold reality of human life when we discover the private basis of public acts.' It is not enough to know that Rousseau suffered from paranoia, that Napoleon had partly atrophied sex-organs, that Alexander, Caesar, and Blücher were alcoholics, that Calvin was plagued by eczema, migraine, and kidney-stones, that Bismarck was hysterical, Lincoln a depressive, and Marat a sufferer from arthritis, diabetes, and eczema; we want to know what specific psychological motivations brought them to choose the particular field of politics. As Alex Comfort has shown in his book *Authority and Delinquency in the Modern State*, power-loving and delinquency are closely related:

The chief factor which makes any overt act 'delinquent' is the assertion in it of the right of the actor to behave without regard for others. He may do so by burglary or murder and take the consequences or he may find a place in the social pattern which licenses him, within certain limits, to make his assertion unchallenged. The opportunities for this kind of accepted and acceptable delinquency lie almost entirely within the pattern of power.

People have an unfortunate tendency to select those positions for which they are objectively least suited, and of delinquency amongst those whose job it is to enforce the law H. von Hentig says that:

... the police force and the ranks of prison officers attract many aberrant characters because they afford legal channels for pain-inflicting, power-wielding behaviour, and because these very positions confer upon their holders a large degree of immunity. Yet these are only the crassest instances, those which cannot be smoothly concealed behind the screen of means justified by the end.

The private motives of those who occupy positions of power of which they may themselves be unaware, are a legitimate object of study to which sufficient attention has not as yet been given. Nevertheless, it would be wrong to think that leaders of any kind either become leaders solely because of their own personal traits, or, as the Marxists would have it, are purely the result of historical circumstances. Obviously the men who ruled Germany during the Nazi period were driven towards politics by their personal peculiarities; Hitler had, indeed, almost all the above-noted qualities of the man who, by reason of his weaknesses, is motivated to impress himself upon his society. He was an Austrian not a German, of humble but not working-class origin, an ex-soldier with a chip on his shoulder, hysterical, a paranoiac, and above all a failed artist. Also failed creative artists were Goebbels (the drama, the novel, and poetry), Rosenberg (architecture and philosophy), von Schirach (poetry), Funk (music), and Streicher (painting). Peter Viereck observes that '. . . almost all were failures, not only by the usual vulgar criterion of success, but by their own artistic criteria'. Their artistic and literary ambitions 'were originally far deeper than political ambitions: and were integral parts of their personalities'. It might truly be said that in his nuclear personality Hitler was the epitome of those attitudes which existed in the peripheral personalities of Germans as a result of the situation in which they found themselves after the First World War; he was by nature what they had become by circumstance and the group invariably selects, not the leader who is theoretically best suited to deal with its problems in a practical way, but the one who most closely mirrors its own feelings of the moment. A sick group chooses a sick leader. Hence Hitler's traits could not have made of him a leader in any situation but only in that particular situation and he made Germany into a Nazi state primarily because many Germans were willing to support him and eager to join his party. Without the latent and enduring public opinion that existed in Germany he could not have been successful so to that extent he was the creation of circumstances, but without him and his organization German public opinion on national and international issues might have changed quite differently, moving, for example, towards Communism. That Hitler succeeded rather than the Communists was due to his intuitive understanding of what the German people really felt and therefore he was able through his propaganda machine to tell them what they wanted to hear.*

One of the weaknesses of the democracies is their failure to understand, as Hitler did, some of the less rational facets of human nature. It is assumed that most people want political doctrines explained to them rationally, that they cannot stand being bamboozled, that they prefer an easy life to a hard one, and that they inevitably prefer pleasure to pain, love to hate. This may be true under ideal conditions, but in the circumstances of 'quiet frustration' in which most lives are lived it is not true at all. In the first place, frustrated people are more credulous than those who are not frustrated; 'one is well-minded to understand Holy Writ when one hates oneself' said Pascal, and during the period before Hitler came into power Stresemann said of the Germans: 'They pray not only for their daily bread, but also for their daily illusion.' An effective doctrine is not one which is rationally understandable (for even Lenin did not obtain power by appealing to dialectical materialism but by his impassioned oratory); rather is it, as Pascal said of effective religion, 'contrary to nature, to common sense, and to pleasure'. Communists distinguish between propaganda and agitation, a distinction based on the definition of Plekhanov that 'a propagandist presents many ideas to one or a few persons; an agitator presents only one or a few ideas, but presents them to a mass of people'. Lenin accepted this view and takes as an example the treatment of unemployment. A propagandist would explain this in terms of Communist economic theory – that it arises as a result of the recurrent crises which are inevitable under the capitalist system, the causes of which he would then go on to explain. The agitator, on the other hand, would choose some easily comprehended and emotional fact – e.g. that an unemployed worker's family had died of starvation – and work upon the feelings of the masses. Lenin appealed to the Russian crowds as an agitator, not (in terms of the above definition) as a propagandist.

* The potency of Hitler's propaganda, however, has been grossly exaggerated. Democracy had failed, and the only real choice open to the Germans was between Communism and the Nazis. In a situation in which nationalist feelings had been vastly intensified by the Treaty of Versailles Communist internationalism had little chance of success.

Secondly, frustrated people want to suffer and sacrifice themselves to the cause; hence they respond, not to promises of an easy victory, but, as Churchill understood and Chamberlain did not, to promises of 'blood, sweat, and tears'. Having submerged their hated individuality in the crowd, they cling on to certitude for dear life, even to the extent of giving up their lives to demonstrate to others their role of defender of the holy cause. They no longer care, as once they did, for the opinions of others outside the cause; in fact, they positively desire enmity, since it confirms the correctness of their beliefs. Hitler said that the National Socialist should seek and deserve the violent hatred of his enemies. The promise of self-sacrifice in the name of a cause draws more from people than all the promises of ease and comfort.

Thirdly, apart from their natural credulity, frustrated people enjoy being bamboozled; like Tertullian they account it a virtue to believe 'because it is impossible', and one recollects how Goebbels would frequently interject during his speeches in which he was making the most incredible claims: 'Of course, this is all propaganda!'

Finally, frustrated people need to hate because hatred when shared with others is the most potent of all unifying emotions; as Heine wrote: 'What Christian love cannot do is effected by a common hatred.' Psychologically speaking, what happens is that, when an individual is frustrated in his attempt to reach a goal, aggression naturally arises, probably with the original function of massing all his energies to overcome the obstacle. But when this cannot be done, the aggression must be turned in one or both of two directions: inwardly against the self, or outwardly against a substitute object. Hence the frustrated person both hates himself and has the latent tendency to find external objects for his hatred, joining in comradeship with those who share his views. Anger is the great solvent of depression (which is self-hatred). Frustration also leads to regression – that is, to a reversion to more primitive behaviour and less constructive actions, as is seen in the frustrated individual's already-noted ready acceptance of absurd statements. All this Hitler intuitively understood, whilst his Communist opponents did not, and these were the foundations upon which his propaganda was based.

But, since the results of propaganda depend upon the nature of the target towards which it is directed as much as upon the power of the propagandist himself, it is necessary to consider the more fundamental reasons why the Germans proved a peculiarly suitable target for Hitler's propaganda. For it is impossible not to see that Fascism in other countries did not, apart from its right-wing nationalism and general economic structure, show at all the same characteristics as German Fascism so far as its psychological aspects were concerned. It is true that Mussolini glorified war and used much the same type of slogans as the Nazis ('The Duce is always right'), but the Italian people had enough innate cynicism not to take them too seriously, and, apart from professional politicians, the freedom to express unorthodox views in conversation was never so completely suppressed in Italy as in Germany. Anti-semitism was not a natural growth in Italy but one forced upon her during the course of the Second World War by the Germans which was never accepted in its doctrinaire forms by the bulk of the people. In Britain the leader of the Fascist party showed himself true to type by shifting from one party to another before plumping for Fascism, and his followers were an assorted group of cheerfully brutal types, psychopaths, renegade Tories, and eccentric members of the minor aristocracy or from the armed services retired list. This last is a body which can always be relied upon to produce a rich crop of oddities with the tendency, as Rebecca West says of one particular British Fascist, to be foredoomed to follow strange by-paths so that a variation in circumstances would have found them just as happily spiritualist mediums or believers in the lost ten tribes of Israel. But the German Nazis were imbued with traits which arose, not from their military defeat and economic collapse alone, but from that peculiar German national character which alienated it from the West from 1806 to 1945. This character had been basically authoritarian, not merely in the form of its government but throughout the whole social structure from the family up; Prussian society in particular had always been founded on a kind of 'pecking order' such that the reward for being pecked by someone more powerful was to peck in turn someone who was weaker. The years of the Weimar Constitution which followed the revolution of 1918 were for most Germans years of frustration, during which, used to commands from above and respect for authority, they found democracy all confusion and chaos. They were, says Theodore Abel, shocked to realize 'that they had to participate in government, choose a party, and pass judgement upon political matters'. The basic personality traits of the average German have tended to be those described by the psychiatrist as obsessional ones, the obsessional character (based, according to Freud, upon a stringent upbringing in relation to bowel training) being deeply concerned with such supposed virtues as obedience, cleanliness, punctuality, efficiency, and hard work. Freud's thesis would appear to receive some support from the correlation in the German character between these traits, and an even more overt obsession with bowel movements such as is found, for example, in Martin Luther to a pathological degree, and the national tendency towards jokes which are about the lavatory rather than, as with other nations, about the relations between the sexes. The obsessional virtues are not such as would be regarded by the rest of the world as unconditional ones, as they are in Germany; obedience and efficiency, for example, would be regarded as good or bad according to the ends towards which they were directed. But Germans have commonly regarded them as ends in themselves, as when those who had committed particularly horrible acts during the Second World War were genuinely surprised when they were asked whether they accepted personal responsibility for them, believing that the fact that they had been ordered to do them by higher authority was sufficient reason in itself for carrying them out. Again, most other nations have been guilty at one time or another of mass murder, but it is difficult to conceive of anyone but the Germans solemnly arranging for the processing of the pathetic remains (hair, tooth fillings, clothes, etc.) with such ghastly efficiency and industry. Lastly there is the truly appalling ability for self-pity which goes with a total inability on the part of the German to put himself in the place of another. Indeed, this has been one of the fundamental reasons for the almost complete failure of German propaganda either in war or peace to impress anyone outside Germany – the propagandists were quite unable to put themselves inside someone else's skin and, in spite of Hitler's dictum about being indifferent to the hatred of the enemy, nothing could be more typical than their constant wasting of valuable time by being so touchy as to be unable to resist the temptation to reply thereby spreading the enemy's propaganda to an even larger audience.

Hitler traded on all these characteristics; he reassured the nation that the War had not been lost by the army but by a stab in the back from Jews and Communists thus giving back a measure of self-respect and reassurance; he played on the theme that everybody had been unfair to Germany. The British had continued the hunger blockade for months after the armistice, the Versailles Treaty was grossly unjust and a breach of American promises, the German colonies had been stolen, and Germany was encircled by enemies. Then there was the appeal to national arrogance which, whilst assuring the Germans that their achievements were unsurpassed by those of any other nation in the world, affirmed that for this very reason they were the object of jealousy on the part of the British, French, and Slavs. Furthermore, the National Socialist Party claimed to be the party of the little man and upheld the claims of the shopkeeper, small trader, and craftsman against those of big business or 'monopoly capitalism'; it demanded the destruction of the 'bondage of interest' and stood for relieving these members of the population from their debts to banks and other moneylending people or institutions. Thus it appealed to individual greed, although when it obtained power the big monopolies were to become more powerful than ever under National Socialist bosses. More concretely, it cured unemployment by absorbing the unemployed into the new armaments industry and those who were not so absorbed were employed in the clearing of land, building of cities, or even mere marching; for as Hermann Rauschning remarked: 'Marching diverts men's thoughts. Marching kills thought. Marching makes an end of individuality.'

The youth of the nation was especially drawn into the movement, fitted into uniforms, and taught the new ideology such as it was. For it must be remembered that Fascism, being a revolution of nihilism, has really no ideology in the sense that Communism has. It upholds the power of the nation, rewrites the history school-books to show its greatness, and remodels science into a preposterous fandango of nonsense to demonstrate the superiority of the supposed national type of man (in the case of the Germans the 'Aryan' type); it has countless enemies and is against many things but, concretely, it is *for* nothing. Books and other art forms were censored, but, again unlike the Communists, there was little positive use made of films and plays to state the Party's point of view because, apart from conquest, it had none. Nor did Hitler make the Germans anti-semitic because like many other nations they were so already; but, as has often happened before, he used the Jews as his nation's particular scapegoat with unspeakable consequences to the Jewish people and the self-respect of all other Europeans. The national pleasure in submission to authority and in military or paramilitary spectacles was satisfied by giant rallies, marching, and torch-light processions (even today the torch-light procession is peculiar to Germany), and none of those who recall, either from actual experience or in radio broadcasts, the frenzied voice of the Führer and the barbaric chanting of his followers *'Sieg Heil! Sieg Heil! Sieg Heil!'* is likely to forget the terrifying and hypnotic impression it made. Certainly Madame de Staël was right when she pointed out over a century ago that the Germans were ideal material for mass movements.

The Germans [she wrote] are vigorously submissive. They employ philosophical reasonings to explain what is the least philosophic thing in the world, respect for force and the fear which transforms that respect into admiration.

Whatever may be the superficial resemblances between the two, Fascism and Communism are essentially different. Fascism is nationalist, Communism is international; the former is not for export, the latter is. Fascism has no coherent doctrine, Communism has. Dialectical materialism or Marxism–Leninism, although a curiously metaphysical doctrine for convinced materialists, is a perfectly coherent one which has been, and is, held by highly intelligent people and extends into every sphere of thought. It sees politics everywhere: in biology, in history, in psychology, and even in prehistoric archaeology and linguistics. Moreover, whilst the avowed ends of Fascism run counter to what has been held to be good by the great majority of political and ethical philosophers from the earliest times, the avowed ends of Communism (internationalism, peace, comradeship, a fairer distribution of wealth, and hatred of injustice and tyranny) are such as might appeal to any reasonable person. Dictatorship, which is described as 'the dictatorship of the proletariat', is regarded as a means to an end not an end in itself, and since the death of Stalin the 'personality cult' is strongly disapproved of. Nevertheless, the similarities exist; there are the same mass meetings, the same processions, the same contrived 'spontaneous' demonstrations to suit the purposes of the government at any given moment, the same use of slogans, the same identification of enemies – in this case the imperialist war-mongers, colonialists, and capitalists. Goebbels's propaganda was deliberately lying and often inconsistent, whereas Communist propaganda is, broadly speaking, in the light of its doctrine, true – it is its interpretations rather than its facts which repel others. The Communist belief is a secular religion, which has its doctrine and sacred books, its group of high priests to interpret the doctrine according to present needs, its heroes and heretics (the dogmatists and revisionists, formalists and objectivists, the Trotskyites etc.), and its power to punish those who hold false beliefs, formerly at any rate in the most barbaric way. Religion is persecuted, as under the Nazis, although in a much more consistent and fervent manner and atheism is the avowed dogma of Communism.

In spite of the fact that there is nothing basically irrational about Marxism–Leninism or dialectical materialism, it is held in an irrational way and Marxists are not permitted to criticize current interpretation of its doctrine once it has been enunciated. Hence, so far from giving an impression of reasonableness which is open to discussion and confidence that the results of any rational debate will turn out in their favour, in argument Communists are often curiously evasive. Like the convinced Roman Catholic, they will argue rationally up to a point but no further. Thus a Communist shop-steward will argue his point reasonably (in the light of his beliefs); but when asked point-blank whether he gets directives as to what industrial action he should take, he will shut up like a clam and either refuse to answer or evade the issue. One of the most pathetic examples of this evasiveness was when during the Lysenko controversy foreign Communist geneticists had to perform comical manoeuvres to reconcile their scientific knowledge with their political beliefs. Some discovered for the first time that they had been believers in the new highly controversial viewpoint represented by Lysenko (which adhered to the previously discarded belief in the inheritance of acquired characteristics) all along. Others, such as Professor J. B. S. Haldane, had to engage in prolonged soul-searching. Few of them saw that the real issue was not which school of thought was right but the academic freedom to think what one pleased. In fact, the whole of orthodox genetics had been outlawed in Russia for political reasons and its supporters suppressed.

The curious mingling of science with politics, and the strange belief that a scientific theory is to be judged, not by its correspondence with the facts, but by the degree to which it accords with dialectical materialism, is well shown in the following extract from *Pravda* (No. 240) dealing with the Resolution of the Praesidium of the Academy of Sciences on 26 August 1948:

Michurin's [a predecessor of Lysenko] materialist direction in biology is the only acceptable form of science, because it is based on dialectical materialism, and on the revolutionary principle of changing Nature for the benefit of the people. Weismannite-Morganist idealist teaching is pseudo-scientific because it is founded on the notion of the divine origin of the world and assumes eternal and unalterable scientific laws. *The struggle between the two ideas has taken the form of the ideological class struggle between socialism and capitalism on the international scale,* and between the majority of Soviet scientists and a few remaining Russian scientists who have retained traces of bourgeois ideology on a smaller scale. There is no place for compromise. Michurinism and Morgano-Weismannism cannot be reconciled.

The love of slogans and incantations, which makes Communist propaganda so unmistakable, can be seen in the words with which the Praesidium closed its meeting (to the accompaniment, of course, of 'tumultuous applause, turning into an ovation'):

Long live the Party of Lenin and Stalin, which discovered Michurin for the world and created all the conditions for the progress of advanced materialist biology in our country. Glory to the great friend and protagonist of science, our leader and teacher, Comrade Stalin!

It would be difficult to imagine a meeting of the Royal Society closing in a corresponding manner, or, for the matter of that, any other 'capitalist' organization; but the reader of Communist propaganda inevitably finds himself confronted by strange forms of speech, strange epithets, and words which are given different meanings from those which he usually supposes them to have. Thus, at the World Congress of Intellectuals held at Wroclaw in August 1943, Fadeyev the Russian novelist announced that 'if hyenas could use fountain pens, and jackals could use typewriters, they would write like T. S. Eliot'; and apart from these zoological epithets there are the 'rotten' capitalist warmongers, and the 'lickspittle lackeys of the bourgeoisie'. Some of these terms are to be found in the writings of Marx and Engels, but most of them were coined by Lenin from whom they were taken over by Stalin. As for the odd meanings given certain terms, these are part of Communist 'double-talk' which must be discussed later. It is, however, interesting to note how the use of apparently innocuous words or phrases often give away to the sensitive observer something of the political and emotional sympathies of the speaker or writer. Thus, for some unknown reason, the apparently innocuous adjective 'Hitlerite' is almost exclusively limited to Communists, and at the other end of the scale the use of such words as 'the organic society', 'the soil', 'the folk' and their 'handicraft', makes one wary of the otherwise excellent F. R. Leavis and Denys Thompson. D. H. Lawrence's 'thinking with the blood' and the highly regarded C. G. Jung's use of the words 'soul' and 'soil' as in 'the Germanic soul' and his belief that 'soil' could influence character, are likewise code-words for what, in this ideology-obsessed world, one can only describe as extreme right-wing tendencies. Those who use the words 'blood', 'soil', 'soul', the 'folk', to mean anything other than the liquid in the body circulated by the heart, ordinary earth, a concept employed in theology, and people (i.e. other individuals) are regarded with suspicion by the wise as likely to have tendencies, possibly unknown to themselves, which ultimately lead in the direction of Hitler's '*Blut und Boden*', '*das Volk*', and the eternal German '*die Seele*'. The use of the suffix '-ism', although obviously not limited to Communists, is a tendency to which they are especially addicted – hence 'bourgeois nationalism', 'cosmopolitanism', 'democratic centralism', 'deviationism', 'dogmatism', 'economism', 'formalism', 'fractionism', 'imperialism', 'neutralism', 'objectivism', 'opportunism', 'practicism', 'socialist realism', 'subjectivism', 'tailism', 'voluntarism', and many others. Doubtless, these otherwise irrational-seeming conjunctions and preferences will, at some future date, become the subject of a more serious psychological study.

Communist control over literature and the arts is much more thoroughgoing than ever was the case in Fascist countries, where the control was mainly negative; for example, in the case of Nazi Germany, films were affected by the removal of Jewish producers and directors or actors, but, except in the case of the notorious *Jud Süss* and the films of the Nuremberg rallies and the Olympic games, there was relatively little positive propaganda in the arts in favour of Nazism. This is not the case in the Soviet Union where the most minute control is exercised over art and literature. As Alexander Werth says, if the Government and the Party approve of a play like Simonov's *The Russian Question*, it will not only be played in 600 theatres throughout the country but will also be turned into a film to be shown by thousands of cinemas. Fadeyev's novel *The Young Guard*, described by Werth as a 'dreary hack-work with the literary finesse of Ethel M. Dell', sold two million copies throughout Russia because, if the whole propaganda machine of the State boosts a book and it is distributed more or less free to every school-child, it is hardly possible to avoid being a best-seller. Many serious artists from Mayakovsky onwards have committed suicide and others have been silenced, such as the humorist Zoshchenko (for his 'cheap hee-hawing' at Soviet reality) and Anna Akhmatova ('half-nun, half-harlot') the poetess. In all the Central Committee's cultural reforms since the War, up to the time of Stalin's and his own death, its spokesman was the late Andrei Zhdanov, and his most startling criticisms were those relating to the reform of music, at the beginning of 1948. For here idols were knocked down who had been built up and worshipped for years by the Party and Government press – notably the music of Shostakovich, Proko- fiev, Khachaturian, and Miaskovsky which, it was said, had merely been praised by 'a clique of sycophantic critics'. The sin of which they were guilty was 'formalism' because 'discarding the great social role of music, they [were] content to cater to the degenerate tastes of a handful of estheticizing individualists'. Politics, of course, had to be dragged into the argument, and A. Goldenweiser (Professor at the Moscow Conservatoire) said on the second day of the Conference: 'When I hear the clatter of false chords in some of our new symphonies and sonatas, I am horrified to feel that they are akin to the decadent ideology of the West – or even of Fascism – and not to the healthy nature of Russian, Soviet humanity.' The composers, of course, duly ad- mitted their failings, Shostakovich concluding: 'I have always listened to criticism, and have always tried to work harder and better. I am listening to criticism now, and shall continue to listen to it, and shall accept critical instructions . . .' In his final speech Zhdanov reprimanded them in the following words:

Comrades, if you value the high name of Soviet composer, you must prove that you can serve your people better than you have done so far. A severe test lies before you. Formalist tendencies were severely con- demned by the Party twelve years ago. In the interval the Government has conferred Stalin Prizes on many of you, including those who sinned in the formalist direction. We did not consider when we gave you these prizes, that your works were free of faults, but we were patient, and waited for you to choose the right road. Now, clearly, the Party has had to intervene. If you continue on the road you have hitherto followed, our music will win no glory.

Not only do Communists have their own vocabulary, but there is frequently a contrast between their use of ordinary words and the same words as used by non-Communists. This is what has been described as double-talk. Thus 'peace', which ordinarily means a state of friendly relations with other countries, is inter- preted by Communists to mean the state of affairs in a Com- munist country since capitalist countries are assumed to be in a state of open class war and of at least potential hostility amongst each other in their competitive struggle for survival. In a state of 'peaceful coexistence' the non-Communist powers are interpreted as being not yet free to wage a war of 'aggression' against the peace-loving Communist powers either by reason of internal weakness or because of the threat of a class-war or revolution at home. Wars carried out by Communist powers are either wars of 'liberation' coming to the aid of the peace-lovers in the capitalist countries, or wars of 'self-defence' to forestall capitalist plans for aggression. 'Democracy' is the right of a people to government by its own representatives (i.e. the Communists) who pursue a Communist policy; a 'people's democracy' is one in which, for the time being, the Communists are assisted by other 'progressive' elements before the latter are dismissed and real Communist 'democracy' is in power. Anyone who is prepared to join a Communist-led 'Popular Front' is a 'progressive', anyone who is not is a 'reactionary'. Freedom similarly means freedom to live in a Communist society, because in any other form of society only the ruling class enjoys freedom, the remainder being composed of the oppressed and exploited masses or the dupes and lackeys of the ruling class. The freedom in the 'bourgeois democracies' is a sham because the parties between which they are able to choose are all controlled by capitalists and warmongers.

What appear to non-Communists as inconsistency and frequent changes of policy which a party that by definition must always be right can ill afford are seen by the loyal Communist as exemplifying the 'dialectic' element of Marxism as derived from Hegel. It does not seem to him to be inconsistent to hold one opinion one day and an entirely opposite opinion on the next. Thus in its early stages a loyal British Communist supported the last war as a war against Fascism until the official doctrine became the belief that it was an 'Imperialist War' because Russia had asserted her neutrality when he had to hold the view that it was wrong to cooperate in the war effort. Then when Germany attacked the Soviet Union it became once more the correct doctrine to support the British government and to insist upon the early opening of a Second Front. Similarly, following the 20th Congress, when Khrushchev denounced Stalinism, the loyal Communist was expected to change his views overnight and hold that Stalin had exemplified the now first-mentioned heresy of the 'cult of personality'.

The non-Communist cannot help but be surprised at the Soviet Encyclopedia re-writing history as each new edition comes out, so that the article on Beria, for example, which had been laudatory, had to be eliminated following his arrest and subsequent execution, and Trotsky is rarely mentioned at all. But not to re-write would mean to be guilty of the heresy of 'objectivism' (an excessive attachment to pure facts regardless of whether they fit in or not with the dogmas of Marxism). As an article published in *Culture and Life* of 20 August 1947 entitled 'On the Soviet Encyclopedia' declared: 'A Soviet encyclopedia cannot be a mere collection of information presented in an impartial, neutral, and politically indifferent manner. It should present all aspects of human activity and knowledge from the standpoint of a militant Marxist-Leninist world outlook.' The trouble about Marxism is not that it tells lies on the model of Dr Goebbels who was a calculating liar (it has already been pointed out that most Communist propaganda tells the truth *as it sees it*); its real danger is that it attacks the faculty of being capable of distinguishing between truth and falsehood with the result that most Communists have lost this faculty or regard it as being an outmoded relic of a decadent bourgeois culture. It is true that in his *Concerning Marxism in Linguistics* Stalin declared that 'no science can develop or flourish without a battle of opinion, without freedom of criticism'; but this is meaningless as long as it remains an article of faith that only that which assists the policy of the Party is 'true'.

The unit of the Party's structure, at any rate up to about 1924, was the Communist cell with ten or more fanatically dedicated members (here again use was made of the morale-building properties of the primary group) whose function was to act as a 'ginger group' to the rest of society. Communism is not only intolerant of other political parties on its right; it is even more intolerant of the heretic who once shared its views but has now strayed from the orthodox path possibly moving further to the left. Agitators have the duty of explaining to the ordinary man or woman the recent changes in policy and justifying them by reference to quotations from Marxist literature, which, of course, can always be found, and there are organizations within the hierarchy which pass on the policy from the inner group which decides it right down to the level of the local branch. Since expediency is the only issue, the Communist does not feel that he is being in the least dishonest in changing his attitude from time to time, and the ordinary citizen who may sometimes be confused is thereby made all the more ripe for listening and accepting what he has been told. He neither can nor wants to think for himself, after a lifetime of believing what he is told. But Communist propaganda has not been uniformly successful, and has failed even in the Soviet Union itself notably in the religious field; for in the census of 1937, after nearly twenty years of Communist rule and at a time when persecution was at its height, some fifty million Soviet citizens declared themselves to be 'believers' in one or other of the many religions of the Soviet Union. Yet even at the 22nd Congress in 1961 one of the tasks set the members of the Party was 'overcoming religious prejudices' among the Soviet people, i.e. teaching them to become atheists through the anti-God propaganda which has been a prominent feature of Communist society since it first began. Today it is estimated that the number of practising Christians belonging to the Russian Orthodox Church alone is between twenty and thirty millions and to this must be added other groups of Christians and millions of people belonging to nations which traditionally believe in Islam, Buddhism, or Judaism. The scale and vigour of the campaign to suppress religion, which has included every conceivable method from the firing squad to public lectures on the merits of materialist philosophy, has been documented by Walter Kolarz in his book *Religion in the Soviet Union*. Kolarz notes that the 1,470 Roman Catholic priests in Lithuania in 1945 had been reduced to 741 by 1954 and are still fewer today. At the other end of the scale it is recorded that the number of atheist lectures given in the Soviet Union increased from 120,000 in 1954 to over 300,000 in 1958 without, apparently, producing any significant effect.

Another sphere in which Soviet propaganda has failed has been amongst the older members of the populations of the satellite countries and it is widely recognized that those who were thirty or more when the Communist régimes were set up are almost all unteachable. They have to be dealt with by force rather than by words. Propaganda can help, however, by spreading threats which terrorize the weaker into passivity, giving them the feeling that they have no hope of rescue. To quote Lindley Fraser:

It is agreed by many people who have had to live in the Soviet Zone in Germany or in a satellite country that this last technique [i.e. the badgering with slogans, banners, and loudspeakers so that nobody is allowed an opportunity for meditation or relaxation] is the most difficult to endure. Terrorism may stimulate defiance; the sense of isolation can be overcome by listening to Western radio stations; but the perpetual nagging of Communist propaganda slogans involves a soul-destroying boredom which only the stoutest and most patient spirit can withstand. Life in the satellite countries even more perhaps than in the Soviet Union itself is bathed in propaganda from morning till night. One cannot escape from it.

All plays and films, until the 'thaw' which set in following the death of Stalin, were slanted in favour of Communism and even standard classical plays were interpreted in Marxist terms; it is still not clear just how far this loosening of censorship has gone, but it is very far from being completely lifted. It is difficult or impossible to get other than Communist-approved news or books, and attendance at parades, mass demonstrations, and indoctrination classes is still more or less compulsory. The fear of the midnight knock at the door, described so eloquently by Ilya Ehrenburg in the latest instalment of his memoirs in the literary magazine *Novy Mir*, when '. . . in the circle of my acquaintances no one knew what tomorrow would bring, [and] at night the whole house lay awake listening for the sound of the lift', may have been removed, but the expression of unorthodox views can still have quite unpleasant consequences. Propaganda cannot convert the older citizens, but the state holds enough power to stun them into inertia. With the youth of the satellite countries, or anyone born after about 1930, the results are likely to be different; for all of these have spent the greater part of their lives in a totalitarian atmosphere of the right or left, and for this reason are apt to accept such conditions as the natural state of affairs. Western propaganda directed to these countries, even when transmissions are not jammed, has very often been singularly inept, and it is probable that its main results have been the introduction of beatnik mannerisms, a thirst for modern jazz, and the cult of pop singers and American film stars. The Polish writer Czeslaw Milosz describes in his book *The Captive Mind* how even those Polish intellectuals who find it difficult to settle down under Communism feel about the West: they ask themselves '. . . what goes on in the heads of the Western masses? Isn't Christianity dying out in the West, and aren't its people bereft of all faith? Isn't there a void in their heads? Don't they fill that void with chauvinism, detective stories, and artistically worthless movies? Well then, what can the West offer us? Freedom *from* something is a great deal, yet not enough. It is much less than freedom *for* something.'

In relation to countries outside the Soviet bloc, propaganda must obviously be different. In those nations arrayed against Communism, agitators will be employed to bring about as much discontent as possible, particularly in the field of industry. Of course, so far as Britain is concerned, only a minority of strikes are Communist-inspired, but the Communist parties of the West are specifically committed to disrupting the industrial life of the nation whenever they can. In doing so they are only following the famous exhortation from Lenin himself:

The leaders of opportunism will resort to every trick to prevent Communists from getting into the trade unions. It is therefore necessary to agree to any and every sacrifice and even, if need be, to resort to all sorts of stratagems, manoeuvres, and illegal methods, to evasions and subterfuges, in order to penetrate the trade unions and to remain in them, carrying on Communist activities inside them at all costs.

Thus in the case of the 1961 trial against the Electrical Trades Union and its officers for ballot-rigging in the election of union officials during the 1959 election, when the candidates were John Byrne, a non-Communist, and Frank Haxell, a Communist, it was found that the latter together with his colleagues had diligently followed Lenin's advice. In the words of Mr Gardiner,

Q.C., the defendants not only adopted all their usual methods, but actually excelled themselves.

There was, as usual, only one Communist candidate, and as was customary they arranged for as many nominations from the branches as possible – there was more canvassing than ever. They had already trumped up a charge against Mr Chapple, a non-Communist. They thereafter had an extra 26,000 voting papers printed and sent to Communist supporters, these votes being simply fraudulent votes. They altered some of the branch returns. But even so, in spite of these practices, they found that when the votes came in Mr Haxell had plainly lost the election – Mr Byrne had won by a substantial majority. There was only one way out left, and that was to disqualify as many non-Communist branches as possible.

Naturally, in this sort of manoeuvre Communists are helped by the political indifference of their opponents and their own fanatical discipline, but it is probably true to say that the number of Communists holding power in a union is in direct proportion to the number of real and justified complaints of the members which have not been satisfactorily dealt with by management. This is less true of countries such as France and Italy, where the Communist parties are relatively large and there has long existed an extremist tradition in politics which makes it seem creditable to be a revolutionary and where the unions have from the outset been politically motivated.

Another Communist line in the West is to appeal to people of good-will, belonging to other parties or to none, to join them in fighting some social or political evil; examples are the Popular Front of the 1930s and their present infiltration of pacifist, nuclear-disarmament, or anti-militarist bodies (for which the writer has nothing but mildly-qualified respect). The trouble about this kind of alliance is that, as with the Catholic's prayer for church unity, any compromises arrived at are necessarily uni-directional; the pacifist or the Presbyterian are not going to influence those who already know the absolute truth. Yet Marxism–Leninism has been seriously mistaken in its predictions, notably in predicting that Communism would come first to the highly-industrialized countries, whereas it has been effectual only in the least industrialized areas, and even there has gained a minor degree of power. In fact, such spread of Communism as has taken place has been, not by popular support, but by force of arms. It was also predicted by Lenin that capitalism was doomed to collapse both by reason of its internal stresses and by colonialist wars among the rival capitalist powers. Hence, when India was given her freedom, Russia would not at first believe that any colonial power would willingly part with its Empire, and Mr Nehru, formerly a favourite, was regarded as a traitor and a reactionary British stooge. Again, the fact that Communism is a supra-national philosophy is not likely to appeal to those countries which are gaining their freedom through nationalist movements, and in these areas the full doctrine of Marxism is imparted only to a few fervent followers whilst to the rest the Communists pose as the friends of the local nationalist movements. These, of course, are to be regarded purely as tools to be discarded when the time is ripe and, once their object is attained, they will be subjected to Communist pressure along the same lines as the older nations.

Much of this has changed within recent years, particularly in the greater freedom for criticism and self-expression. Thus *Literaturnaya Gazeta*, the organ of the Writer's Union, recently substantiated many of the criticisms already quoted from Werth, declaring that 'there is no branch of our economy with so much fortuitousness, disorganization, lack of planning, chaos and stupidity as the book-publishing business'. It is now admitted that, in spite of the Russians' claim that they publish more books than any other country, very large numbers, 'worth hundreds of millions of new roubles remain unsold. This is partly due to duplication of titles and to the fact that the choice of book published bears little relation to the demand.' Various writers now criticize the Stalin régime and even the existing bureaucracy, but Pasternak's *Dr Zhivago* remains unpublished and Mr Khrushchev tells abstract painters that they 'must understand their faults and work for the people'. In the field of politics we still have the same tortuousness of mind as 'Yugoslavia' (Russia) conducts its controversy with 'Albania' (China), and the same duplicity as when Mr Frol Kozlov tells the 1962 Italian Communist Party Congress that the Chinese aggression in India 'seriously damages the interests of the Chinese people and the interests of the people of friendly India' – forgetting, perhaps, that Mr Khrushchev himself had said at the Moscow conference in 1960: 'We support them (the Indians) as the rope supports the hanged man. When the time is ripe, we shall cut the rope and bring them down.' Nor, unfortunately, (at any rate in China), has the excruciating jargon shown any sign of disappearing, and their journal *Red Flag* in early 1963 produced an article titled 'Defend the Purity of Marxism/Leninism' containing this gem: [Communists must work hard] 'to raise their ability to distinguish Marxism–Leninism from revisionism, to distinguish the way of opposing dogmatism with Marxism–Leninism from that of opposing Marxism–Leninism with revisionism under the cover of opposing dogmatism, and to distinguish the way of opposing sectarianism with proletarian internationalism from that of opposing proletarian internationalism with great-nation chauvinism and narrow nationalism under the cover of opposing sectarianism.'

However, whether Russia or Communism has changed since the death of Stalin is no concern of this book, although obviously of the greatest possible significance to the future of mankind. All we have been concerned to do is to take Communism as it has been up to the present time and study it as a specimen of the control of minds by propaganda and physical force. There is no great mystery as to how Communism gained control in Russia, where it took over control in a revolutionary situation just as Fascism did in Germany. Nor is there anything mysterious about how Communism retained power, since it did so both by positive propaganda backed by physical force and by that most potent of all propaganda weapons, the negative form of censorship which refuses people free access to information as to what is going on outside the country. Perhaps basically it succeeded because it was the only party capable of forcing Russia rapidly enough in the direction the larger part of the civilized world had already taken, that of industrialization. Outside the Communist world the most striking feature of Marxism has been its relative failure to attract adherents in those countries and amongst those people to whom it might have been expected to have the greatest appeal.

It is not the highly industrialized capitalist areas nor the industrial workers who have accepted Communism, but the agricultural parts of the world, the peasants, and a small fraction of the intelligentsia of Europe. In no part of the world has it gained control by constitutional means, and for all its attempts to gain control by other methods it seems fair to conclude that, apart from military action, the results have hardly justified the effort.

CHAPTER 6

PROPAGANDA AND THE MASS MEDIA

IT is a common mistake to confuse mass communication with the mass media of television, radio, the cinema, modern newspapers, and cheap books or magazines, which are the instruments by which it is largely transmitted today. The problem of mass communication has existed for a long time, and, although technological developments did give it an immense impetus, the increased wealth, leisure, and literacy of the lower classes which has occurred throughout the history of the industrialized nations would undoubtedly have brought about a great expansion of cultural consumption of varying quality even without the new means of communication which arose largely during the present century. Socrates, in Plato's *Phaedrus*, is reported as having held much the same opinion about the invention of writing as is now held by many at the present time in relation to other media such as radio and television:

... it will create forgetfulness in the learners' souls because they will not use their memories; they will trust to the external written words and not remember of themselves. They will appear to be omniscient, and will generally know nothing; they will be tiresome company, having the show of wisdom without the reality.

But the real expansion of mass communication by means of the printed word began in eighteenth-century England with the rise into power of the middle classes; for it was at this time that the writer first became dependent for his financial support on the public instead of on aristocratic patronage, the reading public became the population at large instead of being limited to scholars and members of the privileged classes, and the author became a professional writing on commission for the rapidly expanding booksellers' trade. Soon almost every one of the literary products that are familiar to us today were offered to the purchaser, from the newspaper, the family magazine with columns giving advice to those with personal or other problems, the weekly news review, magazines retailing the gossip of the theatre and stage, book digests and the rest, to the eighteenth-century equivalents of modern pulp magazines of the *True Stories* type. The novel became increasingly popular and latterly came to be presented in pocket-book size and three volumes so that it could readily be carried about and it was common practice to bring out fiction in weekly instalments in news sheets as a serial story with illustrations, as (at a much later date) Dickens was to bring out his *Sketches by Boz* with illustrations by George Cruikshank. The anthology or selections from modern and classical writers, cheap reprints, remainder sales, and secondhand bookstalls were all part of the eighteenth-century scene, and the bookseller, who was often the same person as the publisher, took great pains to ensure that his wares were sold; book blurbs (then described as 'puffery') accounted for at least half the advertisements in magazines. Catchy titles, endorsements of the book by eminent public figures, and even bribery of book reviewers in reviews which were owned by the bookseller or in which he had controlling interests were amongst the less unscrupulous methods employed. The first circulating library opened in 1740 and by the end of the century at least a thousand such libraries existed in London and the provinces; these, too, were often controlled by booksellers who, in addition, encouraged the many book clubs and literary societies which had sprung up all over the country. The largest such library was opened by a bookseller named Charles Edward Mudie; at its height his firm had about three and a half million books in circulation and, for those customers unable to call in person, Mudie had his 'famous door-to-door van service' which daily kept eight vehicles in operation.

By 1850, the modern form of mass society had taken shape in both Britain and America and the middle classes were dominant. In face of the flood of popular literature the creative artists such as Stendhal had begun to feel themselves isolated and, in self-defence, began to proclaim the doctrine of 'art for art's sake', an art which could only be understood by the élite and must remain forever closed to the masses. The aristocracy, fearful at the results of the French Revolution, responded by causing the reproduction of large numbers of moralistic and religious tracts for the special consumption of the lower orders, but their efforts were nullified by new technical innovations which were capable of producing an even greater flow of modern literature which completely swamped the trashy and 'improving' tracts. In this struggle the most eminent British writers took one side or the other, for or against the Establishment versus the common people. In his Preface to the second edition of his *Lyrical Ballads*, Wordsworth wrote of the threat of 'frantic novels, sickly and stupid German tragedies, and the deluge of idle and extravagant stories in verse' which tend to reduce the mind to 'a state of almost savage torpor', whilst Matthew Arnold, more concerned about the loss of spiritual values, attacked the producers of literature for mass consumption:

Plenty of people will try to give the masses, as they call them, an intellectual food prepared and adapted in the way they think proper for the actual condition of the masses. The ordinary popular literature is an example of this way of working on the masses.

He even indicted games and sports which, although they may result in the production of a 'better physical type for the future to work with', in fact have the result that 'our generation of boys and young men is in the meantime sacrificed'. William Hazlitt took a similarly gloomy view:

The public taste is therefore necessarily vitiated in proportion as it is public; it is lowered with every infusion it receives of common opinion. The greater the number of judges, the less capable must they be of judging ... and thus the decay of the arts may be said to be the necessary consequence of its progress.

The Royal Academy, even then under attack, was described as 'a society of hucksters' and, Hazlitt added:

A fashionable artist and a fashionable hairdresser have the same common principles of theory and practice; the one fits his customers to appear with *éclat* in a ball-room, the other in the Great Room of the Royal Academy.

Two men who, although very different in their other qualities, took the side of the masses were Sir Walter Scott and John Wesley. The latter, in fact, might almost be described as one of the pioneers of the cheap book and the education of the common people as well as of the religious propagandist magazine. When he saw a book he thought likely to be useful, he edited and published it. So he gave to Methodists Young's *Night Thoughts*, Thomas à Kempis, Brooke's *Fool of Quality*, and caused to be poured from his presses works of history, medicine, biography, and science, many of them written by himself. Scott made no secret of the fact that he wrote for popular consumption and for the money he could earn thereby: 'I care not who knows it – I write for general amusement.' For, he added, '... it has often happened, that those who have been best received in their own time, have also continued to be acceptable to posterity. I do not think so ill of the present generation, as to suppose that its present favour necessarily infers a future condemnation.' But, as an anonymous writer to the *Edinburgh Review* wrote in 1837, it was the newspaper which held the key to the immediate future:

Books, how cheap soever, and however popularly written, are not likely to be read by the uninformed. ... But all men will read THE NEWS; and even peasants, farm servants, country day-labourers, will look at, nay pore over the paper that chronicles the occurrences of the neighbouring market town. Here then is a channel through which, alongside with political intelligence and the occurrences of the day, the friends of human improvement, the judicious promoters of general education, may diffuse the best information, and may easily allure all classes, even the humblest, into the paths of general knowledge.

These 'friends of human improvement' were to be confronted by a new situation in 1870, the year of the Elementary Education Act, but by this time the original innovators had already grown set in their ways; for the public for which they catered was essentially a middle-class public. It was, as Francis Williams says (*Dangerous Estate: the Anatomy of Newspapers*, Grey Arrow Books), the public of the ambitious *petite bourgeoisie* making its way in the world. Although aping their social betters, such people could neither afford nor digest *The Times* and the *Morning Post* was too aristocratic and High Tory for their taste: a paper for dukes – or their butlers. What they wanted was a respectable cheap substitute for the daily reading matter of the superior classes looking, as all the best substitutes do, as much like the original as possible but easier on an unsophisticated palate. Thus there was the *Daily Telegraph* which had shed its original radicalism; the Conservative *Morning Standard*; the Liberal *Daily News*; and the *Daily Chronicle*, which appealed to Liberal Unionists of the shopkeeper class. All such papers were for men established in their station in society or on the way to being so and were heavily political, long-winded, and restricted in interest – in short, they were extremely dull and totally ignored the fact that women too could read. Also ignored by the editors and proprietors of these papers were the new products of the Board Schools, a lower-middle and working-class public seeking to educate and amuse itself. In an earlier age Cobbett had written for this group, as had Hetherington with his *Poor Man's Guardian* and Charles Knight with his *Penny Magazine* which, appearing in 1832, had sold 200,000 copies a week. There were the ½d. evening papers started by Edward Hulton of Manchester to cater for the new interest in sport which had arisen with the first Association Football Cup Tie of 1871, the first Australian Test Match in 1878, and the beginning of professional football in 1885.

However, the important newspapers did not concern themselves with this public, and it was left to George Newnes of Manchester to bring out a new type of paper for popular consumption. Sitting with his wife one evening, reading a paragraph from an evening paper, he remarked: 'Now that is what I call an interesting titbit. Why doesn't someone bring out a whole paper made up of titbits like that?' 'Why don't you?' she replied, and the result was called *Tit-Bits* (from All the Most Interesting Books, Periodicals, and Newspapers of the World). This was, in fact, a kind of low-brow *Reader's Digest* and proved an unqualified success together with its more stable companion the *Strand Magazine*. Within three months *Tit-Bits* was selling 900,000 copies – three times as many as the *Daily Telegraph*.

Six years after *Tit-Bits* appeared, T.P. O'Connor produced the first of the modern evening newspapers, the *Star*, to appeal to the same audience, and Alfred Harmsworth (later Lord Northcliffe) had brought in *Answers*, a weekly of the same nature as *Tit-Bits*, described as 'a weekly storehouse of interesting information'. Although beginning slowly, *Answers* soared to success when Northcliffe offered a prize of £1 a week for life for the best guess of the amount of money in the Bank of England on a given day; 700,000 people went in for the competition, and the paper became known to millions. It was followed in 1890 by *Comic Cuts*, the first 'comic' ever to be produced, *Home Chat* for the housewife, the *Sunday Companion*, the *Boy's Friend*, and many others.

The first daily newspaper to mark this decisive change in the relations of press and public, the triumph of the sensational in daily journalism, was the *Daily Mail*, brought out by Northcliffe on 4 May 1896; it was a halfpenny paper of eight pages with advertisements on the front page and was described as 'A Penny Newspaper for One Halfpenny' and 'The Busy Man's Daily Journal'. Within were short domestic and foreign news items, an instalment of a serial story, a column of political gossip, society news, sporting news, Stock Exchange prices, and a number of features for women. Amongst other ventures in Northcliffe's vast newspaper empire were the *Evening News*, the *News of the World*, and the *Daily Mirror* which, beginning as a paper 'written by gentlewomen for gentlewomen', transformed itself shortly into the first popular picture paper. By 1959 one of every two younger citizens read the *Daily Mirror* and one in three at a higher age-group Lord Beaverbrook's *Daily Express*; in 1961, the directors of the *Daily Mirror* group could take decisions on the editorial policy of women's magazines read by eight out of every ten British women and girls. This was mass circulation with a vengeance.

Broadcasting in Britain began with the formation of a limited company, the British Broadcasting Company, which, combining the interests of six large radio and electrical manufacturing firms, was granted a licence by the Postmaster-General in 1922. Its revenue came from the receiving licences bought at the post office and from royalties on the sale of wireless sets. In 1927, on the recommendation of the Crawford Committee, a public corporation, the British Broadcasting Corporation, was formed as a monopoly granted by Royal Charter. As such the BBC has certain obligations to the government (e.g. any government department may demand that it transmit information considered important to the public) but it is neither controlled nor operated by any branch of the government, being headed by a Board of Governors appointed by the Queen through the Prime Minister and operated under a Director General and a professional staff who are employees of the Board. It is financed by the money from licences and to some extent from the sale of the *Radio Times*, its weekly programme paper. The BBC provides four main services for home listeners: the Home Service (with which are linked six Regional Home Services covering Scotland, Wales, and Northern Ireland, and the North, Midland, and West of England which may substitute their own programmes for some of those of the basic Home Service), the Light Programme, the Third Programme designed for the serious listener, and Network Three designed for a specialist minority which, using Third Programme frequencies, was introduced towards the end of 1957. Originally, the BBC was committed to a policy of cultural enlightenment for the average listener and each of these programmes represented a level in a hierarchy in the hope that the listener to the Light Programme would elevate himself to the higher level provided by the Home and ultimately, perhaps, to the dizzy levels of the Third and Network Three. But this policy appears to have been given up in recent years.

The first Royal Charter was renewed in 1937, after Parliament had considered the Ullswater Committee's report, and the BBC was further entrusted with television broadcasting, which had originated with the world's first high-definition television service from Alexandra Palace on 2 November 1936. Television, like radio, was a BBC monopoly until 1954, when Parliament (after much lobbying from pressure groups) approved the setting-up of the Independent Television Authority, which began competing with the BBC in 1955. Programmes for the ITA are provided by privately-financed programme contractors, who sell advertising time. In cultural level the ITA corresponds to the

Light Programme of the BBC radio, whilst the BBC television corresponds roughly to its radio Home Service.

In America, according to a UNESCO survey, there is almost one radio set per person and at least one television set for every five viewers. The broadcasting stations are privately owned and function as profit-making organizations, but since 1927 the Federal Communications Commission has issued licences, which must be obtained before a station can be set up, allocated wavelengths, and decided the hours during which a station may operate. Each radio or television station is responsible for choosing the material that it broadcasts: some of this it originates itself, but many stations also have programmes distributed through one or other of the regional or national networks with which they have become affiliated. In the larger cities the networks possess stations of their own, but the affiliated stations themselves supply their greatest number of outlets by putting aside a certain number of hours for network programmes. There are four major broadcasting networks in the U.S.A., the largest being the Mutual Broadcasting System (MBS); others are the National Broadcasting Company (NBC), the Columbia Broadcasting System (CBS), and the American Broadcasting Company (ABC). Television stations operate in much the same way, and out of the 500 or so stations about twenty-two transmit educational material, being run by funds supplied by private grants from foundations or other bodies. Money for most stations, however, comes from the sale of time to advertisers, some from local sponsors who deal directly with the station, but on the national level most of them deal with the networks through the advertising agencies of Madison Avenue in New York. The advertiser may buy time for 'plug' announcements, as with Britain's ITA, or he may sponsor particular programmes, some of which originate within the station itself, some come from independent producers, and others are created by the advertising agencies. Unlike the state of affairs in British commercial television, therefore, the advertiser frequently has the power to control the actual content of the programme. Broadcasting is completely free to the public and, since there is open competition to catch the public ear, the programmes tend to be of a more sensational nature than those of the non-competitive BBC, especially as in recent years many have been advertiser-sponsored and therefore practically out of the control of the network and its stations. Since the advertising agencies are not actually engaged in broadcasting, they are not subject to the regulations of the Federal Communications Commission. In all these ways the American system differs from the British one and those in the majority of European countries, which are dependent on the money from the sale of licences.

In the Soviet Union broadcasting comes under the U.S.S.R. Ministry of Communications, its policy being shaped by the radio committees of each republic. The whole system differs strikingly from those in other industrialized countries; thus radio receiving sets as we know them are less common than wired wireless, for which in 1957 there were 30,000 relay centres connected with sixteen million individual loudspeakers, which permit the choice of only a few stations relayed from the centre: it was planned to double that number by 1960.* There are three national programmes: Moscow Home, with a foreign service in thirty-six languages (in 1957), the Alternative Programme, and the Third Programme. Secondly, the system is planned and operates under a philosophy committed to the Party Line, therefore its content is unlike that of the non-Communist countries in a number of ways: the concept of news, if this be defined as the objective and rapid reporting of current events, hardly exists, and it is replaced by a highly selective editing of past and present events interpreted in terms of Soviet ideology;† high priority is given to the transmission of Soviet culture, including material which is not only cultural in the broad sense of social norms, but also selected artistic material (more than half of the broadcasts consist of music, most of it classical); entertainment plays a relatively small part unless it can be shown to improve the mind of the listener or viewer. Lastly, the local programmes show a high degree of specialization, carrying, for example, special programmes for farmers linked by a particular network of wired

---

* According to *Izvestia* the number of plug-in sets in 1960 was 62,500,000.

† For example, many important events, such as the crisis over Cuba or the Chinese aggression in India, are not made known to the Soviet citizen until days after they have occurred and government officials have decided how to present them.

receivers. Soviet broadcasting is therefore an instrument of propaganda, designed to shut out external influences as far as possible, to inculcate a particular ideology and indoctrinate the people with a particular attitude towards current events as they occur, and to raise the people's cultural level in the educational sense.*

So far we have briefly discussed three of the more important mass media, and more will be said of these elsewhere; but it is now necessary to turn to the actual process of mass communication – its audience, content, and social effects.

Broadly speaking, mass communications fall into four main functional categories: (1) the surveillance of the environment, or supplying the *news*; (2) the commentaries on current issues or news, which take the form of *editorial* or *propagandist* activities; (3) the transmission of the social heritage or *education*, whether in the sense of formal education or the provision of social norms; (4) *entertainment*.

News, as Charles R. Wright puts it, is a tool for daily living, but too much news may have the undesirable effects described by American sociologists as 'privatization' or, in other cases, 'narcotization'. In the former type of response the individual feels overwhelmed, and turning away from unpleasant reality proceeds to 'cultivate his own garden', ignoring what is going on round about him. In the latter, the mere possession of news becomes an end in itself without leading to any useful action. Hence the editing of news and the interpretation of events is of great importance to society, since the vast majority of people are not in a position to understand the significance of bald statements of fact. For example, the fact of an epidemic of poliomyelitis is alarming and it is obviously valuable when a medical man through the mass media tries to give the public a balanced account of the real state of affairs and thus prevents panic action and enables people to take reasonable steps calmly and rationally.

* The systems of TV and radio control described above correspond to Raymond Williams's classification in his Penguin book *Communications*: the authoritarian (Soviet Union), the paternal (BBC), and the commercial (ITA and U.S.A.). Williams's fourth category, rather oddly described as 'democratic', involves complete public ownership combined with syndicalist workers' control and he regretfully admits that so far, 'we can only discuss and imagine it'.

The educational and entertainment aspects of mass communication arouse much more controversy and will be dealt with later. But to most of us the burning question is whether, as some would maintain, they raise the general standard of culture in the population and provide harmless amusement which is selectively used, or whether, on the contrary, by providing endless diversion, they weaken the willingness of people to pay attention to serious thought, and, by providing positively harmful material, lead to delinquency. This is not a question to which any simple answer can be given, since clearly mass communications can have vastly different effects upon different types of people. For example, a study which compared two groups of white-collar workers seemed to show that the group with the more skilled and interesting work was discriminating in its use of the media, whereas those who had monotonous work showed two extremes of behaviour, either engaging in an excess of mass media activities by being glued to the radio or television set or visiting the cinema unselectively several times a week, or, at the other pole, retreating into isolation which either took them to the public bar or led to an impoverished home life. From the standpoint of the creative artist, mass communications must have an effect too; he is not likely to starve, but he is not always paid for performing his most creative function. Mass man, Priestley's 'admass', is alleged to be unreceptive to contemplation; to have brought about a complete separation between artistic production on the one hand and occupational and community life on the other; and to have made it less and less clear for whom the creative artist is working, with the result that he is often restricted to addressing himself to a small group of experts. It is Paul Lazarsfeld's complaint that the mass media

... emphasize the fleeting events of the moment and weaken people's connexion with the past, as it is expressed in myths and the kind of symbolism which epics or the Bible provide. This has grievous consequences for the artist, for his creativeness consists essentially in providing new variations on pervasive themes.

People are said to have lost the ability to take cultural issues seriously – a view expressed in T. W. Adorno's statement that 'radio has made of Beethoven's Fifth Symphony a hit tune which is easy to whistle', implying that popular culture has made of the classics something to be consumed rather than understood.

But what is mass communication? It has been defined as communication directed towards a relatively large, heterogeneous and anonymous audience. It does not necessarily cover every occasion on which the mass media are used; for example a small audience of doctors watching a surgical operation on closed-circuit television or a family watching holiday films on a home cinema are not involved in mass communication. By a 'large' audience we mean one exposed during a short time only and of such a size that the communicator could not interact with its members on a face-to-face basis. The term 'heterogeneous' excludes communications to a specialized or élite audience, and means those aggregations of individuals occupying a great variety of positions within the society in respect of sex, age, class, occupational group, religion, nationality, level of education, geographical location, and so on. Finally, the criterion of anonymity implies that the individuals in the audience remain personally unknown to the communicator; it does not mean that all members are necessarily unknown to each other, although under certain conditions many of them will be. The individual, however, may listen to the radio or watch television in the company of his or her family, small groups may listen to the radio in public or semi-public places as in the Soviet Union and elsewhere; and even when he is for the time being physically isolated, each member of the audience is likely to be linked to a number of primary or secondary groups which will ultimately modify in varying degree the communicator's message. But, so far as the communicator is concerned, his message is open to whoever cares to listen or look. Mass communications are addressed to the public in general and are likely to be rapid and transient; rapid in the sense that they are meant to be utilized in a comparatively short space of time, unlike such works of art as buildings and paintings or sculpture which may exist for centuries; and transient in the sense that, although films or recordings of them may be made, they are ordinarily regarded as for immediate consumption. For the most part, or so it has usually been thought, the mass audience is composed of anonymous individuals who have very little inter-action with each other and are loosely organized. A crowd, too, is composed of anonymous individuals, but for the time being they interact and are organized at least to the degree that they are sometimes capable of concerted action. Of course there are rare occasions, such as the panic reaction following the Orson Welles broadcast of an Invasion from Mars, which many believed to be a news report instead of merely a story, when collective action may follow mass communication although still lacking the unity of purpose that marks a crowd, but interaction has ordinarily been believed to be the exception rather than the rule.

However, observation and research has tended to discredit this view of the non-interacting and loosely-organized mass audience; for, apart from the obvious fact that the audience of a cinema, for instance, is taking part in a group experience, there is plenty of evidence that the group-affiliations of the members of audi-ences affects their selection and response to mass communication. For example, John and Matilda Riley found that children who got on well with other members of their age-group had less interest in radio and television shows depicting action and violence and, in so far as they had any, tended to make use of the material for aiding their group play. On the other hand, socially isolated children not only preferred such stories but were likely to dwell upon their more morbid 'creepy' or horror aspects. Nor is it true that mass communications always come directly to the individual, because they frequently arrive indirectly from others who pass on the message. Those people who pass on messages in this way are the so-called opinion leaders of a group who hand on information by word of mouth or, more indirectly, incorporate it in the advice they give to those within their circle of influence.

Some interesting observations were made by Paul Lazarsfeld and his colleagues on a panel of 600 people representing the population of Erie County, Ohio, during the American presid-ential campaign of 1940. The primary objective was to find out why people vote as they do, and the research was carried out by means of interviews with the selected panel, which took place once each month from May to November, that is prior to, and throughout, the election campaign. Thus it was possible to study the development and change of opinions and attitudes of members of the representative group and to determine the impact of the political campaign and the effect of the mass media in influencing voting intention. The fundamental finding was that there was very little evidence of direct influence of the campaign in changing people's votes, and that the main effect of the mass effort was to reinforce the original voting intention of some citizens and to arouse the latent predispositions of others. People were found to be very selective and for the most part paid attention only to that material which reinforced their original views. Republicans listened to Republican propaganda and Democrats to Democrat propaganda. The study showed again and again that people voted in groups, that is that people belonging to the same church, family, or social club tended to vote alike. Apparently this was not so much due to the fact that such individuals were likely to belong to the same environment and share the same interests as to the fact that, as the interviewed individuals admitted, private political discussions had influenced them more than exposure to radio or the printed word. By questioning it was found out who were the main opinion leaders of the group (the technique by which this was done is irrelevant to the purposes of the discussion), and some further interesting facts emerged: (1) opinion leadership was found to be distributed throughout the social structure, showing that personal influence flows not only from above down but also horizontally amongst members of the same social class or status group; (2) the opinion leaders, as might be expected, turned out to be especially alert, interested, and active politically; (3) opinion leaders were more exposed to the mass media campaign than those who were not leaders; (4) there was evidence that the opinion leaders used the information they obtained in this way in the information and advice they passed on to their followers. One of the functions of opinion leaders is to mediate between the mass media and other people in their groups and it is not true, or was not true in this piece of research, that individuals obtain most of their opinions direct from newspapers, radio, and other media as is usually thought. This suggestion that information flows from the mass media to opinion leaders and from them to the mass audience is described as the 'two-step' hypothesis of the flow of information.

A further study of opinion leaders was carried out by Robert Merton in a small Eastern American community of about 11,000 people, the opinions in this case being of a more general nature than in the last one. From this it appeared that there are two different kinds of opinion leader, described as *local* and *cosmopolitan* types, the former being preoccupied chiefly with community affairs, the latter with the larger world outside the community. The localite is more likely to be a native of the community whilst the cosmopolite is likely to have travelled and come as a relative newcomer to the town; local influentials such as shopkeepers are naturally concerned with knowing a large number of the members of the community whilst the cosmopolitan ones are more restrictive in their associations and tend to form friendships with those on the same status level. Both groups use the mass media more than other people and both, for example, use magazines more than the average member of the population, but the cosmopolitan reads more, especially news magazines such as *Time* and *News Review*, which are an important link with the outer world and provide information that helps to reduce his relative social isolation and enables him to maintain his leadership on non-local subjects. He also reads the large New York newspapers rather than the local journals which are favoured by the localite. Furthermore, whilst the opinions of the local opinion leader are likely to be asked on a large number of topics, the cosmopolitan's influence is more likely to be restricted to the field in which he is regarded as an expert, which might be fashions, national or international affairs, business, or some other subject.

The importance of face-to-face relationships in influencing opinions has been demonstrated again in a study by Katz and Lazarsfeld conducted among a random sample of 800 women in Decatur, Illinois, a town of about 60,000 people. They were able to show that personal contacts had greater influence than any of the mass media in themselves, of which radio was the most influential and newspaper and magazine advertising the least so, in determining the choice of fashions, films selected, and market goods bought. Lazarsfeld suggests five reasons why personal communication is a more effective means of persuasion than direct mass communication: (1) personal contacts are more casual, more difficult to avoid, and apparently less purposeful than mass communications in which, as we have seen, people tend to be highly selective; (2) face-to-face contact permits of greater flexibility in that the content can be varied to suit the resistance of the audience by the communicator modifying his line; (3) the direct personal relationships involved in face-to-face relationships can enhance the rewards for accepting the message and the 'punishment' for not doing so; (4) people are more likely to put their trust in someone they know than in an impersonal mass communication; (5) by personal contacts the communicator can often achieve his purpose without actually persuading the audience to accept his point of view; for example it may be possible to get a friend to vote in an election without in fact altering his interest in the campaign or his position on the issues.

A considerable amount of audience analysis has been carried out in the post-war period and this has generally shown a tendency towards an 'all-or-nothing' exposure to mass communication. That is to say, people who use one medium a good deal are also likely to make use of the others, and those who avoid one are likely to restrict their use of the others. Of course, the various media compete with each other to some extent (e.g. the cinema and television, television and radio), but the fact remains that some people are more media-minded than others. The most striking observation, perhaps, is the degree of self-selection which takes place: those with political convictions read the papers that correspond to their opinions, and those with particular interests read the sections of the newspapers which report most fully on these interests. The same items which have already been heard on the radio are read about in the papers. Interests are conditioned more by social role than by any distinguishable psychological characteristics: university-educated people read more books and magazines than others, a large part of the regular cinema-going public consists of young people who are less well-educated, serious programmes (classical music, discussions, etc.) appeal most to older individuals and those with more formal education and least to the young with less education. This is not due to the greater reading ability of the highly educated; for the preferences are still evident in radio and television. Lazarsfeld concludes:

. . . in general, then, people look not for new experiences in the mass media but for a repetition and an elaboration of their old experiences into which they can more easily project themselves.

This selective attitude applies even more clearly, in other contexts, to outright propaganda: a 1947 public-information campaign in Cincinnati, Ohio, presented information about the United Nations and world affairs. This was initiated by several public organizations including the American Association for the United Nations. For six months the people of Cincinnati were bombarded with propaganda and information about the U.N. – meetings and speeches were arranged, pamphlets, leaflets, and posters were handed out, features were run in all the newspapers and over the radio; but the net result was that, whereas prior to the campaign 30 per cent of adults had no idea of the general purpose of the United Nations, after it 28 per cent were still in the same state of ignorance – a net gain of 2 per cent. 'The campaign failed,' comments Charles R. Wright, 'because it did not reach those most in need of its message from the point of view of the sponsors. That is, it did not reach the ill-informed, apathetic, or hostile people in the city.'

A striking example of selective interpretation is provided in a study by Patricia Kendall and Katherine Wolfe of Columbia University's Bureau of Applied Social Research in relation to anti-racial-prejudice cartoons. These showed the adventures of a character named Mr Biggott who was satirized as showing gross hostility towards a number of American minority groups and were presented to 160 men who were subsequently interviewed for from one to three hours to discover their understanding and reaction to the cartoons. The interviews demonstrated that about two-thirds of the men had misunderstood the message, and a large number had even reversed its meaning, believing that the cartoons were designed to *create* racial prejudice.

All these examples demonstrate that political propaganda is much less effective than has often been thought and that, in particular, the mass media play only a very small part in changing people's attitudes. Their function is limited to reinforcing or crystallizing *existing* voting intentions, and it is events rather than words which prove effectual. Thus the recent Liberal revival in Britain had no help from the media and, in fact, occurred a year after the only Liberal newspaper in the country, the *News Chronicle*, had closed down, while the United States persists in electing Democratic Congresses in complete opposition to the media which are eighty per cent Republican. We have already noted the inability of the Communist countries and the Communist party, in spite of intensive propaganda, to gain power constitutionally anywhere else in the world, and the failure of their anti-religious campaign. Indeed, not only have they failed, but there have been spontaneous revolts in countries where the media have been a government monopoly for years: in Hungary and Poland in 1956, in East Germany continuously, and the cultural revolt which is so evident amongst Soviet youth today. The Pilkington Report is discussed later, but it is worth noting that its belief in the 'immense power of television' was based solely on the unsupported impressions of a number of oddly assorted organizations which not only had no specialist knowledge of the subject but made no reference whatever to the vast body of research of which we have been able to give only a few examples above. Shortly we shall come across the view expressed by such writers as Raymond Williams in *The Long Revolution* that, in the cultural sphere, the media condition and brainwash the sturdy workers into preferring Westerns and crime programmes to Ibsen, variety programmes to symphony concerts, and Radio Luxembourg or ITA to the BBC. This is done, it is alleged, by the 'advertisers and mass psychologists, the pseudo-scientists of the new society', who press upon the public their 'unalterable vulgarity' and whose talk about the sovereignty of the consumer 'reeks of dishonesty'. Of course, the media simply do not possess this overwhelming power to manipulate our tastes and deprive us of free choice. As Barbara Wootton very sensibly says (*New Society*, 4 October 1962): 'As we all know to our cost, one of the major problems of complex, modern, professedly democratic communities is the difficulty that the ordinary individual experiences in making himself heard. Ordinary individuals have reason therefore to applaud the invention of contemporary polling techniques inasmuch as these make it possible for every shade of opinion on any topic to be accurately measured and assessed. Incidentally this is, no doubt, one reason why these techniques tend to be unpopular with politicians.' These being the methods whereby the media select their programmes, it is strange, as Lady Wootton points out, that the Pilkington Committee almost wholly ignored the fact, repeatedly established by audience research, that a majority of viewers actually preferred I T A programmes to those of the BBC. It is unfortunately the case that, although Mr Williams repeatedly extols the working-class and socialist virtues of solidarity, community, and traditional neighbourliness, he fails to see that these may well conflict with the opposite (and equally socialist) values of democracy as exemplified by opinion polls, freedom of choice, and freedom of criticism. What Dr Leavis and Messrs Thompson, Hoggart, and Williams appear to wish is the power to impose their own cultural standards of a 'common culture' and 'socialist realism' on a totally unwilling majority.

Numerous investigations have been made into the effects of TV programmes upon children which, since four out of five British homes possess television sets, are generally assumed to be profound. What influences it has to the good are not usually discussed, although talking to children certainly gives the impression that they are better-informed about the world in which they live than formerly; nor is it usual to consider what *indirect* effects it may have in setting social norms as to how to behave in relation to others. For example it might be the case that the constant presentation of people living in more luxurious circumstances than their own or the impact of television advertising may be one of the influences stimulating some children towards a more competitive attitude to life and the less successful to a life of crime in order to obtain these luxuries. From what we know about the rearing of children in the home it is apparent that what they learn is not so much the overt lessons taught them by their parents but rather derives from the concealed implications lying behind their parents' attitudes and their own social background; the child who is punished *may* learn that it should not commit the same act again, or, on the other hand, it may learn the other lesson that 'thou shalt not be found out', and it might be argued that the same is true of television or the other mass media. On the face of it there seems to be no more reason why normal children should be turned into criminals by watching television crime than they would be turned into pirates by reading *Treasure Island*, but we have noted that nobody simply perceives – he interprets what he perceives in the light of his own past experience and upbringing. Yet if certain abnormal children have actually imitated behaviour seen on television or observed in comics and hanged themselves or died trying to fly like Superman, these are in a very small minority; and although many investigators believe that scenes of violence which may leave the average adolescent unharmed might stimulate an emotionally disturbed child or gang and reinforce their delinquent tendencies, others believe on the contrary that such scenes are actually a deterrent to delinquency, permitting youth to work off its aggression vicariously. The popularity of detective stories amongst intellectuals suggests that it is not only children who feel the need to let off steam.

Hilde Himmelweit has analysed the actual content of children's television plays or films in relation to their attitudes to acts of violence and makes a distinction between 'Westerns' and 'crime plays', suggesting that the difference lies in the stylized 'goodies' and 'baddies' of the former in contrast with the complexity and 'realism' of the latter.

The central lesson of Westerns is that good triumphs over bad through violence – the manly, as well as the only, course of action. The villain's case is never stated, no sympathy is invited for him, and the hero never gains anything from his deeds. There is no suggestion of internal conflict or indecision.

In crime stories, there are three kinds of explicit values:

First, that crime does not pay. . . . Second, that the activities of criminals and the law are not in fact dissimilar. Both sides bully and cheat as necessary. . . . Third, that appearances are deceptive; a person may look harmless and yet be a criminal (though hardly ever the other way round).

A final important difference is that in Westerns 'the impact of violence is dulled because there are no close-ups at the kill and also because the emphasis is on opposing sides rather than individuals', while in crime plays 'there is no attempt to evade the consequences of violence, the camera stays with the man who has been hit; we see blood on his hands and beads of sweat on his face'.

However, the general tendency of most of the investigations which have been carried out concerning a possible connexion between television violence and delinquency has been, in effect, to conclude that, although such influences may be undesirable in themselves, there is no proof that they have any effect on the normal child although they may have a different effect on the maladjusted child. The report *Citizens of Tomorrow* sponsored by King George's Jubilee Trust concluded that

... the power of these extraneous influences is often exaggerated, and we have no evidence that a boy or girl not previously disposed to law-breaking has been started on a life of crime solely by gangster films or reports of violent behaviour.*

Dr Mark Abrams, asking whether 'the abundance of this noxious material in the mass media' creates a general climate of undesirable values in ordinary average children, takes another view:

The available evidence from research on these points among children is slight and often negative. It appears that when maladjusted and well adjusted children are exposed to identical amounts of violent mass-media content, the former, unlike the latter, show a marked preference for such material, derive distinctive satisfactions from it, and, in the process of consumption, their problems are sustained rather than resolved.

He concludes that the strength of the case for removing such material depends upon how large a proportion of our children are maladjusted and frustrated. If it is very low, e.g. one or two per cent, then the introduction of censorship could hardly be

* The Nuffield study of television and the child concludes even more positively that 'the influence of television on children's leisure, interests, knowledge, outlook, and values proves to be far less colourful and dramatic than popular opinion is inclined to suppose'.

justified; but if it were high, e.g. twenty or twenty-five per cent, the case for censorship would seem to be unanswerable. 'Unfortunately, . . . we do not know whether it is two per cent or twenty-two per cent.'

Regarding the actual content of TV shows we can obviously have much more accurate data. Thus it has been calculated that in 1954 most television time in New York was given up to entertainment (about 78 per cent), and from 1951 to the end of 1954 about 17 per cent of total programme time was devoted to information programmes and 5 per cent to orientation (i.e. public events, religion, etc.). In Britain during one week of January 1956, the comparable BBC figures were, entertainment 67 per cent, information 24 per cent, and orientation 9 per cent, whilst for the ITA presentations the figures were, entertainment 78 per cent, information 14 per cent, and orientation 8 per cent. During one week in 1954 on New York television someone was injured or threatened with violence once in every six minutes of programme time. However, these rather grim-sounding figures are less alarming if they are further analysed: it was shown that only one fifth of the acts of violence actually occurred in a tension-producing or thrilling context, one third were in a humorous context, and the rest occurred in a neutral setting of 'normal' violence not accompanied by tension-producing stimuli. In children's programmes relatively little of the violence occurred in a tension-producing context and 59 per cent of it occurred in a humorous situation.*

A great deal of the discussion about the effect of scenes of violence upon children is beside the point because it does not take account of the real nature of the child as revealed by modern psychoanalytic techniques. We notice that children listen to fairy tales such as those of the Grimm brothers and Hans Andersen with an air of fascinated horror, or even with gusto, and often ask for the reading to be repeated although the gruesome figures of these tales sometimes enter into their nightmares. Surely this would seem to be an indication for avoiding them, and yet, as the child psychologist P. M. Pickard points out (*I Could a Tale Unfold: Violence, Horror & Sensationalism in Stories for Children*,

* For present trends see p. 160.

Tavistock Humanities), we find that young children *spontaneously*, both consciously and, still more, unconsciously, create for themselves the same images of horror and terror without ever having heard a fairy story, much less seen TV violence or read horror comics. She writes:

Children are innately capable of anger; this anger can appear in the earliest months; during anger, thought is phantastically horrible and far more fierce than during anger in adults. If we accept these findings of modern research, then some of our difficulties are cleared away. The argument that we have to condition children to horrors is now seen as fallacious; there is no question of introducing them to horrors, because the horrors already known to them are far in excess of anything we experience as adults.

Thus the wicked devouring witch with iron teeth is the bad aspect of the mother whom the child once had fantasies of devouring himself, and the bad giant may represent the unpleasant aspects of the father. Indeed, the telling of these tales, which already correspond to something in the child's experience, has a reasurring effect when seen against the context of the safe fireside and mother's reassuring smile; they are sought by the child as a form of self-therapy. Even at a later age, normal children *are* self-assertive and aggressive; thus in a group of 100 children with ages ranging from six to twelve and characters ranging from the normal to the delinquent and neurotic, it was found that, on the whole, the normal children had strong self-assertive trends, lively conflicts with their parents, and ambivalent swings between love and hate for their brothers and sisters. In contrast, the neurotic children showed an abnormal degree of attachment to their families whilst the delinquent ones showed a corresponding degree of detachment.

Most people have very little idea about the real nature of aggression and the various ways in which it can be handled. In fact, it is almost universally assumed that what is a perfectly natural and innate drive is, without qualification, evil. But, as Dr Anthony Storr points out in an article on 'The Psychology of Aggression' (*New Society*, 11 October 1962): 'One can blame aggression on the Devil; or attribute it to the Fall; or indulge oneself in fantasies of a past when it was not, or of a future in which it will have no place. But all these ways of regarding aggression are attempts to deny it or get rid of it, and, as such, are doomed.' Actually, as Dr D. W. Winnicott the eminent psychoanalyst has stated: 'At origin aggressiveness is almost synonymous with activity.' Thus we talk about 'attacking' a problem; 'struggling' with, and 'overcoming' a difficulty; 'mastering' a subject or 'getting one's teeth into it'. With young children their bloodthirsty and aggressive games and imaginings are an expression of their desire to overcome their feelings of dependency in order to attain freedom of choice and adult self-determination; in addition, as we have already seen, they are a form of self-therapy and it is more than probable that the continued and intense absorption in horror-producing scenes in comics or TV when later years have been reached is a sign that these conflicts have not been resolved. If this is true, then, so far from TV violence leading to delinquency, the child with problems who behaves in this way is unconsciously trying to resolve his delinquent tendencies by working them out vicariously. In the case of the normal child, as Dr Storr points out, aggressive themes, as in so-called horror films, may actually be harmless channels for expression. The real danger of aggression lies in quite another direction from that assumed by those who wish to deny or get rid of it, and, says Dr Winnicott, 'If society is in danger, it is not because of man's aggressiveness, but because of the repression of personal aggressiveness in individuals.' Normal children and adults are normal because they express their aggressiveness as it arises within the bounds acceptable to society (or at least not wholly unacceptable). The dangerous individual is the one who denies or represses these emotions with the result that they may be turned against the self, leading to melancholia, against a scapegoat rather than the original object, or suddenly explode in an outburst of violence. He is the delinquent or the neurotic.

These observations, which we have no space to enlarge upon, obviously have considerable bearing upon the misplaced sympathy which is wasted upon children so far as the mere exposure to horrid scenes is concerned. What is important to the child is not the incidental horror but the necessity for a satisfactory ending to the tale, in which the good are rewarded and the bad punished. Indeed, anyone who has watched a young child looking at unpleasant fantasies on TV or listening to gruesome fairy stories cannot help but be struck by the sort of things that move it to emotion; the killing and the cutting-off of heads pass by with hardly a sign of passing interest, but the lost little girl or dog moves the child to tears because he or she identifies himself or herself with them. Nor have they much bearing upon the problem of the so-called 'horror comics' directed at much older children and adolescents of all ages, the worst traits of which are probably their indescribable idiocy, vulgarity, and sex-obsessed bad taste. It is to these we must now briefly turn to see whether there is any likelihood that they are capable of influencing those who read them in the direction of sadism or delinquency.

As was mentioned earlier, it was Alfred Harmsworth, later Lord Northcliffe, who in 1890 published the first comic, entitled *Comic Cuts* and originally intended, not for children, but for working-class men and women. Allegedly it was intended as a counterblast to the 'penny dreadful' with its tales of horror, and soon *Comic Cuts* was found to be a great favourite with children and became the first of many such ventures on the part of Harmsworth and others. Whatever may be said of the modern British comic, nobody by the wildest stretch of imagination could suppose it to do any harm; such papers as *Topper*, *The Beezer*, *Beano*, and *Dandy* are innocuous and amusing while those intended for older children, *Girl*, *Eagle*, *Judy*, and *Bunty*, are often highly informative into the bargain. But comics in America had quite a different history, although they too were at first intended for adults. The first American papers in this genre were for the entertainment of the foreign-language communities, whose knowledge of English was poor and had to be supplemented by pictures, or for those whose native language was English but were below average ability so far as reading was concerned. At first these tales were harmless enough stories of the early settlers, but soon they became infiltrated with all the elements of the Gothic novel of an earlier period: ghosts, ghouls, vampires, spectral riders, pointless murders, and sinister relationships between the sexes. Unfortunately, they too were taken up by children although to this day they are still read by back-ward adults and were supplied to the American forces abroad as part of their essential supplies – a source from which they finally penetrated to British children at a time when many of the British comic papers had closed down owing to the war. According to Dr Frederic Wertham, the Director of the Lafargue Clinic, in his book *The Seduction of the Innocent* (Museum Press, London), these comics contain such material as the following: '. . . one girl squirting fiery "radium dust" on the protruding breasts of an-other girl ("I think I've discovered your Achilles' heel, chum"); white men banging natives around; a close-up view of the branded breast of a girl; a girl about to be blinded.' Dr Wertham reported to the Joint Legislative Committee to Study the Pub-lication of Comics (1949) that such books sold forty to eighty million copies monthly (although this is a minute proportion of the actual readers since the books are handed around from one person to another and later sold second-hand); the hero is nearly always 'regular-featured and an athlete, a pure American white man' whilst the villains, on the other hand, are 'foreign-born, Jews, Orientals, Slavs, Italians and dark-skinned races'. He cited one comic in a boy's possession which contained nineteen mur-ders (ten by shooting, nine by strangling, stabbing, and being beaten in the face) and forty-five threats of murder with a gun, and seventeen deaths by hanging and being dropped alive into acid. Dr Wertham comments in his book:

Whenever I see a book like this in the hands of a little seven-year-old boy, his eyes glued to the printed page, I feel like a fool to have to prove that this kind of thing is not good mental nourishment for children.

Studying some of these comics which had arrived in this country, P. M. Pickard substantiated Dr Wertham's claim that they contain every known form of sexual perversion, right down to the obscurer forms of vampirism, etc. She points out that researches in Britain and America show that at least 98 per cent of children read comics,* and the peak period is at eleven years. From a large group of children Miss Pickard found that fears

* Not all horror comics, of course.

over comics were admitted by 26 per cent and bad dreams by 18 per cent, and comments: '. . . it becomes patently clear that what they disliked was having back their own horrid nightmares of evil faces, skeletons, bad men, ugliness, and murder, without any assistance towards surmounting them' – because, of course, the intention of such books is not to resolve suspense and tension but to maintain it. Most authorities are extremely doubtful whether there is any straightforward relationship between comic books and crime and express themselves as concerned lest this over-simple attribution of delinquency to comics should draw attention away from its true causes. Nevertheless, there can be no doubt about the undesirability of such publications and their possible effect of instilling an unpleasant code of values in those who are already predisposed.

What is most striking about much of this research work* is its failure to take into account what good the mass media may do, and the obvious fact that teaching people to become more selective is at least as important as any question of changing or censoring the content of the media. The common belief that sinister élites are forcing rubbish upon the inoffensive individual simply does not bear careful scrutiny – on the contrary, they give people what they ask for, and very often a good deal better material than they demand. Norman Collins of ITA has said:

If one gave the public exactly what it wanted it would be a perfectly appalling service . . . The overwhelming mass of the letters we get are illiterate, they are ungrammatical, they are deplorably written, and what is more distressing, too, they evince an attitude of mind that I do not think can be regarded as very admirable. All they write for are pictures of film stars, television stars, or asking why there are not more jazz programmes, why there cannot be more programmes of a music-hall type. I hold the teachers very largely responsible, if that is the attitude of people in their teens and early twenties. If we provided simply that it would be deplorable.

The head of the *Mirror* group of papers, Cecil King, takes a similar view:

The trouble is the critics imagine the great British public is as educated as themselves and their friends, and that we ought to start

---

* cf, too, the Pilkington Report (1962).

where they are and raise the standard from there up. In point of fact it is only the people who conduct newspapers and similar organizations who have any idea quite how indifferent, quite how stupid, quite how uninterested in education of any kind the great bulk of the British public are.

So far as Britain is concerned the answer must be that we have for long been divided into the 'two nations' described by Disraeli; universal education is of comparatively recent growth, and, as Raymond Williams points out in his book *Communications*, to many working-class people it is still the case that education is identified with childhood whereas the world of mass communications is identified with the greater freedom of the adult. In objective fact, Beethoven and Shakespeare are as available to the masses who listen to radio or watch television as are 'Wagon Train' or 'Dr Kildare' but high culture has come to be associated in the minds of the masses with both 'education' and the class minority which in the past has been identified with it. There is a snobbery on the other side too, amongst those intellectuals who seem to assume that the high traditional culture is the only one and reject musicals such as *West Side Story*, films such as *A Taste of Honey* or *Saturday Night and Sunday Morning*, and science fiction, which, on their own level, are equally 'culture' and as good as, or better than, that of the past. The intellectual who never reads a detective story or enjoys a Western on television is either maladjusted to the world in which he lives or a complete myth. Thus it is difficult to agree with Williams in the obvious distress he feels at the fairly obvious discovery that in women's magazines the theme of 'marrying the boss' or at any rate someone of higher social status than the heroine plays a major part in their stories or serials. But this has been a theme of great literature from *The Arabian Nights* and fairy tales to Richardson's *Pamela* and beyond, because fantasy plays an important part in everybody's life. It is perfectly natural for people who have worked hard at a dull job all day to want to escape, and *Pickwick Papers* or *Don Quixote* are as much escape literature and fantasy as *Peg's Paper*. Nor is it even true that this is the sole interest of the women who read this type of publication; for television serials such as 'The Rag Trade' and 'Coronation Street' are every bit as popular in spite of, or because of, the fact that they deal with everyday working-class life.

Mention has been made of the complaint that radio and television limit the scope of people's interests and that, instead of getting what they 'really' want, they are given the sort of rubbish they have been conditioned to want. Thus Himmelweit writes:

After all, people like Westerns, we put Westerns on. But because we have this trend study extending over a period of years you can see that this kind of taste is to some extent – not of course entirely – an artificial one, a taste produced by the programme planners and producers.

The first statement, that choice of programme subjects is limited by the producers, is rubbish; for over the past few months in Britain anyone could have seen the whole range of Shakespeare's historical plays, the plays of Ibsen, Chekhov, or Strindberg, learned Russian, Italian, German, or French, heard theologians debate with atheists, and Communists and the other political parties stating their case, and discovered what is new about practically every other subject under the sun. The problem is that most people have rather low tastes, tend as they grow older to have certain fixed or relatively fixed interests, and, on the whole, do not look for new experiences. There is no evidence of what people 'really' want except in what they say they want and it has been noted that you cannot start a trend or reverse it, but only accentuate one that exists. As the Head of BBC Audience Research has said: 'You cannot reinforce something that is not there.'

In support of her belief that a taste (for example, for Westerns) is to some extent an artificial one produced by the programme planners and producers, and is therefore a function of supply, Himmelweit in a more recent survey ('Television Revisited', *New Society*, 1 November 1962) quotes the following example: 'In 1956, especially on ITV, a spate of crime programmes were shown e.g. *Dragnet*, *Inner Sanctum*, *Highway Patrol*, with BBC adding *Fabian of the Yard* and *Dixon of Dock Green*. Then, it was the crime programmes which received the top vote. In January 1960, both sides offered large numbers of Westerns, so

Westerns attracted most votes with crime programmes taking fourth place among grammar-school pupils.' Now if this is to be taken to mean that people ordinarily make their choice from what is most available, the results of the trend study are almost a truism. But it can be of small consolation to the moralists who, after all, are contending that television can create *good* taste and that the planners and producers are failing in their duty in making little attempt to do so; for obviously the change from crime programmes to Westerns is merely a substitution of one type of programme for another *at the same cultural level.* If Dr Himmelweit is seriously contending that the television authorities could forcibly change taste in the direction of *good* taste – for example, in the direction of serious plays, the classics, educational subjects and documentaries, regardless of the preferences of the audience – then surely all experience shows her to be mistaken. Thus, after many years of sound broadcasting throughout a major part of which there was a deliberate attempt on the part of the BBC to educate popular taste, there was no evidence, when this policy came to an end, of any change in the form of a shift of audience from the Light to the Third programme. Undoubtedly an immense change in taste is occurring and will continue over the years, but, as will be argued later, it is coming as the result of better education and changed attitudes, causing people to become more selective within the limits of their own interests. Popular taste is always shifting, although not to any significant degree in response to television policy, which, as has been suggested, is the slave rather than the master of its consumers. For example, although in the same article it is stated that 'ITV this autumn [1962], *in response to the Pilkington Committee's strictures,** has reduced the number of Westerns and crime programmes it shows', it is odd that similar changes have occurred in America without the blessing of the Committee. In response to public opinion alone, Westerns have been a dying category for years and crime programmes are to a considerable extent being ousted by the comic or serious programmes of family life represented in Britain by such productions as 'Coronation Street' and 'Steptoe and Son', or by those dealing with

*My italics – J. A. C. B.

160

medical life such as 'Dr Kildare', 'Ben Casey', and 'Emergency Ward 10'. Finally, it is worth while noting that figures giving the hours of 'crime' or 'Western' programmes shown at any given time can be highly misleading in so far as they are supposed to indicate the amount of violence to which the audience is exposed. It seems quite clear that they have often been compiled by those who have never seen the programmes in question. Thus two of the currently most popular crime series, 'Perry Mason' and 'Sam Benedict', are basically legal stories centred around the courtroom and rarely show any violence at all. Again 'Dixon of Dock Green' shows violence but rarely and is simply an account of the usually minor comedies or tragedies seen at a police station in a working-class area; the police are represented as helpful and benign characters and the series has a highly moral tone, making the point that the police are there to aid and protect and should be supported by the public. Nor is every programme which takes place against a Western background an orgy of slaying and gunslinging: 'Lassie', for example, is about a dog. It may well be that all these programmes are not improving, but that is no reason why they should be misrepresented. The basic fact, however, is that changes in taste, such as the disappearing Western and the current shift in Britain towards the B B C, do not happen by regulations or government intervention; certain programmes gradually drop out, neither by intervention nor because they have deteriorated, but simply because we have progressed past them.

The fact is that the mass media are there to be made use of, and what use is made of them depends upon the individual himself. He can drug himself into insensitivity or use the media selectively – and the ability to do so must begin with education, when it comes to be regarded, not as a childhood activity, but as a process continuing throughout life. Indeed, there is evidence all around us that people are looking at more good pictures, hearing better music, and, with the paperback revolution, reading more and better books than ever before in the history of mankind, and that this is not a temporary phenomenon but a progressive trend. Even Dr Himmelweit points out that '. . . in America librarians and teachers report that the cultural values communicated by TV programmes are responsible for much wider exploration of the world of books by children than in pre-TV days', and that while in England at first '... TV adversely influences reading and reading skill, yet in the long run it increases book-reading (as opposed to "comic" reading) with an increased range of books and no loss of skill'. These results are not achieved by forcing culture on the children, but by allowing them a wide choice of programmes from which they can select according to their interests and level of education. TV can intensify interests and open up new vistas but only for those who are willing and prepared to receive them.

So far as the horror comic is concerned, it may very well be true that this is an undesirable form of literature for children or, for the matter of that, for adults. But it never seems to have occurred to the critics that, although all classes of children read such books, delinquency is the result, in the view of nearly all authorities who have been concerned with the problem, of basically social factors. Many delinquents come from broken homes, but the vast majority belong to a specific social class and live in specifically delinquent areas. In other words, the typical delinquent is the individual who, especially when family tensions lead to frustration, has delinquency open to him as an outlet because in the particular area in which he lives this is a socially acceptable form of behaviour. The middle-class child, on the other hand, does not have such outlets in the area in which he lives, and in similar home circumstances is more likely to become a neurotic. It is also true that, although there is no reason to suppose that such publications are less read by middle-class than by lower-working-class children, the former tend to be interested in them for a much briefer period than the latter who may in some cases go on reading them into adult life. It is more than doubtful whether delinquency would be influenced even in the slightest degree by the withdrawal of violence on TV or of horror comics. But horror comics are only a minute fraction of the output of the mass media as a whole and the conclusion we have reached about the media in general is that they can be a powerful force for the bettering of society, but are inevitably only a short step ahead of public taste which can be improved only by better education and time. Except in a totalitarian country, the mass medium cannot rise too far above or fall too far below the cultural level of the people at whom it is aimed.

Although we have tried to take their propositions seriously, there is something verging on the comical about many critics of the mass media; these range from the ruling classes, who feel that their high culture and elegant style of living is being rudely destroyed by crowds of vulgar, noisy, and newly affluent people egged on by the mass media, to the disillusioned leftists, who want to blame the media and their capitalist bosses for the loss of a warm working-class culture and craftsmanship or, in the case of the more politically minded, for the workers' apparent loss of militancy and revolutionary fervour. The fact that the ruling classes (if by that one means the aristocracy, landowners, and, later, the industrialists) have never had – at least since Elizabethan times – any culture worth mentioning to lose, and that the workers' 'organic society' is largely a figment of the imagination is completely ignored. The critics rarely argue, they merely *assert* that the media corrupt moral standards, are a cause of juvenile delinquency, encourage 'keeping up with the Joneses' or greed for possessions, and debase artistic taste. Yet it is quite clear that snobbery and social emulation, as C. A. R. Crosland has pointed out, were at least as evident in the world of Jane Austen, the worship of success in the days of Samuel Smiles, and money-obsession in the days of the Forsytes or of Newport and the American Baroque. Again, most of these attitudes have nothing to do with the mass media as such, but with the process of industrialization and democratization *of which the media are themselves just one symptom*. The proof of this statement is apparent in the fact, completely ignored by the critics, that the same attitudes can be observed in countries where the media either do not exist, or, as in the Communist countries, are not commercially controlled and there are no wicked capitalists. The Soviet Union is just as much concerned with juvenile delinquency as every other modern industrialized country, because there, as here, teenagers are socially emancipated, reach puberty earlier, and have money to spare and far wider possibilities for success or failure than their parents. Furthermore, the desire for emulation and material possessions is arising all over the world, not because of commercial advertising which is only there to provide for an existing need, but because, as the Industrial Revolution has gathered momentum, millions of people for the first time in history have the possibility of increasing their living standards beyond the level of mere subsistence. They are simply demanding the luxuries which the ruling and the middle classes have always taken for granted. We shall deal elsewhere with the suggestion that popular taste is declining, but the thesis that people are uncritical of the media and accept whatever they bring has been shown to be contrary to reality. C. A. R. Crosland, in the article already quoted ('The Mass Media', *Encounter*, November 1962) has this to say of the latter belief: 'The theory of the passive, captive audience seems eccentric in the light of the intense and active family life in working-class areas, with its immense range of hobbies, do-it-yourself activities, gardening, house-repair, and (the greatest change of all) family travel; we may take different views about the desirability of the shift to *home-orientated* leisure activities. But it is certainly not a shift to a drugged, undifferentiated passivity.'

CHAPTER 7

ADVERTISING AND INDUSTRY

IT is possible, if not particularly profitable, to trace advertising back in some form or another to very early days. There are, for example, the small stone printing stamps (some of which are to be seen in the British Museum) which were used by the quacks of Roman times to impress a message on the surface of their salves and ointments. One such, found near Hereford, mentions 'T. Vindaius Ariovestus' and his 'unbeatable' ointment made of a 'preparation of aniseed' and called 'Chloron, the green salve'. But advertising in the modern sense is a product of the mass society inasmuch as it comes into being only when people can no longer do most of their communicating face-to-face and begin to require some other method of describing where and what they supply. Also there must be a surplus of goods, especially luxuries, since man's basic needs will always sell themselves: countries which live near subsistence level have little need for advertising since want is their salesman. In the small village or town the shoe-maker, weaver, potter, or provision merchant has no need to trumpet the virtues of his goods because the information gets about by word of mouth and his local fame or disrepute is established in this way. It is only as towns grow in size and the masses become a reality that he is in danger of becoming forgotten. Nor is advertising an easy matter without a medium whereby it can be disseminated; hence the importance of the newspaper or periodical which carries advertisements as part of its services to the public. However, the first regular publication, Nathaniel Butter's *Weekly Newes* brought out in 1622, contained no advertisements; the first paper to do so was the *Mercurius Britannicus*, which, three years later, carried one of the earliest known examples in a periodical:

An excellent discourse concerning the match between our most Gracious and Mightie Prince Charles, Prince of Wales, and the Lady Henrietta Maria, daughter of Henry the Fourth late King of France . . . with a lively picture of the Prince and Lady cut in bronze.

Since the main purpose of these early advertisements was simply to draw the reader's attention to a particular product or service, they generally took the form of a bald statement of fact, as in this example from the same periodical on 30 September 1658:

That excellent, and by all physicians approved *China* drink, called by the Chineans *Tcha*, by other nations *Tay* alias *Tee*, is sold at the Sultaness Head Cophee-House, in Sweeting's Rents, by the Royal Exchange, London.

But these comparatively subdued efforts were not to last for long, and Daniel Defoe in his *Journal of the Plague Year* describes how during the plague of 1665 the public was assaulted by advertisers, so that:

. . . even the Posts of Houses and Corners of Streets were plastered over with Doctors' Bills, and Papers of Ignorant Fellows; quacking and tampering with Physick, and inviting the People to come to them for Remedies.

When the Great Fire followed the plague, those whose businesses had been burned out were invited to advertise their new addresses in the public sheets, although these had a comparatively restricted readership because of the general illiteracy of the greater part of the population. The world of the seventeenth- and eighteenth-century newspaper or periodical was the world of the coffee-house frequented by merchants, lawyers, captains of ships, writers, gamblers, and clergymen, and there, as in cafés on the Continent today, the papers could be read, business transacted, and messages left. From the point of view of advertising, the important name of the latter part of the seventeenth century was John Houghton, who, seeing a great future for the profession, brought out the first paper of note published almost exclusively for its advertisements. This was known as *A Collection for the Improvement of Husbandry and Trade*, which, appearing in 1682, carried not only commercial advertisements, but also 'situations vacant', 'situations wanted', 'lost and found', and other announcements. Books were read and recommended free, booksellers reproved for putting new titles on old books, and finally Houghton introduced a matrimonial column.

Throughout the eighteenth and nineteenth centuries newspapers relied, to a greater or less extent, on some income from advertising; this was at its highest point of importance in the middle of the eighteenth century and at its lowest in the latter half of the nineteenth. Such advertising was mainly of what is now usually known as the 'classified' type (i.e. specific individual notices) and one element of all modern advertising was noticeably absent – there were no advertisements for household goods. These did not make their appearance until the first quarter of the nineteenth century had passed and the advertising methods of Henry Colburn began to attract the adverse comments of the more respectable papers such as the *Athenaeum* and *Frazer's* which expressed themselves as disgusted that he should advertise shoe-blacking and tooth powder on the same lines as literature. The former periodical pointed out that 'by dint of eternal paragraph' even the 'stupidist cluster of trashy papers could be forced into sale' and that '. . . it could not otherwise happen that Day and Martin, Rowland, Eady, Warren, and those after their kind could lavish so much money in the praises of their oils, their books, their pills and their polish if there did not exist a class of human beings who are greedy of belief'. Nevertheless, Colburn (who was the publisher of Disraeli, Mrs Shelley, Hood, and Fenimore Cooper) continued to flourish and in a single year spent as much as £9,000 on advertising. The Warren mentioned above is generally supposed to have marketed the first nationally advertised household article, Warren's Shoe Blacking, and the Mr Rowland was none other than the maker of the famous Rowland's Macassar Oil for the hair which replaced the bear's grease of earlier days and was on sale until quite recent times. The mass market as we know it now was rapidly developing and advertising began to employ tricks of the trade familiar to the present day: the jingle or verse of doggerel recommending a product, the use of repetition, and the employment of neologisms to give the reader an impression of erudition and scientific accuracy whilst flattering his supposed knowledge. Hair dye was an 'atrapilatory', hair cream and tonic an 'aromatic regenerator', pills for the chest 'pulmonic wafers', and so on.

Not all the wealthy merchants of the country were convinced that newspapers were the best medium for advertising their products; for the great mass of the public never read newspapers and yet were, in varying degrees, capable of reading. Bills posted on walls could be made to appeal to these, and an additional advantage was that posters were not subject to the advertisement tax. In the early and middle years of the nineteenth century bill-posting became a large and organized trade. All kinds of buildings were used, often without consent, and soon London was almost submerged in posters and they had begun to spread out into the countryside. The Metropolitan Police Act of 1839 made it an offence to post bills without the consent of the owner, but the law was difficult to enforce, until in 1862, special hoardings were organized by the Billposters' Association. Street leaflets and handbills were also employed and thrust into the hands of passers-by who were frequently shocked to find that many were concerned with cures for venereal disease, and other methods employed were 'sandwich men' (a title supplied by Charles Dickens) who carried large placards back and front, and vehicles carrying columns with bills or models of the article advertised. By 1848 omnibus passenger transport had begun the familiar advertising within its coaches, and new developments followed: balloon and skyline advertisements, electric signs, and even the firing of leaflets from guns.

Because advertising had gained for itself a reputation for vulgarity and untruthfulness, the more reputable firms returned during the latter part of the century to the mere repetition of the name of their product, as 'Hot Bovril', 'Pears Soap', 'Stephens Ink', sometimes on the metal plaques which can still be seen in our older railway stations. One of the notables in the field of advertising at this time was Thomas J. Barratt of Pears' Soap Company who, on taking over the old business (the soap had been marketed originally in 1789), raised his expenditure on advertising to the then astronomical figure of between £100,000 and £130,000. His first aim was to link the name 'Pears' indissolubly in the public mind with soap, or with a frequently-used phrase. The latter gave rise to the catch-word *'Good morning! Have you used Pears soap?'* which soon became so familiar that the more sensitive citizen would fear to wish his acquaintances a good morning lest the infuriating catch-phrase should be aroused in the other's mind. Barratt was also the first to employ reputable artists, or rather to gain possession of their works for advertising purposes, as when he bought Sir John Millais's famous (if overrated) painting *Bubbles*, which depicted a small boy in a green suit blowing bubbles. Although this aroused considerable public indignation with vociferous complaints of 'degradation of art', the genuine poster artist began to come into his own and the crude prints of former times were replaced in favour of simple, bold, and well-produced colour posters. The influence came from France after the process of colour lithography had been perfected in Britain, and the posters of Jules Cheret and Toulouse-Lautrec's posters commissioned by the Moulin Rouge are still famous.

Finally, from the 1880s the new kinds of display advertising began to influence the press at a time when changes in marketing and the development of the retail trade had begun to alter the whole basis of advertising. Such men as Lord Northcliffe saw how display advertising could be made to lead to increased revenue and enable them to cut the price of their newspapers to the public. By these means Northcliffe hoped to gain a large circulation; and, publishing his own circulation figures, he challenged his rivals to do likewise. The results of this policy were to alter the whole structure of the press in our time; for while the typical nineteenth-century newspaper tried to attract advertising revenue, it was not dependent upon it; but in the twentieth century a paper might be dependent on advertisements to the extent of half its total revenue, with the result that those papers which are unable to attract this amount may have to close down whether they have popular support or not. In his use of this type of advertising, Northcliffe was supported by the new advertising agencies which had started to develop both in Britain and the U.S.A. at the same period. The original advertising agent had been a man who worked either for the company which wished to buy advertising space or for the journals which sold it. He was, in fact, a kind of liaison officer, and although he might often be prepared to help an advertiser to prepare his material, it was not until the 1880s that he began to see this as his main job. Henceforth it was no longer necessary for companies to maintain their own advertising departments; the work was done for them by the agency and being an 'ad-man' became a profession. It would be an exaggeration to say that everyone regarded it as a highly respectable profession, and, indeed, as Martin Mayer points out, advertising occupies today in the public mind the social position hurriedly abandoned by the stockbroker in 1929 – it is seen as glamorous, financially rewarding, and somehow not quite honest.

Most ad-men would claim that there is a genuine science of advertising psychology, comparable, for example, with industrial psychology. Whether or not this claim is justified will be discussed later, but the first text-book on the subject to arrive in Britain was written by Professor Walter Dill Scott, Director of the Psychological Laboratory at the North-Western University in Chicago. This appeared in 1909, and the writer enunciated a number of principles, most of them obvious to the point of platitude, of which the most fundamental was the long-familiar principle of association; not only should words come to be associated together so that 'Pears' comes to stand for soap and 'Hoover' for a vacuum-cleaner, but an attempt should be made to associate the product with the individual's basic motivations. These included the maternal instinct, greed, emulation, the desire for health and good looks, the desire to be appreciated by others, and so on. Advertisements should not be ugly or show, even in jest, unpleasing figures, and the wealthy and prosperous should be depicted rather than the poor and undistinguished. Humour was frowned on because advertising is a serious business, and unless very well done humour is apt to create a wrong impression. The appeal to basic 'instincts' was for long the general foundation of advertising psychology, which later came to justify it in terms of the theories of McDougall, although this is now an outdated concept which has been replaced by that of a few relatively undifferentiated biological drives moulded by society from a very early age. It was not until the late 1930s that advertising discovered Freud and little came of this discovery until the late forties and early fifties. However, whether or not advertising is a 'science', the advertising agency employing trained psychologists, sociologists, psychoanalysts, and social anthropologists is now an established reality in the United States and rapidly invading Europe.

That skilful advertising produced dramatic results even before the advent of these more subtle methods is beyond doubt, but those concerned with the modern profession, apparently from some latent sense of guilt or perhaps embarrassment (there is something a little shaming in the picture of an adult writing drivel about 'yummy' sweets and similar baby-talk), must needs justify their actions by an appeal to the social benefits conferred upon the rest of us by advertising.

Thus it is claimed that advertising cheapens goods by increasing the sale of an article which in turn lowers prices. This, of course, does not apply to basic goods and services; but in the case of non-essentials such as cigarettes it often happens that the product could be sold more cheaply if wasteful competition between firms did not cause the cost of advertising to be passed on to the public. *Which?* (the journal published by Consumers' Association Ltd) has pointed out that aspirin, unbranded, can be had for twenty-five for 4d., whereas the same formula, advertised at a cost of half a million pounds a year, costs 1s. 8½d. for twenty-seven. Elizabeth Gundrey (*Your Money's Worth*, Penguin Books) quotes the case of a kettle which went up in price from 23s. to 37s. 6d; when the manufacturer was asked the reason, he wrote: 'An extensive national advertising campaign is being conducted on it, and the price has been lifted mainly owing to the advertising charges.' In fact advertising may either raise or reduce prices.

Secondly, it is contended that advertising justifies itself economically by its function of bringing knowledge of desirable goods to the customer, and it is, of course, useful to know what is on at the local cinema, the date of a sale, or even that certain types of goods are available. Unfortunately the great bulk of advertising is much more than merely informative and a good deal is positively misleading. This is especially true in the case of patent medicines: to say, for example, that glucose gives you energy is not entirely untrue, since glucose is indeed the body's natural source of energy – what is not true is the advertiser's claim that people are tired because of lack of glucose, since nobody under any conceivable natural conditions suffers from any such deficiency. The claim that 'rheumatism' (a term which is pretty vague even to most doctors) is caused by unspecified 'impurities' in the blood which can be 'washed away' by the use of certain salts is either plain lying or the result of downright ignorance. Purgative manufacturers, in particular, are guilty not only of telling people untruths and scaring many out of their wits when they become constipated, but of doing positive physical harm, as any doctor can testify; there are no known diseases resulting from constipation (unless it happens to be secondary to some more serious condition which would certainly be worsened by taking purges), nor has constipation any specific symptoms, as is usually asserted; but there are quite dangerous diseases caused by the regular use of purgatives – colitis, for example.

When, as in the above instances, advertising seeks to give specific information about factual matters, it is very often misleading or lying. This is almost as true of the detergent manufacturers as of those who make patent medicines. Thus a 1959 issue of *Shopper's Guide* made the following comments on their claims after chemical analyses: the 'new magic ingredient' was carboxymethylcellulose, which, if new to this product, was currently used in all synthetic detergents; the 'fabulous new ingredient' was fluorescer, found in other detergents; and the 'special ingredient' with 'oxygen bubbles' which 'ease out stains' was perborate, also in other detergents. It would take a pretty stupid person to believe that all the detergent 'tests' carried out on television were genuine; and television advertisements often deceive the public in other ways. Thus, in a polish advertisement black glass was used instead of wood to give the effect of gloss; and in a cats' food advertisement, fresh liver, because the cat refused to oblige by eating the tinned product. A. S. J. Baster (*Advertising Reconsidered*) comments:

The major part of *informative* advertising is, and always has been, a campaign of exaggeration, half-truths, intended ambiguities, direct lies, and general deception. Amongst all the hundreds of thousands of persons engaged in the business, it may be said about most of them on the informative side of it that their chief function is to deceive buyers as to the real merits and demerits of the commodity being sold.

Finally, it is said that advertising brings about an improvement in the quality of goods and a sustained reliability, because, according to Dorothy Sayers:

> The advertiser's reputation is in the long run his livelihood. An anonymous purveyor may sand his sugar or put paper in the soles of the shoes he sells; but if the advertiser of branded goods does so, his victims will talk; his bad name will be bandied about.

By and large this may be true, but it would be an optimistic person who would be ready to claim that the quality of, say, groceries, has improved over the years, that packed and branded cheese let alone 'processed' cheese is as good as the unwrapped product, or canned or frozen vegetables as good as fresh ones. Poor quality goods *can* be sold and E. A. Filene has written:

> Poor values can be sold by large persistent advertising. It is simply a question of psychology – the hammering into people's minds of a certain idea until finally they accept it. If the sacrifice to accept it is not so big as to make a constant reinvestigation necessary, they will submit to the suggestion that a certain thing at a certain price is the best on the market.

Indeed, it might very well be argued that advertising has been largely responsible for a decline in popular taste in certain fields over the years by making people willing to accept the second- or third-rate. Compare, for example, the ghastly imitations of 'contemporary' furniture sold in cheap furnishing stores with those made by the craftsman for the poorer classes in bygone days and there can be no doubt which is the better and more durable. Many advertisers are willing to admit that their work consists largely in the creation of imaginary differences between products which are, for all practical purposes, the same. Thus only a small minority of cigarette smokers are capable of distinguishing between one brand and another when they are blindfolded and the cigarette is smoked through a holder. More-over, the emotions to which they appeal are by no means the most pleasant: fear, social embarrassment, greed, hypochondria, emulation in keeping up with the Joneses, and the rest. There is the appeal to social embarrassment in advertisements relating to bad breath, body-odour, facial blemishes, the state of one's W.C., and so on; the appeal to greed of the football pools and the food (especially confectionery) advertisements; the pseudo-scientific nonsense of patent medicines, 'health' foods, or 'tonic' wines which trade on hypochondria and personal insecurity ('By the time I left the office, I felt finished . . . younger men than me were coming on in the firm', etc.); and the desire for emulation in buying an unnecessary new car or living in a house in a partic-ular part of the country which is regarded as being in accordance with one's social status.

Some examples of what the more conventional type of adver-tising was capable of achieving during the 1920s and 1930s are quoted in Denys Thompson's book *Voice of Civilization: an Enquiry into Advertising*. First is the case of 'Curly Top', a hair-curling preparation for babies, the manufacture of which was begun towards the end of 1935 in the rooms of a house in Bury, Lancashire, when the work of mixing and bottling was carried out by a man and a boy. Advertising on an ascending scale was employed, and three years later the Vosemar Company needed a factory of 100,000 square feet to handle all the orders. Another product, '232' flannel trousers, was put on the market in 1922 and sold 3,000 pairs a year without advertising. In 1923, £800 was spent on advertising in the *Daily Mail*, following which sales rose to 60,000 pairs a year, and by 1930 over half a million had been sold.

Still more spectacular is the manner in which Britain was caused to buy a brand of packaged raisins because the American Raisin Growers' Association had to get rid of a surplus. Every-thing seemed to be against the Association because Britain had previously been supplied by certain interests which controlled the bulk market and bought from South Africa, Australia, or other areas where they could buy to the best advantage. How-ever, the American farmers spent two hundred and fifty thousand dollars in sixteen weeks in London alone; front pages were used in all the main newspapers, and posters for Sun Maid seedless raisins appeared on hoardings, in buses, on the underground, and even on goods trucks. The result, according to Stanley Q. Grady, was that '. . . at the end of three weeks we had seven thousand retail accounts. Then the jobbers had to come in, and that little five-cent package blazed the trail. The big packages followed, and twenty thousand tons were sold in Great Britain in a year.'

But there is no mystery about these results, which, for the most part, would appear to be due to the informative aspect of advertising: people were told of the existence of a particular product which they needed little encouragement to want to buy at that particular time. Mothers, for some unknown reason, like their babies' hair to be curly, and this was the first time that a product had been offered for this specific purpose; the 1920s were the era of 'flannel bags' and men who already wanted to buy them would be interested in a particular make which was thrust upon their attention; the 'gimmick' about Sun Maid raisins was that they were seedless and presented in an attractive packet. Moreover, it was suggested that they could be eaten as a health-giving sweet – a novel idea to those who had previously thought of raisins only in terms of cooking.

These victories were gained by the use of a simple and rather old-fashioned psychology which, in spite of the use of market research, took a great part of its inspiration from the intuition of the expert – 'a good ad-man is born and not made' was the generally accepted belief. But with the belated impact of Freudian psychology many ad-men came to believe that they had discovered a much more potent instrument than simple market research, which had been based on the assumption that direct questioning would indicate customers' attitudes and that their answers could form the basis for a more effective campaign. In fact, it was proved beyond doubt that people very often do not know what they want, that even when they do know they often lie, and that many of their motives in buying a particular product are unconsciously motivated. To discover by new techniques what these unconscious motives are became the basis of a new applied 'science' described as motivational research or motivational analysis, which is now in use by more than two thirds of America's hundred largest advertisers. But the method is not confined to the commercial world of the ad-man and is, indeed, just one aspect of the 'social engineering' approach made use of by those who are attempting to raise funds for charities, by executives seeking to influence their employees in the desired direction or in the selection of management, by politicians wishing to make the most appropriate appeals to their electorate, and even by churches hoping to raise their attendance. In other words, this procedure assumes (a) that by new methods one can discover what a person 'really' wants, his 'real' motivations, and (b) that, on the basis of this knowledge, it is possible to manipulate him even without his being aware of the fact. Many books have been written, from William H. Whyte's *The Organization Man* to *The Hidden Persuaders* and other volumes by Vance Packard, which suggest that this hidden manipulation is potent, scientific, sinister, and immoral, and, since manipulation is what we are concerned with here, it is necessary to deal with it in all its aspects as far as motivational research is concerned. Although its main use is in advertising in the widest sense (for obviously the church seeking more worshippers or the politician seeking more votes are both advertising for *something*), other circumstances in which attempts are made to manipulate the individual through his unconscious must be considered as well, and perhaps the best way to do this is to state the case for those who regard the process as dangerous and a potent weapon for evil.

We have seen that amongst the several reasons which have driven prominent advertising agencies into motivational research was their discovery of psychoanalysis since those who make practical use of psychology are bound to end up sooner or later by considering the uses to which Freudian depth-psychology can be put. If it be true that the sources of many everyday actions lie outside consciousness, as Freud and others have maintained, so that the ordinary individual is a great deal less logical than he believes himself to be, then it is obviously important to know what these motivations are. But even apart from this, it was becoming evident that the market-researcher's method of asking simple questions of a selected panel representing particular age, class, occupational, or sex groups on the assumption that they knew what they wanted did not always work. For example, they genuinely might not know, might not tell the truth, certainly did not know their unconscious motivations, and were liable to say what they felt they *should* want rather than what they actually preferred.

The prestige of a product has a powerful influence upon what people admit to liking, so that if one accepted their answers to a direct question it might well be assumed that the relatively high-brow *Atlantic Monthly* is America's most-read magazine and some of the 'true-story' confession magazines the least-read, whereas the latter have at least twenty times the readership of the former. A brewery making two kinds of beer, the light type and the cheaper regular one, made a survey in order to discover what kinds of people drank each product. To the astonishment of the directors, more than three people to one voted for the light brand although for years, in response to consumer demand, the firm had been brewing and selling nine times as much of the regular as the light. It was evident that the seemingly foolproof question carried a quite different implication to those questioned, to whom it meant in effect: Do you drink the kind preferred by those with discriminating taste or do you just drink the regular brand? Psychologists at the McCann-Erikson advertising agency asked a group of people why they did not buy the product of one of their clients who sold kippers. Direct questioning revealed that most of those asked did not like kippers. Yet a more subtle approach demonstrated that 40 per cent of those who gave this reply had never tasted a kipper in their lives. Similarly, the Colour Research Institute, suspecting the reliability of people's comments, gave women who were waiting for a lecture the choice of two waiting-rooms. One was a modern Swedish room furnished in contemporary style, whilst the other was a traditional room filled with period furniture of a familiar type. It was found that virtually all the women went spontaneously into the Swedish room, yet when asked after the lecture as to their real preference, 84 per cent said that the traditional room was the nicer one.

What people think and what they say or do are not necessarily the same thing; but there is an even greater gap between what people believe themselves to think and the unconscious desire or fear that in the last resort motivates their actions. Thus common sense might lead one to suppose that most of us brush our teeth for reasons of dental hygiene, to prevent decay, or to make our teeth look clean, and these were therefore the motives upon which toothpaste manufacturers hammered for years in their advertisements. But investigation has shown that most people brush their teeth once a day and the time they choose is the least logical – immediately on rising, because what they basically seek is to start the day with a fresh mouth. Hence the subsequent emphasis on the 'clean mouth taste' and the 'tingle-tongue taste' because a majority of individuals are more worried about the way their mouth feels after a night's sleep or the social effects of bad breath than they are about the fate of their teeth.

Two other reasons for the advent of motivational research in America were the crisis of over-production which made manufacturers desperate to sell the multitude of goods turned out by their factories, and the fact already noted that all the brands of a particular product are becoming more and more alike. Increasingly manufacturers began to talk of creating 'psychological obsolescence' because it became absolutely essential in their eyes that goods should not last too long. Products are not only caused to have a high turnover by psychological obsolescence created by advertising so that people become dissatisfied with a perfectly efficient old model; there is in many cases a deliberate attempt to manufacture an article which will have a limited life-span, if only by making it impossible after a few years to obtain spare parts. Increasing standardization leads to increasing sameness between products; and the greater the similarity the smaller part does reason play in the choice between one brand and another. This, again, immediately suggests the use of a psychology based on the concept that man is not fundamentally rational. It is obviously impossible to appeal to common sense by truthful advertising which relies on giving factual data if the brands from which the customer is expected to choose are alike in all essential qualities. As the president of a large advertising agency, David Ogilvy, is reported as saying:

There really isn't any significant difference between the various brands of whisky or the various cigarettes or the various brands of beer. They are all about the same. And so are the cake mixes and the detergents and the automobiles.

Two men have made claims to be the originator of the depth approach: Ernest Dichter, President of the Institute of Motivational Research Inc. and author of the book *The Strategy of Desire*, and Louis Cheskin, Director of the Color Research Institute of America. Dichter was born in Vienna and in the United States works with a 'psycho-panel' of several hundred families all composed of individuals who have been thoroughly investigated as to their emotional make-up. Whether they are secure or insecure, ambitious or non-ambitious, neurotic or relatively normal is all recorded on Dichter's card-index system and, by finding their responses to a particular product, advertising can be geared to appeal to the fears of the hypochondriac or the hopes of the ambitious. Depth interviews are conducted with individual people on the basis of the free-association method of Freud with the exception that the subject is given the stimulus-word of the product and asked to think aloud by saying whatever thoughts come into his mind without regard to rational sequence. Sometimes group reveries of ten members are employed as in group psychotherapy and in this permissive atmosphere the members are able to express even those thoughts of which they were previously unconscious. Also employed are the tests known to psychiatrists as 'projection tests' in which the subject is unaware of the real motive behind the testing and believes that he is being tested for quite another reason. All of these have in common the fact that the testee is presented with an 'unstructured' picture or design and asked to tell the investigator what he imagines he sees in it. Since the picture itself gives no clue, being deliberately vague, what the subject says is a projection of his own hopes, fears, and other emotions from the deepest recesses of his personality. Used by the psychiatrist, these tests more or less reliably uncover such traits as latent homosexuality, paranoid trends, emotional insecurity, and other sources of mental conflict. Amongst the tests thus employed are the Rorschach 'ink-blot' test, the T.A.T. or thematic apperception test with its blurred outlines of human figures about whom a story must be told, and the Szondi test. The latter shows a series of photographs of various people and the testee is asked to say which of them he would prefer to sit beside on a train journey and which he would least like to be alone with. What he is not told is that the photographs are all pictures of mentally disordered patients such as homosexuals, manic and depressive types, paranoiacs, hysterics, sadists, epileptics with mental disorder, and catatonic schizophrenics. It is found that the choices of the subject are made on the basis of an unconscious rapport with or revulsion from the types selected and that these give important clues as to his real problems.

Amongst other aids to probing the testee's emotional states may be mentioned the lie-detector, which detects changes in tension by recording such physiological responses as blood-pressure, an increased heartbeat, the amount of nervous sweating, and so on; the hidden camera which records the rate of eye-blink as a clue to tension or relaxation; and the employment of hypnosis. One subject under hypnosis when asked why he always bought a particular make of car was able to recall an advertisement which had taken his fancy twenty years before and, although long forgotten, still influenced his choice.

As an example of the allegedly deadly accuracy of such tests, Donald Armstrong claims to have diagnosed on the basis of Rorschach results exactly what brand of cigarette was smoked by each of a group of eighty smokers known to have a strong loyalty to a specific make: '. . . just looking at [the test results] you knew immediately the brand the poor devil *had* to smoke. We were right eighty times in a row.'

Basically [says Pierre Martineau, one of the leading experts in the field] what you are trying to do is create an illogical situation. You want the customer to fall in love with your product and have a profound brand loyalty when actually content may be very similar in hundreds of competing brands.

The best brand image is the self image which enables the customer to project himself into the product so that what he actually buys is a projection of his own traits. Thus it is said that the way a person draws a picture of a car tells what brand of petrol he will buy just as his personality reveals what brand of cigarettes he will smoke.

The researchers are, it need hardly be said, practical men in whom such matters as the health of the individual or the nation arouse little sentiment. One agency acting on behalf of the whisky distillers employed the Szondi test to discover why those who drink whisky do so. The reason behind this investigation was the known fact that heavy drinkers account for most of the whisky consumed, 85 per cent of the volume being drunk by only 22 per cent of the drinkers. Testees were tested before and after three large whiskies and the conclusion (hardly an earthshaking one) was that heavy drinkers are seeking a personality change that alcohol can bring about, making, for example, the meek man into a temporarily tough one and so on. This, again, could be employed in advertising appeals to the heavy drinker, as the basic supporter of the industry, to drink more.

Neither in selling whisky nor cigarettes must one adopt a negative attitude which implies 'this won't kill you'. It is much better not to refer to such unpleasant subjects at all. As Martineau suggests:

I can't imagine a whisky advertiser in folksy, confidential tones telling people to 'guard against cirrhosis of the liver' or proclaiming that 'a ten-month study by leading medical authorities showed no cases of acute or chronic alcoholism'.

Another group of manufacturers was disturbed by the decline in the sale of sweets because, as it appeared, people had guilt-feelings about indulging themselves or bringing about tooth decay or obesity. Dichter was called in and was soon able to dispel the nation's guilt-feelings by pointing out to the firms concerned the folly of meekly accepting the statement that sweets are bad for the teeth and fattening instead of telling the public that they are a delightful, wholesome, and nourishing food. The plan was to urge them to emphasize 'bite-size' pieces within the large packages; for, as Dichter pointed out, this would provide the excuse the consumer needs to buy a bar of candy: 'After all, I don't have to eat all of it, just a bite and then put the rest away.'

But he added: '. . . seriously we doubt whether the rest will be put away.' Another researcher had the brilliant idea that sweets in childhood become a reward-symbol for being a good little boy or girl and hence the adult consumer might well be asked to reward himself in the same way. The new message was: 'To make that tough job easier, you *deserve* M. & M. Candy'; and, according to the company, sales soon doubled in the test areas.

There might appear to be more cause for uneasiness in the use of these techniques outside the field of advertising, in politics and industry, for example. The national chairman of an American political party indicated his acceptance of the new approach during the election campaign of 1956 when he spoke of his candidates as products to sell, and Rosser Reeves of Ted Bates's advertising agency was employed to run the television campaign for Eisenhower in 1952 by means of twenty-second plugs written by himself. Reeves studied all of Eisenhower's speeches and then contacted George Gallup to discover from the opinion polls what issues were most important to the public, his scripts being written about these. In all the plugs there was the same introduction, an announcer saying, with suppressed excitement: 'Eisenhower Answers the Nation!' Then the voice of 'an ordinary citizen' would ask a question such as: 'Mr Eisenhower, what about the high cost of living?' And the General would reply, in this instance: 'My wife Mamie worries about the same thing. I tell her it's our job to change that on November fourth.' And then would follow a formal disclaimer to the effect that 'what you have just heard is a paid political announcement'. The technique of the 'spot' or 'plug' was used so that people would have little choice but to listen to a statement which came to them without warning in the same way as the commercials; for the same reason the time occupied was too short to make it worth while for an opponent to turn it off, and the carefully selected messages, cast in a 'folksy' form, were expected to achieve maximum penetration by this means.

In the field of industry, one trade school in California recommends its graduates as being 'custom-built men' tailored by social engineering to have the right attitudes from an employer's point of view, and, as W. H. Whyte has shown in *The Organiza-*

tion Man, many large concerns employ the tests already described to pry into the innermost recesses of the minds of prospective candidates for management. The modern business executive is not satisfied with the mere knowledge of the external facts of a candidate's past life in respect of his practical qualifications and so on, or even with his past work-record; he wants to know *all* about him. Refusal to cooperate makes little difference since, as Whyte has pointed out:

Testers have learned ways to attach great significance to the manner in which people respond to the fact of the tests, and if a man refuses to answer several questions, he does not escape analysis. Given such a man, many psychologists believe that they can deduce his suppressed anxieties almost as well as if he had cooperated fully.

Nor are the tests limited to the screening of new applicants, but also to check on those already in the organization. At Sears', one of the largest corporations, Whyte found that no one had been promoted for the past ten years until the chairman of the board had checked his test results. It can hardly be pleasant for the manager to be aware that his president knows more about him than he does himself.

During 1956, the *Sunday Times* published an account of what appeared to be a new threat to the integrity of the human mind. This was 'subliminal advertising', thought out by Jim Vicary, an American market researcher, who arranged with the owner of a New Jersey cinema to install a second special projector which flashed on to the screen whilst the main film was in progress such phrases as 'Coca-Cola' or 'Eat Popcorn'. The words were either flashed so quickly or printed with such weak intensity that the conscious mind could not see them superimposed on the actual film even when the individual was told that they were about to appear. Films treated in this way were alternated with untreated ones throughout the summer of that year and on those evenings when the subliminal effect was used Coca-Cola sales went up by about one-sixth, popcorn sales by more than a half. Although Vicary himself is of the opinion that it is unlikely that such a stimulus can produce any response at all unless the prospective customer already has in mind the idea of buying the product, subliminal advertising aroused a storm of protest in the American press as it was later to do here. In this country the British Institute of Practitioners in Advertising went to the trouble of publishing a booklet (*Subliminal Communication*, 1958) and imposing a ban on the use of this method by any of its 243 agencies, saying:

> The free choice by the public to accept or reject is an integral part of all forms of professionally accepted advertising and does not appear to be available to recipients of subliminal communication.

Aldous Huxley in a TV interview quoted an investigator as holding the view that 'once you've established the principle that something works, you can be absolutely sure that the technology of it is going to improve steadily'. From this Huxley drew the Orwellian conclusion that it would be possible by about 1964 to manipulate people politically and otherwise, and warned his audience of the danger that they might be persuaded, below the level of choice and reason, to vote for a candidate during an election in total ignorance of the fact they were being persuaded.

So much for the theories. But what are the facts about the 'Hidden Persuaders'? Since the publication of Walter Dill Scott's book, many others have made the assertion that advertising is, or can become, an exact science, and in 1923 Claude Hopkins published his *Scientific Advertising* which made just this claim. But Hopkins was dealing with only one aspect of the problem, namely mail-order advertising, which is, in fact, the unique area for which such claims can be made. Obviously, if two different advertisements for the same product are published in the same edition of the same newspaper so that one half of the edition contains one version and the second half the other, both being accompanied by a coupon and the request to send a dollar if the article is desired, then the version which brings in most coupons and dollars is the better advertisement. Sales, in this case, are an accurate measuring rod of efficiency. But selling by mail order is more typical of the United States than here, is only applicable to quite a narrow range of goods, and is on the decline even in America where the isolated customer or members of a relatively isolated community, originally the main supporters of this type of salesmanship, are being engulfed in larger communities with all the facilities of the city. Moreover, whatever 'scientific' lessons have been learned in this field are almost totally irrelevant in the much wider field of general advertising, where the problem is not to sell a relatively unique article on a single occasion, but to make regular customers for an article which is almost indistinguishable from similar products carrying different brand names.

There is, in fact, with this single exception, no such thing as scientific advertising and, as Martin Mayer has conclusively shown in *Madison Avenue U.S.A.*, no general agency can prove the efficacy of its methods to anyone who wishes to apply rigorous standards of proof. Advertisers may claim to employ scientific principles; but what their work is actually based on is intuition, hunches, and a background theory of advertising which varies widely from one agency to another. This is not to deny that they employ scientists in plenty: analytical chemists to test a product so that the claims for it will pass the demands of the Federal Trade Commission, psychologists for testing the validity of motivational research, psychoanalysts to discover the deep-seated significance of a product to the consumer, and so on. But the social scientists at any rate are not all employing the same discipline: some work along Adlerian lines in terms of power-seeking as the basic drive, some along Freudian sexual lines, and others on the basis of Riesman's thesis that the reference group is the main source of the individual's opinions.

Adding to the complexity is the fact that each agency has its own unprovable philosophy of advertising which, in Madison Avenue, ranges from the USP (Unique Selling Proposition) of Bates and Company, through the 'brand image' of David Ogilvy, to the 'empathy' of Norman B. Norman. According to the first of these three beliefs, it is necessary for a product to be able to make a claim which the opposition cannot, or does not, offer. This must be done even when the product differs in no significant degree from its competitors, e.g. Colgate tooth-paste raised its sales by the slogan 'Cleans your Breath as it Cleans your Teeth' although, as Bates confessed, '*every dentifrice cleans your breath while it cleans your teeth – but nobody had ever put a clean breath claim on a toothpaste before.*' In fact Hopkins (of *Scientific Advertising*) had thought out this technique earlier when he helped to sell Schlitz beer on the slogan 'Washed with Live Steam' referring to the method by which the bottles were sterilized before being filled with beer. He was quite well aware that every brewery employed the same process, but explained that the important fact was not what the industry *did*, but what the individual brewers *advertised* they did. To David Ogilvy, the main appeal is to snobbery: 'It pays to give your brand a first-class ticket throughout life. People don't like to be seen consuming products which their friends regard as third-class.' Hence the philosophy of the 'brand image', which allegedly gives the product a total personality exuding elegance and prestige in the form of such models as Baron George Wrangel of the Russian nobility complete with his black patch over one eye advertising Hathaway shirts, and Commander Edward Whitehead whose aristocratic English accent has been successful in selling Schweppes. The agency of which Norman is the leading light found its solution to the problems of advertising in 'empathy', which by definition would mean the ability to put oneself in the customer's shoes but in practice resolves itself into trying to discover the 'real' reason why people buy these products. Since Norman's orientation is basically Freudian and the main part of his business is concerned with selling cosmetics and lingerie, the 'real' reasons naturally enough turn out to be mainly sexual.

The work of Ernest Dichter with its fairly rigid Freudian approach has been used by Vance Packard in his book to suggest that something sinister is being perpetrated upon the customer, not only by Dichter, but by others using similar approaches. He manages, as one reviewer of *The Hidden Persuaders* puts it, 'to make George Orwell's Big Brother world sound about as blood-curdling as *East Lynne*'. But, as Mayer has pointed out, Packard classifies as motivational research almost the entire field of advertising, from copy-writers' common-sense intuitions to the most Freudian depth interpretations. Thus Bates's work for Colgate, already mentioned, is attributed to motivational research which, in fact, was not carried out until sixteen years later.

Dichter has become something of a legend in his own time and is often credited with work for which he was not responsible. Thus a biographical article credits him with developing 'new, dynamic approaches' for the Chrysler Corporation whose 'Look at all Three . . .' campaign 'proved to be the sales turning-point for this automobile'. But the facts are that this was not a 'campaign', since the advertisement was used only once, and Dichter could not have had anything to do with it because it made its appearance six years before he came to America. The difficulty is to know how much of Dichter's success comes from his supposedly 'scientific' depth approach, and how much from ordinary intuition. Mayer writes that '. . . it is astonishing how often Dichter's motivational analyses lead to copy suggestions which a first-class advertising man should have found without any Freudian explanations.' Some of his most successful and apparently most Freudian research work has led to what can only be described as common-sense suggestions. When, for example, the airline companies came to him for advice, they were attempting in their advertisements to present the argument that air travel is safe and that nobody need be afraid to fly. Dichter recommended that they should give up the safety theme and concentrate on selling to men the idea that flying is the most speedy and convenient form of travel and to women that it would bring their husbands home faster. But this advice is based on the principle dating back to the earliest years of advertising that when you have a potentially dangerous product to sell you must never allow yourself to take the position that it is not really dangerous after all. It is important to stress the positive approach, because advertising against what people believe simply reinforces their anxieties. Another example of a supposedly Freudian interpretation which turns out to be ordinary common sense was Dichter's advice to Ronson's, who had been failing to attract customers with the argument that their lighter was failure-proof. This again was a merely negative approach which was countered by Dichter's analysis that flame is a sexual symbol, that the Goddess of light is associated with Eros. What he actually recommended was that the flame should be shown in close-up rather than the lighter as a whole. The results had nothing to do with sexual symbolism, for the effect of the advertisement on the customer was to show that Ronson's were confident in their own device whilst not making any claim that he was not prepared to believe, since, obviously, no lighter is failure-proof. Also the former negative appeal had been changed to a positive one.

Vicary's 'subliminal advertising' is another case of a storm in a tea-cup because the procedure, in spite of the sensation it aroused, is neither new nor, as Vicary himself admits, likely to be particularly effective. Subliminal perception was mentioned as a possibility by Aristotle, and the philosopher Leibniz dealt at length with the possibility of 'minute perceptions' that are 'little noticed, which are not sufficiently distinguished to be perceived or remembered, but which become known through certain consequences'. 'It is a great source of error,' he added, 'to believe that there is no perception in the soul besides those of which it is conscious.' In 1910, H. Ohms demonstrated a subliminal effect by reducing the loudness of barely audible words, and in 1955 N. F. Dixon obtained evidence that, when stimulus words were presented subliminally and the observers were asked to say the first word that came into their mind, they often responded with words which had a meaningful connexion with the stimulus one. According to the booklet on the subject issued by the Institute of Practitioners in Advertising:

R. Jung showed that even in sleep psychogalvanic responses (i.e. physiological changes measured by instruments which indicate emotional responses) may appear not only with loud noises, but also with faint but significant sounds such as the whispering of the observer's name. This may happen without the observer waking, or if he does wake, he does not remember what stimulated him. Thus clearly there is a mechanism in the brain which can respond to certain kinds of stimulation, of potential importance to the individual, and although he does not become aware of their precise nature, yet his autonomic nervous system may react to them as to an alarm or emotional threat.

The stimuli comprising the messages passed during subliminal communication are weakened either by reducing their intensity to a level below that at which they can be consciously perceived or by restricting their duration to very short periods of time. It is impossible to disagree with Vicary's own conclusion that the only people who are influenced by subliminal advertising are those who are already predisposed to buy the product, although, in fact, in the vast majority of people no evidence has been produced to show that they perceive the message at all, either consciously or unconsciously. We have already seen that the whole idea of insinuating into the mind an idea which runs contrary to its basic trends is absurd; for such ideas or experiences are either rejected or, as in the case of traumatic experiences or hypnosis, dissociated and thus shut off from the mind as a whole, where if their content is unpleasant, they may lead to anxiety but not to action. Like other forms of propaganda, advertising can accelerate or retard trends, but it cannot reverse them. Mayer, for example, writes:

Advertising is of little use in combating a trend against a kind of product – brewers spend more than 100 million dollars a year to advertise their beer, backing the ads with the full panoply of motivational research, but *per capita* beer consumption goes steadily down – because advertising cannot add values great enough to overcome primary factors which lead consumers to find less and less satisfaction in using a product. Here, as on the political scene, advertising is the wind on the surface, sweeping all before it when it blows with the tide but powerless to prevent a shifting of greater forces.*

Neither market research nor motivational research can be scientific, because, as Alfred Politz has pointed out, so far as general advertising is concerned:

Any one specific piece of consumer behaviour goes back to a multitude of psychological and mechanical causes. It is the specific combination and the relative strength of the various causes which lead to a specific purchase. If we do not know the relative strength of these causes we cannot compute the effect of a particular marketing action. One can perform a useful function in marketing by getting a good idea. But not everything that is good must be called 'research'.

* Further evidence of the comparative helplessness of the advertiser or propagandist to influence established trends for good or ill is shown by the fact that, in spite of the cancer scare, cigarette sales in the USA have gone up 26 per cent since 1950. On the other hand, the sale of pipe tobacco, like that of beer, has gone steadily down from 210 million pounds in 1920 to 75 million pounds in 1961. Neither health propaganda in the former case, nor the efforts of the advertising agencies in the latter, have had the slightest effect.

Or, as Mayer expresses it:

Out of the hole left by the disappearance of 'scientific advertising' [there has grown] a large crop of advertising philosophies.

So far from the new methods being either as successful or as sinister as Vance Packard would have us believe, there is plenty of evidence that, like many other messages which reach people over the mass media, the total result may be to cause them to be unresponsive and increasingly critical. A Gallup poll in 1958 found that the majority of shoppers thought that too much money was being wasted on advertising; an American survey during the same year found that 50 per cent of women associated advertising with exaggeration whilst 86 per cent thought it positively dishonest; and in Canada a survey revealed that belief in advertisements was declining. A British survey has shown that only 11 per cent of those questioned believed that celebrities use the products they recommend in advertisements.

Advertising differs in certain important respects from propaganda in general, basically in that the needs it satisfies are either so superficial as to be trivial or so deep-seated as to be universal. Also, the appeal is tailor-made for the particular customer or groups of customers. This is not true to the same degree in political or religious propaganda where the appeal is neither trivial nor wholly universal in respect of a particular party or sect, nor can the propaganda be radically altered without changing that group's essential nature. The politician or priest tells people what they ought to think, and, although either may attempt to show that their message conflicts with none of their audience's fundamental beliefs, it is accepted or rejected according to the individual's basic personality traits or perhaps his group affiliations. The advertiser, on the other hand, is virtually told by people what they want and endeavours to supply it. It is obviously much easier to get people to accept something which has been created for the purpose of satisfying a widespread need and carefully investigated with this need in view, than to get them to accept a ready-made belief which may or may not fit in with those they already possess. Advertisers gear their message to the particular group from which, under existing circumstances, they can expect the greatest response. Thus in Britain the population has long been divided by the agencies into five groups or classes: (A) the top people; (B) the minor professionals; (C) the white-collar workers; (D) the great mass of working-class people; and (E) the relatively deprived, such as old-age pensioners. But it has recently become evident that Group C can be subdivided into two quite different sets of people, the white-collar man on a fixed income, and the new comparatively prosperous skilled manual worker. The latter, which has come to be known as the C2 group, is pre-war working-class, but as one market researcher remarks, he is now '. . . solidly in the market for washing-machines, spin-driers, the lot . . . this C2 group, often living on subsidized premises, with fewer commitments than the white-collar man, is the main market we aim at'. Hence, as David Ogilvy has pointed out, 'most copy is written below the average intelligence'.

On the whole, the verdict on advertising as at present carried on must be an unfavourable one. Most advertising is, if not wholly untruthful, at any rate designed to create false impressions; its claims to be 'scientific' or even sinister have been exposed; and the great bulk of it is culturally repulsive to a reasonably educated person. Of course, much the same could be said of some other products of the mass media: the bad films, television shows, radio programmes, and periodicals. But these can easily be avoided, whereas there are very few people who can avoid contact with advertising. However, with the exception of a few fields (such as patent medicines), it is doubtful whether it does anyone any harm, and it is even possible to claim that it may have done a certain amount of good; for, if often verbally repel-lent, its visual art is sometimes of a fairly high standard. Many people by way of posters may have been brought to accept the work of Braque and Picasso more readily than they would other-wise have done; and, like others of the so-called élites who control the mass media, it is possible that advertisers frequently give people a good deal better from the aesthetic point of view than popular taste, if left to itself, would demand. Finally, and again on the positive side, it is not inconceivable that advertising, so far from leading to conformity as its critics claim, is an impor-tant force in creating diversity of taste since its very existence depends on product differences, whether these are real or imaginary. It is mass production methods, not advertising, which create the real uniformity in goods. Conformity in taste is the burden of the impoverished community without the money or the opportunity to express itself, but, within wide limits, the prosperous modern community is able to indulge its individuality as never before in history. It is true that there are social and psychological forces in the mass society which act in the opposite direction in favour of ideological conformity, but by no stretch of the imagination could these be attributed to commercial advertising.

As for the supposedly sinister projection tests, these are used and will continue to be used in psychiatry, since most psychiatrists, although by no means all of them, regard them as giving trustworthy results. But their employment in business for management selection is quite another matter; for in this case they are a perfect example of the fallacy of employing rigidly scientific methods to grossly unscientific ends. Of course, much older types of test are used to discover a person's specific practical skills, such as manual dexterity, speed of reaction, or the absence or presence of visual defects such as colour blindness, and these are usefully employed in the selection of air-line pilots, engine-drivers, and so on. But the reason why such so-called aptitude tests are useful is *because we know what we are looking for* in a pilot or driver. This is not true of the job of management in industry, since nobody knows what it is that makes a good manager good. If it were possible to know every single detail of an individual person's private life, we would still not have the faintest idea of whether or not he would make a good manager in a particular firm. The concealed fallacious assumptions behind the use of projection tests in industry are (*a*) that we know what makes an individual a good manager, and (*b*) that the normal person is more efficient than the abnormal. The facts, however, are quite otherwise; for all the indications are that most of the greatest leaders in industry have been highly neurotic. It is their neuroticism which gives them their drive in situations where a truly 'normal' individual without mental conflicts would simply sit down and do nothing. Because some neuroses make people incompetent at work, we are liable to assume that those without a neurosis would be competent, whereas the truth is that it is only the incompetent neurotic who is seen by the psychiatrist and, since neurosis is socially defined, we ignore the great bulk of brilliant people who are successful precisely because they are neurotic.

An even more forcible argument against the use of such tests outside psychiatry is that it is easy to cheat at them, and, in fact, there are at least two books in existence which tell the reader in detail how to do so. The rules are simple, because all that is necessary is to give conventional responses to the tester based on the thesis that one is moderate in all things, has no unduly strong feelings either for or against parents and relatives, has conservative views in politics and religion, and has been good (but not too good) at all the tasks one has undertaken throughout life. In other words, that, except for a desire to get on in life, one is simply an unspeakable prig and bore. However, even in this field, there are welcome signs that industrialists in America and elsewhere are beginning to see the fallacies involved in tests other than those which are directed towards discovering specific aptitudes in manual work. It is becoming increasingly clear that the man who gets things done is not the pallid conformist, but the man with drive, ambition, and strong personal feelings. Projection tests are scientific, but the uses to which they have been put in advertising or industry are not.

CHAPTER 8

SCIENTIFIC MIND-CHANGING

ONE field of mind-changing in which intensive investigation has been carried on with generally benign intentions and in a more or less scientific manner for many years is to be found in the sphere of medicine. The problem of mental derangement presented the physician with the necessity of attempting to change back to its original form the behaviour of those whose personality had undergone a malignant transformation. His patient had, to all appearances, become another person, alienated from his true self (hence the name of 'alienist' formerly given to psychiatrists), and the physician's job was to reverse these changes. But before he could do so it was necessary to have some sort of theory as to how the abnormal development had come about.

Of course, such theories have existed from the earliest times, beginning with the belief that the insane were the victims of possession by evil spirits – a belief not now generally held outside the very primitive communities of culturally backward peoples or the highly sophisticated ones of the more orthodox branches of the Christian Church. The contrasting theory that mental disorder has a physical basis arose during the Periclean Age in Greece when Hippocrates 'the father of modern medicine' struck out against traditional views and showed that epilepsy, then known as the 'sacred disease', had a natural cause and was no more sacred or divine than other diseases. Hippocrates believed mental disease to have a physiological basis, being caused by variations in the balance of the four humours within the body which caused the individual to be predominantly sanguine, melancholic, phlegmatic, or choleric (useful descriptions of temperament which are still being employed by the followers of Pavlov and the psychoanalyst, Fromm). The Middle Ages brought a return of demonology and witchcraft, which effectively removed many mental disorders from the medical field until with the Renaissance such men as the Spaniard Juan Vives, the German Cornelius Agrippa, and the Swiss Paracelsus arose to cry out against the stupid brutality practised in the name of religion. In the sixteenth century a Dutch physician, Johann Weyer, wrote a refutation of witchcraft, citing many cases of mental disease which he explained in a remarkably modern fashion, foreshadowing modern psychiatry. But his writings were banned by the Church and indeed remained so until the present century.

However, the true beginnings of modern psychiatry are to be found from the mid nineteenth century onwards, a period when the philosophy of most scientists was a somewhat over-simple materialism which seemed to suggest that all mental disease must be the result of some *structural* defect within the nervous system, a belief now restricted to the more naïve neurologists – those specialists whose particular study is the various pathological conditions to which the nervous system is liable, such as tumours, neuritis, various forms of paralysis, and so on. For just as the true believer hates the heretic whose beliefs are a modification of his own more than the total unbeliever for whom there is always hope, so the specialist in one subject tends to hold views wholly opposed to those of another professing a subject closely related to his own, especially on matters which lie on the disputed borderland between the two. Hence, confronted by a case of writer's cramp, the neurologist will murmur something about 'faulty writing habits' and the need for complete rest from writing, massage, and splinting, whereas his psychiatric colleague will see in it a neurosis with the unconscious intent of avoiding writing to be treated by making the patient aware of this motive and sending him back to his writing as soon as possible. The one sees in the condition something largely restricted to the patient's nervous system, the other a reaction taking place between the patient and his social environment which leads to psychological stresses. The most important of the great nineteenth-century psychiatrists to make this distinction was Emil Kraepelin, a German who made the first fairly complete classification of mental diseases and, in effect, distinguished between those conditions now known as *organic* which are really physical diseases with mental symptoms accompanying them and the *functional* disorders in which structural changes were apparently absent, i.e. what we should now describe as psychological illnesses. Freud and the French psychiatrists Jean Charcot and Pierre Janet were pioneers in the psychological field although all of them attached considerable significance to such organic factors as heredity and constitution.

Paradoxically, Freud, who more than any other worker was to popularize the psychodynamic viewpoint and show that functional nervous disorders such as the neuroses or psychopathic personalities were not diseases in the ordinary sense at all but forms of maladjustment, remained to the end of his life a mechanistic materialist. His psychological theories were apologetically described as his 'mythology' and he was convinced that sooner or later they would be capable of description in wholly physiological terms. This view is both true and misleading; true inasmuch as there is no reason to reject materialism or to doubt that 'mental' states are the subjective aspect of physiological ones, and misleading to the extent that it would be incorrect to suppose that the most complete account of internal physiological changes could possibly afford a satisfactory explanation of a process which involves the whole person in his social setting. But today this older distinction between organic and functional nervous disorders is no longer entirely valid save to indicate in a rough-and-ready manner that the former is basically a physical disease in which structural changes can be detected under the microscope or even by the naked eye, whereas the latter is one in which malfunctioning of the body has been brought about by stress and is, as yet, unaccompanied by structural change. This distinction has largely broken down with the knowledge that prolonged stress with its accompanying malfunctioning at the physiological level can ultimately lead to organic change in the psychosomatic disorders such as duodenal ulcer and high blood-pressure where arteriosclerosis finally supervenes. Stress can be described in psychological terms of anxieties, guilt-feelings, aggression, and other subjective concepts or in physiological terms of muscle tensions, biochemical changes in the blood, and so on, but it cannot be explained without reference to the circumstances in the social environment which bring it about. On the other hand, it can theoretically be attacked at one or all of these three levels: the psychiatrist may alter the patient's environment to remove the external stress-producing situation, he may change the patient's attitudes towards his problems by means of psycho-therapy, or finally, he may by drugs or other means influence the physiological processes which mediate stress stimuli within the patient's body. To take a deliberately over-simplified example: a duodenal ulcer caused by stress at work might be relieved by a change of employment, by altering the sufferer's attitudes towards his job without changing it, by drugs, or by cutting the vagus nerve down which the anxiety impulses flow to the stomach and duodenum.

In reality, the problem is by no means as simple as this because the anxiety-producing source in the external environment is not simply the situation as it objectively is but rather the situation as it is interpreted by the patient in the light of his past experience. Some situations would be intolerable to most people, but the one to which the neurotic responds is one to which he has been sensitized in early life and which therefore has become highly significant to him although often meaningless to anyone else. For instance, he might be intolerant of a perfectly well-meaning figure in authority because of early associations with an over-bearing father, or unable to bear the presence of a mother-in-law because of early associations with his own mother, and in these cases the removal of the patient from the intolerable situation may cause his symptoms to disappear for the time being without in any way altering his faulty attitudes. The proverbial long sea-voyage of former days made the neurotic better, not by giving him an unnecessary rest since there was nothing wrong with the physical structure of his nervous system, but by removing him temporarily from the cause of his stress. In general, the aim of the modern psychiatrist is to alter his patient's subjective attitudes, and changing the objective situation has, from the therapeutic point of view, strict limitations; nevertheless, as will be shown later, drastic environmental change when employed for more sinister purposes can produce dramatic personality changes for the worse. Psychotherapy is directed towards the modification or change of faulty attitudes and is a somewhat elastic term which includes anything from mere suggestion with or without hypnosis, where the intention is simply to increase the patient's confidence and so enable him to face his problems, to analytic psychotherapy, where the intention is to break down old attitudes and allow them to be replaced by new ones more close to reality.

Psychoanalysis, the method of therapy devised by Freud, is the most thoroughgoing of these analytic procedures and also, unfortunately, the most prolonged, necessitating fifty-five minutes every day for five days a week over a period of two or more years. During these sessions the patient lies on a couch and is asked to talk at random, saying whatever comes into his head no matter what its nature, and in due course the free association leads to the basic sources of conflict which are, of course, unconscious. The patient has come to the analyst with various symptoms such as irrational fears or phobias, attacks of uncontrollable anxiety, insomnia, and the like, but these are regarded as being the result of underlying conflicts which arise basically from defects in inter-personal relations. The aim of analysis is to bring such conflicts into consciousness so that they can be dealt with at the rational level in a practical manner. In this process the patient's attitude towards the analyst, the transference, plays a leading part; for it is this attitude which, as it were, forms a representative sample of his faulty attitudes towards significant figures in his early life when the basic conflicts arose. The analyst points out the irrational nature of these attitudes, previously not fully realized by the patient, and the early problems are acted out in relation to the analyst and in this way finally lose their compulsive nature. Since complete psychoanalysis is out of reach to most people for practical reasons of time, money, and general suitability of the method in a given case, attempts have been made to shorten analysis which have for the most part been in one or other of two directions: either an attempt is made to reach the conflicts in the unconscious by means of short cuts such as the use of drugs or hypnosis, or the interpretation of the analyst is active – i.e., knowing on the basis of his knowledge of psychopathology and the general clinical picture what the patient's conflicts are, he will force them upon the patient's attention without waiting for them to appear gradually in free association. Such methods are quite satisfactory when the onset of the neurosis is relatively recent and in direct response to some fairly severe provocation from the environment, or in cases which are monosymptomatic as when the most obvious problem is a single phobia. In fact, they approximate to those used by Freud in the early days of the movement, when a symptom was regarded as the tombstone marking the spot where a traumatic memory lay repressed. Later evidence, however, made it clear that neurosis is a disorder of the total personality even if on cursory examination only a single symptom can be observed, and it is generally accepted that removing a symptom in this way is not in itself tantamount to cure any more than suppressing a troublesome cough is a cure for bronchitis. However, in an otherwise good personality it may be regarded as a satisfactory result, especially if the environmental stress was severe and is unlikely to be met with again. For this reason such short methods are specially useful in battle neurosis where a terrifying memory has been repressed with resultant symptom-formation. In such cases, the patient is given an injection of Pentothal (thiopentone sodium), sodium amytal, or scopolamine which makes him drowsy enough for repression to be relaxed and the memory is brought into consciousness, producing great emotional upset whilst the traumatic incident is re-lived. This emotional crisis is known as abreaction and is therapeutic to the degree that the patient is able to accept the rejected material and integrate it into his ego as part of past history. It is then no longer an undigested mass causing symptoms by reason of repression, but a formerly traumatic memory which has been made a part of consciously-recalled experience and integrated into the rest of the patient's awareness. Similar results may be obtained by the use of ether anaesthesia or hypnosis and the same methods are frequently employed in everyday practice to make a patient aware of his or her problems when they have been partly or wholly repressed. By these means the period of analysis is greatly shortened, although the best results are obtained, as already indicated, in people of previous good personality who have been under considerable environmental stress.

Drugs employed in this way are, of course, what are popularly known as 'truth drugs', and it is necessary to consider how far they are, or can be, employed for other than therapeutic reasons. Can they be used, for example, to extract the truth from unwilling prisoners, whether political or otherwise? All the evidence suggests the contrary. Can they be used, on the other hand, to cause prisoners to make false confessions, as was frequently suggested during the Soviet purges of the nineteen-thirties? Certainly they cannot. The so-called 'truth drugs' are simply ordinary anaesthetics most of which have been in use for many years (ether, widely believed to be the most effective of all in psychiatry, is actually the oldest, dating back to 1847) and in sub-anaesthetic doses they produce much the same effect as amounts of alcohol sufficient to lead to drunkenness. That is to say, they relax conscious control and enable the individual to speak without his usual censorship coming into action. Their use is based on the ancient, if not entirely true, saying: '*In vino veritas.*' Fortunately or unfortunately, as everyone knows, drunkenness does not necessarily cause everyone to tell the objective truth in terms of external reality, otherwise we should not so frequently be exposed to the drunkard's fantasies of how badly he is treated at home and how he was instrumental in winning the last war, or the war before the last. What the good psychologist learns is a great deal of truth not about objective happenings but about the character of the individual himself. This suits the psychiatrist very well, for in the sense that matters to him everything his patient says is 'true' in so far as it reveals his real attitudes to life. When, in his early years, Freud listened to his patients' accounts of how they had been sexually seduced in childhood by near relatives and subsequently found that these happenings were fabricated and had never really happened in the vast majority of cases, he was at first perplexed. But finally he came to realize that the important thing was not whether or not they had happened but rather that the patient felt as if they had.

But this kind of 'truth' is of no use at all to the political investigator who wants to catch his prisoner out and, unfortunately for him, no drug exists which can compel an unwilling victim to tell the truth. The evidence given under the influence of 'truth drugs' is admitted in certain American courts of law provided the accused is willing to undergo the test, but it is well-known that people can lie just as effectively under the influence of a drug as without it and, even when his censorship is relaxed, a prisoner who is on his guard is able to stick to his original story. He may, indeed, have got to the stage where he largely believes it himself. Patients are more susceptible to the influence of such drugs because they are usually ready to co-operate with the psychiatrist in order to lose their symptoms; but even in these instances objective recall is not always possible. 'Truth drugs' have no magical or inevitable power and the writer well remembers a soldier who, during the last war, was able to maintain for more than two years that he did not know his name, unit, birthplace, or any other facts about his past life, in spite of every therapeutically permissible attempt to discover them.

The lie-detector is another method sometimes employed in American criminal practice, being based, first, on Jung's original word-association test for discovering the nature of unconscious complexes, and, secondly, on the long-familiar principle that telling a lie ordinarily leads to anxiety, which can be demonstrated by the physical changes it produces in the body. This fact was allegedly employed by the police of Eastern countries, who, on obtaining a number of suspects, would ask them all to masticate and swallow a small amount of dry rice, the guilty person being recognized by the fact that with the dry mouth of fear he was unable to carry out the order. In the Jung word-association test, occasionally employed in psychiatry, a list of one hundred words is read out slowly to the testee, who is asked to respond with the first word that comes into his head, the reaction time (i.e. the time taken to reply) and the word given in response being noted by the psychiatrist. Most of the words are neutral ones but certain key words are introduced relating to subjects over which conflicts often arise, and a delay in responding or an unusual association often gives a clue to the patient's complexes. The lie detector employs a similar list which includes amongst the neutral words others the significance of which could only be meaningful to one who had been acquainted with the circumstances of the crime. Meanwhile, instead of relying upon such data as the reaction time and the unusual response, the investigator has the testee connected up with a battery of instruments which are capable of indicating anxiety through an increased pulse-rate, raised blood-pressure, increased sweating of the skin, and so on. Thus a robber, confronted by the name of an article which he alone could know was among the stolen goods, may give himself away by his concealed anxiety as revealed by the instruments. This method is now little used in psychiatry but doubtless has some limited application in criminology although even here nobody can be convicted on the evidence of the lie-detector alone, and if the suspect sticks to his story he is in little more danger than formerly.

The subject of hypnosis or hypnotism is a large one concerning which there is considerable divergence of opinion amongst various authorities so far as its therapeutic use is concerned. In treatment, hypnosis can be employed in two entirely different ways: either it may be used as a vehicle for positive suggestions, when it is suggested to the patient under its influence that he is already getting better, that his symptoms will disappear, and so on, or it may be employed solely as a short-cut to analysis, as already described in the case of drugs. The opponents of the former method say that, except in the mildest of cases, the effect of suggestion is bound to be transient since the root of the symptoms has been left untouched, and the inevitable result will be that the original ones will shortly come back or, possibly, be replaced by new ones. Therefore this method, although used by doctors who practise hypnosis in addition to their other work, is not in favour amongst specialists in psychiatry who are more likely to prefer the second method of hypo-analysis where the hypnotic state is merely used as an aid to analysing the basic causes of a neurosis by questioning whilst the patient is in a trance. Even so, hypnosis is not entirely satisfactory since only a minority of patients can be really deeply hypnotized and the use of Pentothal or some other drug is more reliable.

The great advantage of the method from the point of view of

some of those who employ it is that, when results do occur, they are often of a highly dramatic nature. Particularly was this the case in wartime, when the symptoms themselves were frequently dramatic, taking the form of those hysterical manifestations which are now rarely seen in civil practice: hysterical paralysis such that the patient was unable to walk, hysterical aphonia where he could not say a word, and sometimes hysterical blindness. Such patients could often be relatively easily hypnotized (soldiers, being used to authority, are perhaps more prone to suggestibility when coming from an officer, than are other people), and the symptom was often removed in a matter of a few seconds. It must, however, be noted that such symptoms arising from a conflict between the social impulses of duty to one's comrades and the unconscious desire to get away from it all might be removed but very few of those cured ever became able to return to the front line. The life or death nature of the basic conflict had not been changed.

Gullible people, or those who are fond of the mysterious and sensational, are often highly suspicious of the misuses to which hypnosis may be put, and it is therefore necessary to discuss some of the points aroused by this problem. To begin with, it has to be admitted that very little is known about the true nature of hypnosis; certainly it has nothing to do with actual emanations of 'animal magnetism' passing from the operator to his subject, nor is it as was once believed related in any way to normal sleep. All that is known for certain is that it is an induced state of exaggerated suggestibility. Many people are capable of being hypnotized to some degree, but only a minority to the extent of demonstrating the phenomena of deep trance, nor is there any connexion between one's susceptibility and neurosis or a 'weak will' and it would appear that the most readily hypnotizable are intelligent normal individuals. Groups of people can be hypnotized, and experiments by the BBC have shown that the procedure is sometimes effective over television. In general, people cannot be hypnotized against their will or without their knowledge; but this must be qualified by the observation that those who are convinced that they cannot resist can often be hypnotized in spite of themselves.

The phenomena which can be produced in a state of deep trance are extraordinary to anyone who is unfamiliar with them: total anaesthesia can be induced, so that surgical operations can be performed without the patient feeling anything; the subject can be persuaded to 'see' people who are not in the room or not to 'see' persons who are; regression to earlier periods of life can be brought about during which the subject behaves as if he were at whatever age is suggested; blisters can be produced upon the skin on the suggestion that the subject has been burned by the touch of a pen which is represented as a red-hot poker; memories can be recalled which are not recallable in the normal state; and so on. Most interesting, perhaps, is the phenomenon of post-hypnotic suggestion in which the subject feels impelled without knowing why to carry out some act which has been suggested whilst he was under hypnosis; the suggestion has been completely forgotten, but is carried out as ordered at a specific time, bizarre 'reasons' being given for the action. Thus, if ordered to open a window at a specific time (which may be after several days or even longer) the subject will do as he was told under trance but, having no recollection of what happened, will give when asked some such reason as that the room was too stuffy, even when, in fact, it is well-ventilated.

Can such phenomena be put to evil use? In general it seems extremely unlikely that they could be, or have been, used by political manipulators to extract faked confessions or to cause anyone to give fabricated evidence at a show trial because, as has been indicated, hypnosis is extremely unreliable in its effects on any given person and can only rarely be induced in an unwilling or uncooperative subject. This indeed is the main reason for its limited uses in legitimate medicine. Most experiments have seemed to show that even in the deepest levels of hypnosis subjects are unlikely to commit any act which would be contrary to their ordinary moral code but this is naturally a matter of conjecture since, obviously, we are not always in a position to say just what their ordinary moral code happens to be. All that can be said with certainty is that when immoral acts have been suggested under hypnosis they have rarely been carried out except in circumstances where it was possible for the subject to know that the context was one of make-believe. In one frequently-quoted case where a hypnotized girl had been carrying out all sorts of suggestions made to her under hypnosis during a clinical demonstration the subject immediately came out of the trance and slapped the face of a mischievous student who had suggested that she undress in front of the group. In short, the committing of socially reprehensible acts under hypnosis cannot be excluded as a possibility, but it is of far too rare and unreliable a nature to be counted on by those with evil intentions.

When we speak of masses of people being 'hypnotized' by a powerful orator this must not be understood to imply that they have been hypnotized in the clinical sense, but, on the other hand, it is true that they are being drawn into a state of increased suggestibility which is one of the features of the hypnotic state. Furthermore, the methods employed by a certain type of orator are very similar to those employed by the hypnotist and, as Kimball Young has noted: 'Direct suggestion, abetted by rhythm, monotony, stagesettings, and appeals to deep, though unconscious, attitudes and ideas, may well induce emotional states not unlike those found in hypnosis.' The most obvious changes which take place in the susceptible individual when he becomes a member of a crowd are heightened emotionality, heightened suggestibility with decreased self-criticism and intellectual alertness, diminished sense of responsibility or loss of the usual social controls, and a sense of power and anonymity. These changes take place and are brought about by the same stimuli no matter what the basic purpose of this type of crowd and are as common to the political agitator and his public as to the evangelist appealing to sinners – to John Wesley as much as to Hitler. Nor is it only the tub-thumping evangelist who employs them; for what is the function of the semi-darkness, the monotonous chanting, the incense, the rhythmic responses, the religious pictures and stained glass windows of the more orthodox religions, if not to increase the suggestibility of the congregation? Such phenomena together with their causes are discussed more fully in the following chapter, and here it is sufficient to note their existence.

Small groups produce effects upon their members which, whilst in some respects similar to those seen in crowds, in other ways are strikingly different, and these effects are put to therapeutic use in what is known as group psychotherapy or group analysis. It is not easy to describe briefly the processes at work in group psychotherapy, partly because various methods are employed, from the 'Freudian' type of group in which the members are given no specific instructions but told simply to say whatever comes into their minds, to the group which is really very little different from group instruction in its approach. Partly, too, authorities would differ in emphasis as to what actual processes go on in group psychotherapy. For our present purposes it is sufficient to say that neurotics or psychopaths who are treated by this method are people who are basically in rebellion against society, the neurotic by reason of unconscious anti-social impulses, the psychopath by reason of quite conscious ones which, however, are not entirely understood by him. In the simplest type of group psychotherapy the members openly discuss their personal problems (i.e. those matters which, by reason of the guilt attached to them, separate them from society) and also such subjects as their views of other members. Since the fundamental defect in these abnormal conditions is a defect in inter-personal relationships acquired in childhood it is obvious that this type of discussion is valuable in two special ways: the member is able in a permissive atmosphere to express his sense of guilt, which, in effect, is pardoned by the group as the representative of society, and he is enabled to see as in a mirror what are his characteristic faulty attitudes to others as he could not to the same extent in discussion with a single individual. Group attitudes are much more potent than individual ones because, by accepting membership of the group and becoming integrated into it, the person comes to accept its norms, since that is in part what group membership means.

In group psychotherapy the individual confesses his 'sins' and is 'pardoned', becomes integrated emotionally with a social body, thus accepting the norms it painfully works out for itself, and discovers in interaction with others a revelation of himself. All these are useful therapeutic results in those who have hitherto felt cut off from society. But they are employed in other fields too. For example, it has been found in industry that incentive wage plans offering bonuses to individual workers often do more harm than good, whereas group incentives in which the bonus is based upon the work of the whole team are likely to be effective, and even more so when the workers' groups are allowed to discuss plans together and set their own targets of production. The reason for this is that a target which has been set by the members of the group themselves becomes 'ego-involved' for each individual – it is *his* decision he is fulfilling, and the decision of the group with which he identifies himself instead of 'theirs' in the shape of management. But identification with the group naturally results in some flattening out of each member's individual characteristics to approximate towards those approved by the group and this is obviously a desirable end from the point of view of totalitarian social systems, especially when there is added to this the practice of group confession of political 'errors' or moral failings.

Such groups are a regular feature of Communism on the one hand and certain religious movements such as Moral Rearmament on the other. One of the duties of Communist party members as recalled in the revised Party Statutes adopted by the Nineteenth Congress of 1952 in the Soviet Union is 'to develop self-criticism and criticism from below, to expose and eliminate shortcomings in work, and to fight against a show of well-being and against being carried away by success in work'. Criticism in this context means the duty of every party member to bring to the notice of the authorities anything which seems calculated to weaken the régime, and it therefore ranges from denouncing individuals to complaints as to how a factory or collective farm is being run. It must be remembered, however, that such complaints and denunciations must remain within the bounds of accepted doctrine and that a measure may be criticized only until a clear decision has been reached by higher authority, after which criticism is no longer permissible. So although in theory the party member is encouraged to criticize, unwelcome remarks may well be condemned as implying an attack on the established order. How this was regarded prior to the Twentieth Congress is revealed in a cartoon in *Krokodil* showing a large cat addressing a frightened mouse with the words: 'Well! You have made your complaint. And now, what is your defence?' Self-criticism, on the other hand, means the public confession of shortcomings at all levels of the party organization and although its ostensible purpose is efficiency, there can be no doubt that it assists the Party in keeping under constant scrutiny the motives and behaviour of everyone who holds a responsible position. In addition it symbolizes the complete obedience of every individual to the collective will of the party, so that the good Communist must be prepared to confess even when his sole offence was carrying out a policy, now rejected, with which he was entrusted by the very members who are now criticizing him. Thus the public disavowal by leaders of their policies, or by artists, composers, writers, and scientists of their work, commonly takes the form of a self-criticism even although it is also a recantation imposed by higher authority.

There is no need to postulate a peculiar Russian psychology, the use of mysterious drugs or sinister psychological pressures in order to explain these phenomena on the part of people who are simply submitting to a generally accepted Communist principle. This principle may not, of course, apply to the Stalin purges of the old Bolshevik leaders, many of whom confessed to acts they could not possibly have committed, and Mr Khrushchev has already stated that these men were tortured – although, since his aim was to discredit Beria the former head of the secret police, Khrushchev is hardly an unbiased witness. There is, in fact, very little evidence that the Soviet authorities have ever made use of the crude methods of physical torture employed by the French paratroops in Algeria or the Nazis in their concentration camps and, to the writer's knowledge, none of those who have been imprisoned in Russia have ever claimed that they have. The methods used were much more subtle and, some may think, equally cruel, but they did not involve direct bodily torture. Even the most rabid anti-Communist would hardly claim that all the Soviet geneticists who turned their backs on 'Mendelism-Morganism-Weismannism' and welcomed the doctrine of Lysenko were either convinced intellectually by the latter or recanted because of torture, when they simply did their duty as good party members and accepted the decision of the majority.

Hoffer is of the opinion that even the faked confessions of the old Bolsheviks can be explained in this way:

In his purges . . . Stalin succeeded in turning proud and brave men into cringing cowards by depriving them of any possibility of identification with the party they had served all their lives and with the Russian masses. These old Bolsheviks had long cut themselves off from humanity outside Russia. They had an unbounded contempt for the past and for history which could still be made by capitalistic humanity. They had renounced God. There was for them neither past nor future, neither memory nor glory outside the confines of Holy Russia and the Communist party – and both these were now wholly and irrevocably in Stalin's hands. They felt themselves, in the words of Bukharin, 'isolated from everything that constitutes the essence of life'. So they confessed. By humbling themselves before the congregation of the faithful they broke out of their isolation. They renewed their communion with the eternal whole by reviling the self, accusing it of monstrous and spectacular crimes, and sloughing it off in public.

Once one agrees with the principle that the party is always right and with public confession to deviations from the party line, it is a small step to faking additional evidence of crimes which, *as defined by the party*, one is actually guilty of committing. In the Communist party there are no conflicts caused merely by personal differences since all conflicts are raised to the level of ideological differences in which one side or the other must inevitably be wrong. Hence the mildest divergence of views from the official version relating to the correct attitude towards revolutions outside the Soviet Union may be defined as Trotskyism, which is a serious crime, and once this is admitted the details are unimportant to the basic issue. The miscreant, however innocently he may have held his beliefs, must admit to Trotskyism, if the party authorities hold that his views fall within this category; and he will agree, and believe, that they are right. Once he admits to the crime and to having embarrassed the party, why not help it out by making the appropriate confessions? It is not suggested that all confessions were arrived at as simply as this, merely that such might well have been the case with many sincere Communists. The other methods known to have been employed, more particularly with non-Communists, are discussed in another chapter.

In recent years there has been a psychiatric revolution in the use of physical methods of treatment for the mentally ill with the result that many cases of once serious illness can be treated in general hospitals over a relatively brief period or even as out-patients in the psychiatric clinic of a general hospital. It is certain that in the very near future a large number of mental hospitals will have to close down just as the tuberculosis sana-toria have done since the discovery of streptomycin, P.A.S., and other drugs. The break-through in psychiatry dates from the discovery in 1933 by Manfred Sakel of Vienna of the effect of insulin shock (i.e., increasing doses of insulin finally leading to coma) upon schizophrenics and, according to Sargant, two out of three cases of early schizophrenia can be helped in this way. Then followed the discovery of von Meduna of Hungary, now working in the United States, that the production of epileptiform convulsions by the injection of a camphor-like drug could cure certain types of disorder and this method was shortly replaced by the use of electrically-induced convulsions by Cerletti of Italy. Today this treatment is employed for the most part in cases of severe depression and the patient, under the influence of an anaesthetic and the paralysing drug curare, has no actual con-vulsion, but E.C.T. (as it is generally described) is almost specific for this type of illness and produces the most dramatic effects within two or three weeks. In otherwise intractable cases of mental illness the operation of leucotomy devised by Egaz Moniz of Portugal may be performed, a procedure which invol-ves the severing of nerve fibres in the brain which connect the emotional centres of the thalamus at its base with the cerebral cortex on its surface, where the ideational content of the patient's illness may be supposed to reside. The delusions or hallucina-tions are thus cut off from their emotional drive and become of little significance to the sufferer. But if the patient's mental con-dition is often greatly improved by this operation, so that an otherwise incurable case may be able to return home and even to work, there are subtle changes which occur in his personality. The fundamental change is an impairment in the power of moral judgement such that the patient's conscience, his views of right or wrong, tend to become conventional rather than personally important. Religious beliefs once fervently held become of minor significance and expedience becomes primary to sincerity. As Stafford-Clark puts it:

An increased complacency and self-satisfaction with diminished interest in, or awareness of the feelings of others, can be one effect. Tactless and inconsiderate behaviour, usually the result of an attitude which is self-centred rather than deliberately offensive, are not uncommon. Together with the relief from acute self-criticism or despair, there may be a corresponding loss in imagination, sensitivity, and intuition, so that judgement suffers, and while day-to-day intellectual capacity remains unimpaired, the fullest and highest ranges of mental life may no longer be scaled.

Leucotomy is now less frequently used since the discovery of still more effective pharmacological methods: the tranquillizers, the anti-depressants, the stimulants, and the hallucinogenic drugs. In former times the symptom of anxiety, always unpleasant and sometimes almost totally incapacitating, was treated by drugs such as the bromides and barbiturates, which acted by depressing the whole activity of the brain and usually making the subject drowsy, but today the tranquillizers act specifically on anxiety and aggressiveness with little general sedative effect. Thus chlorpromazine (Largactil), to quote a report, can within a few days change many patients from 'raging, combative, unsociable persons to cooperative, cheerful, sociable, relatively quiet persons who are amenable to psychotherapy and rehabilitative measures'. The anti-depressant drugs such as isocarboxazid (Marplan) and imprimamine or chlorprothixene (Taractan) produce dramatic results in 60–75 per cent of cases suffering from certain types of severe depression, whilst stimulants such as amphetamine (Benzedrene) relieve mild depression and increase mental energy, removing all sensations of fatigue.

Amongst the most interesting of the new drugs is lysergic acid diethylamide, known briefly as LSD, which was discovered by Albert Hofmann of the drug firm of Sandoz in Basle. LSD is related to ergot, the fungus sometimes found in blighted rye, which many authorities believe to have been responsible, in the form of infected rye bread, for the outbreaks of Dancing Mania which first occurred in Aix-la-Chapelle in 1374 following the

Black Death. The effects of this drug are to produce an artificial psychosis with delusions and hallucinations often of a particularly vivid nature; in some cases the effects are pleasant, almost amounting to the mystic state (as described by Jane Dunlap in her book *Exploring Inner Space*), but on the other hand they may be terrifying and unpleasant in the extreme. At present, LSD is used in research into the nature of mental illness and as an aid to the analyst, to whom it may give clues as to repressed mental conflicts; or, curiously enough, the drug itself can exercise curative effects in some unknown way, so that those who come out from the hallucinatory state suddenly discover that they have 'found' themselves.

Other hallucinogenic drugs are derived from a Mexican mushroom, *psilocybe mexicana*, long eaten by Indian tribes as part of their religious rites, and now isolated in the form of Psilocybin, and mescaline from the *peyote* cactus similarly used by the Indians. Mescaline depersonalizes, makes minor things seem important (as described by Aldous Huxley in his *Doors of Perception*), and has the unusual effect of translating noise into visual stimuli, so that a knock at the door becomes spots of colour floating in the air. As in the case of the 'truth drug', it must be pointed out that these new discoveries, useful as they are in psychiatry, can play little or no part in the schemes of the malevolent individual or group whose intention it is to manipulate normal minds. It is certain that, so far, no such drugs exist and improbable in the highest degree that drugs have played any part whatsoever in faked trials, forced confessions, brainwashing techniques, or political indoctrination.

Earlier we referred to the useful but, on the whole, rather mild changes in the self brought about by suitable changes in environment. But the lately-developed ability to alter environment in much more drastic ways, notably in the 'weightless state' which is a concomitant of space-travel, and observation of the extraordinary alterations such experiences may bring about in the human personality have led psychologists to ask themselves once again the old question : what is the self and what are the limits of its boundaries? At first such a question might seem to be almost absurd since on the face of it nothing appears to be more obvious than the fact that we are real personalities sharply distinguishable from our surrounding environment; yet such a state did not always exist in the course of our own development, and it has long been known that in the mystic state or under the influence of certain drugs the boundaries of self spread far beyond their usual narrow framework leading to a feeling of 'oneness' with the universe. The very young child has not yet developed the awareness of a self bounded by the limits of his own skin and, if asked to give a foot, will lift it in his hands and present it to the parent just as he would do if he had been asked to give his shoe. The concept of a real and enduring self is not innate but arises in the course of development and relating ourselves to our social and material environment. Basically it originates in the reflected appraisals of other people, so that we learn about ourselves from the way in which others respond to us: an additional source is the constant awareness of those stimuli arriving from the material environment by which we orientate ourselves; and even clothes help to form the sense of individuality. As the American psychologist Gardner Murphy puts it, consciousness of self arises

... through the observation of body surfaces, muscular contractions, the sound of the voice.... By constant comparison of them with other entities observed in other persons, an empirical self is woven and given abiding structure. [This self] represents a relative continuity from the cradle to the grave, is given a name, a social position and a sense of responsibility, and around it in time cluster the goals, values and norms and ideals which give meaningful purposive continuity to life.

So dependent are we upon this continual checking and counter-checking of ourselves in relation to the surrounding social and material environment that the artificial or accidental withdrawal of such stimuli can bring about the most devastating results even in quite a short period of time. Thus, a psychiatrist who volunteered to enter a completely soundproof room was in a few minutes so disturbed that he had to be released and stated afterwards that he had faced something in himself that he had never known about before. Experimental work has shown that total isolation and complete and absolute silence bring about hallucinations of sight and sound, and D. C. Hebb reports that:

... merely taking away from a healthy university student for a few days the usual sights, sounds and bodily contact can shake him right down to the base, can disturb his personal identity, so that he is aware of two bodies (one hallucinatory), and cannot say which is his own, or perceives his personal self as vague and ill-defined; something separate from his body, looking down on where it is lying on the bed, and can disturb his capacity for critical judgement, making him eager to listen to and believe any sort of preposterous nonsense.

The effects of weightlessness in relation to space-travel are well-known in their physical aspects: since not only the passenger but the air surrounding him is without weight, it is necessary to make breathing a deliberate effort by exhaling forcibly and all objects not fastened down will float freely in space; the slightest movement or even a sneeze may propel him violently against the cabin wall and he must drink from a plastic squeeze-bottle to prevent liquid from entering his nose or floating about the cabin. Many psychologists doubt whether a man is capable of tolerating this state for the periods of time necessary if the more distant planets are to be reached without going mad. In a much more trivial way even a change of clothes has some effect on personality, and women have long been aware of the morale-building power of a new dress, whilst, conversely, prisons and the various religious orders have, even if unconsciously, utilized the humbling effects of confiscating an individual's worldly garments and possessions and dressing all in uniform style.

These observations about the influence of environmental changes on the self have, as we shall shortly see, a highly practical significance in the field of 'brainwashing' and political indoctrination. They are indications of means whereby destruction of the original self might conceivably be accomplished.

In the Communist countries Freudian theory is regarded as 'reactionary' and the theories upon which their psychiatric practice is based are those of I. P. Pavlov, the great Russian physiologist and contemporary of Freud who died in 1936. As many writers have been concerned to show, Pavlov's work with dogs sheds a flood of light not only upon the problems of mental illness but also upon the stress reactions of war and the allegedly extraordinary results obtained by the practitioners of brainwashing and 'thought reform'. On the other hand, there is not the slightest evidence that the Russians or Chinese have made deliberate use of Pavlovian theory in this way or that those who carry out such practices have any special knowledge concerning this or any other branch of psychology. Many authoritative papers have made it clear that 'thought reform' is neither mysterious nor even new, and it contains nothing for which the histories of the countries concerned do not furnish ample precedent. Nor, although some would assert the contrary view, does Pavlovian theory at any important point contradict the views of Freud; what it does do is to provide additional evidence at the physiological level of many psychopathological mechanisms. Such concepts as conditioning, fixation, inhibition, repression, regression to more primitive behaviour in response to stress, and the root of neurosis in conflict are common to both theories.

So far as practice is concerned there is no reason to suppose that psychiatric treatment in the Communist countries is in any way superior to the more eclectic methods employed in the West and, in fact, all the new methods described here from the new psychotrophic drugs to E.C.T. and leucotomy were developed by non-Communist nations. A reading of contemporary Russian psychiatric literature reveals a depressingly doctrinaire approach and a concern with theories long discarded elsewhere, such as the assumption that schizophrenia is caused by autointoxication, found to be baseless in Britain and the U.S.A. more than thirty years ago after thorough trials. This is not said in order to discredit the Soviet Union, but simply to show the improbability that Soviet psychiatrists have any access to information not available in the West.

As is well known, Pavlov was extremely critical of the Soviet régime, but his fame and the credit which was reflected on his country by his researches protected him and he was allowed to carry on his work in Leningrad with the active cooperation of the Soviet government. His basic discovery, made in 1901, and of immense importance to psychology, was the conditioned reflex, demonstrated in the following way: if each time a dog is given food a bell is rung simultaneously, the dog becomes 'conditioned' to the sound of the bell and in time salivates on hearing it even though it is unaccompanied by food. Not only sounds, but light, smell, or touch stimuli may condition dogs to salivate when no food is present. The conditioned reflex results if the stimulus occurs before or simultaneously with the original un-conditioned stimulus (food). Thus if the bell is habitually soun-ded two minutes before food is given, the dog inhibits salivation until two minutes after hearing the bell. Moreover, a conditioned reflex can be extinguished as well as established by constantly ringing the bell without presenting food, when salivation is soon inhibited. After being extinguished the conditioned reflex can be brought back in two ways: by spontaneous recovery after a lapse of time, or by reinforcement – that is, by again presenting food with the bell. The degree of response in each experiment can be accu-rately measured by bringing one salivary duct on to the surface of the cheek so that the number of drops of saliva can be counted.

Pavlov's next step was to investigate the effect of stress upon these established brain patterns, but he shortly discovered that all dogs did not respond alike to stress and that there appeared to be four basic inherited temperaments in the animals which he equated with those (mentioned elsewhere) first described by Hippocrates in ancient Greece. The first was the 'strong excita-tory' type which corresponded to Hippocrates' 'choleric' temper-ament; the second or 'lively' type corresponded to Hippocrates' 'sanguine' temperament. Both these types tended to respond to stress situations with increased excitement and aggression, although, whereas the former might become completely uncon-trolled, the latter responded in a more purposeful and controlled way. The other two types met stress situations with passive or inhibitory responses rather than with excitement and aggres-sion. The 'calm imperturbable type' or 'phlegmatic type' of Hippocrates lived up to its name, whereas the 'weak inhibitory type' or 'melancholic type' as Hippocrates described it was reduced by severe stress to a state of brain inhibition and 'fear paralysis'. However, all four types when subjected to more stress than they could deal with ended up in a state of inhibition, which Pavlov regarded as a protective mechanism when the brain was disturbed beyond endurance. The 'weak inhibitory' dog broke down before the others and in response to lighter stresses. Thus the final pattern of behaviour in dogs, and as we now know in man, depends both upon inherited temperament and the degree of stress to which they are exposed.

Pavlov then began to investigate the effect of stress on conditioned behaviour patterns when the dog's nervous system was 'transmarginally' stimulated by stresses beyond its adaptive capacity. These were of four main types.

In the first, a dog which had developed a conditioned reflex to salivate in response to a light electric shock applied to one leg which was the signal for food would be subjected to a gradual increase in the strength of the current. When the shock became more than its system could bear, the dog broke down.

Secondly, a breakdown could be brought about by conditioning a dog to expect food at a fixed time after applying the stimulus, and then increasing the waiting period. Pavlov found that the dog's nervous system broke down when it was subjected to long periods of protracted inhibition as the result of waiting under stress. Some, of course, broke down more readily than others.

The third method of inducing breakdown was to alternate positive and negative stimuli thus inducing a state of confusion. If a dog had been conditioned to respond to one stimulus with salivation because it was associated with food and not to respond to another when food was not given then, if positive and negative stimuli were given one after the other, breakdown occurred. Similar effects might be produced by feeding a dog when a white circle was exposed and not feeding it when an ellipse was shown; if the ellipse was then approximated more and more closely to a circular shape, breakdown happened when the dog could no longer distinguish between the two.

Finally, breakdown occurred when a dog was subjected to long periods of fatiguing work, fevers, and other forms of debilitating circumstance. Even when the three other methods failed to produce much effect in the more stable type of dog, it was found that when they were repeated after castration or an infection of the intestines breakdown inevitably occurred. An interesting observation was that when, after such interference, new behaviour patterns had developed their stability depended upon the type of dog. Thus new patterns of a neurotic nature could be fairly readily removed in the 'weak inhibitory' animal by small doses of bromides whereas in the 'calm imperturbable' or 'lively' types of animal the new patterns were likely to persist with the same tenacity as the original ones. The more difficult it was to change a pattern of behaviour, the more stable was the new pattern once it had been brought about.

There appeared to be three distinct and progressive stages of 'transmarginal' inhibition which made their appearance in the course of Pavlov's experiments: (1) the so-called 'equivalent' phase when the dog responded by producing the same amount of saliva, no matter what the strength of the stimulus; (2) the 'paradoxical' phase when weak stimuli actually produced more active responses than stronger ones, which only increased the protective inhibition; (3) the 'ultra-paradoxical' phase when positive stimuli came to be reacted to as negative ones and vice versa; behaviour during this phase became precisely the opposite of that previously learned. Pavlov also found that transmarginal inhibition led to increased suggestibility in dogs similar to the hypnotic state in human beings so that when one area of the brain was stimulated the rest of the cortex might become inhibited as a result, and conversely when a localized area was inhibited the remainder might be in a state of excitation. He showed too that when one small area in a dog's brain reached what he called a 'state of pathological inertia and excitation' there might develop a stereotyping of certain movements, of the nature of nervous tics in human beings.

Now all these states experimentally produced in dogs correspond to similar conditions found in human mental illness or under the stress of war or political indoctrination, and, it is alleged, the same sort of stimuli are capable of bringing them about. Thus, prolonged periods of waiting, especially when it is not known when the expected event is about to happen, are known to produce great anxiety in certain types of people, and the debilitation produced by undernourishment or illness plays a large part both in political indoctrination and in the phenomena of religious conversion where fasting is often used as a deliberate spiritual technique to induce change. We also know that (like the dog in the 'equivalent' phase of transmarginal inhibition) many mentally ill people reach a stage in which all happenings are received alike without either the natural joy or sorrow normally appropriate to the occasion. Examples have already been given of the apparent reversal of normal patterns of behaviour under stress as in the conversion of Saul to Christianity, and in some cases of schizophrenia negative stimuli are said to become positive and positive ones negative (as in the 'ultra-paradoxical' phase of brain activity): e.g., the sight or touch of a chamberpot is a strongly positive conditioned response to the desire to urinate or defecate from childhood onwards, whereas clothes, beds, and floors are negatively charged in this respect, but the schizophrenic may appear to reverse this order of events and soil his bed or clothing whilst ignoring the bedpan provided. The observation that, when one part of the brain is in a state of excitation, other areas are inhibited forms a basis for what Freud described as 'dissociation' where a traumatic event may lead to loss of sensation or paralysis in some parts of the body and, on the other hand, the converse state of affairs in which a small area of inhibition leads to generalized excitability or anxiety fits in well with Freud's description of the anxiety which may accompany a repressed memory. Pavlov's dogs' occasional repetitive movements when one area reached a state of 'pathological inertia and excitation' has already been noted as similar in nature to the development of nervous tics in human beings, but when a similar condition occurs in the field of thought obsessive ideas may be the result when the individual is unable to get certain fixed thoughts or words out of his mind. If, to employ Pavlovian terms, these occur at the paradoxical or ultra-paradoxical phases of brain activity the obsessive ideas may be the very reverse of those natural to the individual: the fond mother will have thoughts that she may injure or even kill her child and the excessively puritanical character may be unable to stop ruminating on obscene events or phrases. Also, the induction of states of hyper-suggestibility under stress is well-documented in the tendency of frightened or excited people in the absence of accurate information to accept the most incredible statements as literal truth. Hence the phenomenon of absurd rumours, particularly in wartime.

All these are extremely valuable observations which, in the

main, confirm Freudian views on psychopathology. But a Freudian would certainly not interpret them all in the same way. For example, it is simply untrue to say that a schizophrenic's dirty habits are merely a reversal of his previous ones, or that the fond mother's sudden impulse to kill her child is a reversal of a previous state of affairs brought on purely by some external agency as in the case of Pavlov's dogs. Those whose intention it is to show that a technique such as brainwashing can literally reverse behaviour in human beings, just as apparently happens in animals, bring out these examples to prove their point. In fact they prove nothing of the sort, and it is doubtful whether in this instance Pavlov proved his point either; for a dog which, from being friendly towards a laboratory assistant, turns upon him after it has been tormented is not being made in some mysteriously scientific way to reverse its behaviour – it is behaving quite naturally in the circumstances. The schizophrenic who soils his bed cannot be discussed usefully in terms of negative stimuli becoming positive or vice versa; he has regressed to more primitive behaviour just as may occur in the old and senile patient without any stress. The puritanical person may be obsessed with impure thoughts, and the mother feel a compulsion to kill the child she loves, but nobody would guess from the Pavlovian explanation that the forbidden thoughts were there all the time, as can be proved under analysis. The thoughts appear because the patient has previously kept all obscene or hostile impulses repressed in the unconscious until they finally (and not from any external agency) overflow into consciousness. One mother with such impulses known to the writer was a tired and over-conscientious housewife who had to take her little girl every day to the hospital for treatment for a comparatively trivial malady. The ordinary mother would have been able to allow herself to feel irritation at this state of affairs, which involved long periods of waiting in draughty corridors, and the irritation would have been dissipated outwardly. This mother, however, was too dutiful to allow herself this luxury, repressed the hostility, and one day whilst poking the fire the hostility burst its bounds and she was horrified to feel a sudden impulse to hit her child over the head with the poker. When the state of affairs was explained, the deep depression which had brought her to the psychiatrist disappeared almost at once. It is nonsense to talk about unconscious impulses coming to the surface as if it were a mechanistic process of reversal of behaviour capable of being deliberately induced. Indeed the whole idea of, as it were, insinuating an idea or a form of behaviour into the mind, with sinister intentions to produce behaviour contrary to the individual's ordinary way of thinking, is a ludicrous one. Ideas can be introduced, for example, by hypnosis or – as can happen spontaneously in war – an incident may be experienced which the mind finds intolerable. In either case the result is the same: the rejected idea or experience becomes encapsulated like an abscess in the body and can only remain there on condition that the mind as a whole does not recognize it. In other words, it is dissociated and does not become part of the individual's total way of thought. A person under hypnosis can be caused for a relatively brief period to do odd things because he is in a state of dissociation, but we have seen that he is unlikely in the extreme to do anything against his general moral outlook. The war-neurosis case with a dissociated memory will have to have it brought into consciousness so that his mind can finally absorb it. But the notion that subliminal perception, brainwashing, or any other device can introduce permanently into the mind an idea completely foreign to it and thus influence behaviour must be rejected as absurd.

The mind is, to be sure, an instrument for adjusting the organism to its environment. But adjustment means that something is being adapted to something else, which in practice implies that the environment is being interpreted and behaviour adapted *in terms of the personality as it already exists*. Examples have already been given of how, for example, the prejudiced person will actually reverse the meaning of an anti-prejudice message because it does not fit in with his real self. Unwelcome changes in the environment are rejected by the mechanism of denial, or, if taken into the mind, become dissociated and shut off from the main stream of consciousness. Another method of dealing with an environment which threatens the values of the self is that behaviour may be modified appropriately without the individual's basic attitudes being altered in any way. Thus, as will be seen later, the American soldiers who were accused of collaboration with the Communists during the Korean war were, in the vast majority of cases, not converted to Communism. Their behaviour involved what they described as 'playing along with the Communists', i.e., making things easier for themselves by behaving as they were told whilst retaining their true beliefs unchanged. The potent drugs employed by psychiatrists do not act by directly changing the patient's thoughts; what they do is to change his mood so that the unpleasant thoughts become unimportant. Emotions are the subjective aspect of physiological states, and obviously when a depressed individual is made by physiological means into a cheerful one, the idea that he has committed 'the unforgivable sin' which was in part a rationalization to explain to himself why he was so depressed disappears into the background. In short, his mood, but not his thoughts have been altered. Even in the case of a drastic procedure such as leucotomy it would be true to say that, as Allport says of the man in the crowd, 'he becomes himself, only more so'. Naturally, brain damage, like the disintegration produced by diseases such as syphilis or the dementia of old age, causes the personality to change in certain directions but these are in the direction of bringing to the surface usually unpleasant traits which it had previously been possible to suppress. The most difficult thing in the world is to change minds in directions which conflict with the attitudes deeply embedded in the nuclear self.

CHAPTER 9

THE NATURE OF RELIGIOUS CONVERSION

It has been the custom to suppose that throughout history periods of moderation and cerebral control, usually known as Classical, have alternated with periods of emotionalism and impulsiveness, as classical Greece and Rome were followed by the religious fervour of the Middle Ages and the moderation of eighteenth-century Europe by the Romantic movement of the nineteenth. In the specific field of religion Nietzsche contrasted the acceptance of the golden mean in the Apollonian type of religious belief with the ecstasy and excitement of the Dionysian. But whatever broad truth there may be in the theory of periods of alternating intellectual and emotional control, there can be no doubt at all that religions of the predominantly Apollonian or the predominantly Dionysian types can, and do, co-exist. The somewhat cynically held state religion of ancient Greece existed alongside the Dionysiac Mystery religions and the Methodism of John Wesley within the orthodox Church of England, in spite of the contempt in which the latter held the 'enthusiasm' of Methodist services. Indeed, we might not go too far wrong in suggesting that the orthodox religion of the ruling classes has ordinarily tended towards the conventional and conservative Apollonian type and, although emotional and evangelical movements have frequently been initiated by individual members of the ruling or middle classes, their followers have ordinarily come from the toiling masses. In some cases, notably in the case of Wesley's Methodist movement, incipient political revolution on the part of the masses has been replaced by a religious one. The methods by which conversion occurred during these movements were often of a striking and dramatic nature sometimes amounting to collective hysteria and with these manifestations we shall be concerned later in the present chapter since mass movements have characteristics of their own. But, first of all, it is worth while considering the psychological factors involved in the process of individual conversion which have been well documented in the autobiographical writings of those who have experienced it. Dr R. H. Thouless in *The Psychology of Religion* classifies the conflicts lying behind such conversions as predominantly moral, predominantly intellectual, or predominantly social; it is likely that all three of these elements enter into most conversions, but these headings will provide a rough classification, although we cannot promise to adhere strictly to Dr Thouless's explanations.

Obviously, conversion is based upon mental conflict and a feeling of inadequacy, otherwise there would be no point in changing one's beliefs. In this respect it resembles the state of falling in love which the psychoanalyst Theodor Reik explains by showing that the prospective lover first suffers from a feeling of self-distaste – Faust before he meets Gretchen and Romeo before he meets Juliet are both discontented. Love is not a crisis but the way out of a crisis which has arisen from a state of dissatisfaction with oneself. Having fallen short of his ego-ideal, the individual makes use of love as a means of finding it in someone else and, in this way, achieving wholeness. The beloved person is a substitute for the ideal ego, and two people who fall in love with each other are interchanging their ego-ideals. Failing the discovery of a loved object, says Reik, the only remaining alternatives are to 'fall in hate' or to accomplish something creative which gives one back the lost self-respect. To many, conversion is a means to recovering the lost ego-ideal, a process of falling in love, but even hate or the possibility of finding some creative solution can play a part. As Hoffer points out, those who are haunted by the purposelessness of their lives may find a new contentment, not only by dedicating themselves to a holy cause but also by nursing a fanatical grievance, and a religious movement offers unlimited opportunities for both. Martin Luther said:

When my heart is cold and I cannot pray as I should I scourge myself with the thought of the impiety and ingratitude of my enemies, the Pope and his accomplices and vermin, and Zwingli, so that my heart swells with righteous indignation and hatred and I can say with warmth and vehemence: 'Holy be Thy Name, Thy Kingdom come, Thy Will be done!' And the hotter I grow the more ardent do my prayers become.

William James in *The Varieties of Religious Experience* has this to say of the psychology of self-surrender:

There are only two ways in which it is possible to get rid of anger, worry, fear, despair, or other undesirable affections. One is that an opposite affection should overpoweringly break over us, and the other is by getting so exhausted with the struggle that we have to stop – so we drop down, give up, and *don't care* any longer. Our emotional brain-centres strike work, and we lapse into temporary apathy. *Now there is documentary proof that this state of temporary exhaustion not infrequently forms part of the conversion crisis.* [My italics – J.A.C.B.]

But as the reader may remember, nervous exhaustion was experimentally shown by Pavlov to be one of the conditions which apparently led to the destruction of old brain-patterns and their replacement by new ones and it is striking to discover that this finding is confirmed by James from his study of the literature of conversion. Love seeking for an object, hate and anger, worry and despair, and the exhaustion produced either by mental conflict or by physical means are all states which prepare the mind, in suitable environmental circumstances, for religious conversion. St Augustine, it may be remembered, was prior to his conversion being pressed by his mother to give up the mistress he loved:

Meanwhile my sins were being multiplied, and my concubine being torn from my side as a hindrance to my marriage, my heart which clave unto her was torn and wounded and bleeding. . . . . To Thee be praise, glory to Thee, Fountain of Mercies. I was becoming more miserable and Thou nearer.

Pascal was hopelessly in love with a woman of high rank who appears to have been Mlle de Roannez, sister of his friend the Duc de Roannez, and, says Thouless, 'there can be little doubt that the deeply emotional nature of his subsequent conversion was largely determined by his redirection to Heaven of this earthly love'. St Catherine of Genoa and Mme Guyon were both extremely unhappy in their married lives before their mystical conversions. 'Man's extremity is God's opportunity' is the theological way of expressing this need in certain circumstances for self-surrender.

As has been suggested elsewhere, the trouble about Pavlov's work is that, unless we have some knowledge of psychopathology from the subjective standpoint such as is provided by Freud, we are going to be seriously led astray if we are induced to believe that the mind under stress can be wiped clean like a slate and new patterns imposed upon it which have no bearing upon what has gone before – in other words, that a personality can be wholly changed into somebody quite different from the original one. There are no grounds for believing this to be true. Conversion is usually described as being a sudden process and its climax almost invariably is; but it is very easy to see in any carefully studied case-history how the state was being led up to all along. New attitudes are held, but they are held in the same way as the old ones (Pavlov's dogs which were most resistant to the breakdown of the old patterns were also the most resistant to change in the new – they remained obstinate dogs); and often, as we have seen, the 'new' beliefs are strikingly similar in emotional content to the old. Sometimes even after conversion the old beliefs thrust themselves into awareness from time to time, showing that they are not erased from the pages of the mind but repressed into the unconscious whence the 'new' ones originally emerged. Paul may once more be taken as an example; for, as Jung pointed out, the old Saul was never completely extinguished:

It broke forth at times in the fits he suffered from. It is certainly a great mistake to call his fits epileptic. There is no trace of epilepsy in them; on the contrary, St Paul himself in his epistles gives hints enough as to the real nature of the illness. They are clearly psychogenic fits, which really mean a return to the old Saul-complex, repressed through conversion, in the same way as there had previously been a repression of the complex of Christianity.

Or there is the case quoted by Thouless of the unregenerate gentleman who drank excessively but nevertheless lived on affectionate terms with his wife and children; when converted by some religious organization he abandoned them and allowed them so little money that they were reduced to poverty. Two years later he lapsed, but returned to live on the formal friendly terms with his family, taking to drink once more. Once again he was converted, and this time, living on the small salary of an official of the organization, he refused to support his wife and family at all, announced that they were 'living in sin', and sold the house over their heads. He was highly regarded by the other members of the organization, who knew nothing of his personal affairs. Here there was an alternating repression of the 'good' and 'bad' sides of this man's nature.

We must regard every human being as having a large number of groups or complexes of ideas or potentialities which ordinarily he never makes full use of, some, in fact, being repressed into the unconscious in the interests of consistency; for, as both Jung and Anna Freud demonstrated, it is not only socially inadmissible ideas which are repressed but ideas which are inconsistent with the existing organization of the personality. Charles Darwin in his autobiography notes how, as his interests became increasingly absorbed in science, he lost the pleasure in poetry and the plays of Shakespeare which had formerly been a prominent feature of his life and it can be assumed that predominantly intellectual or practical types often repress their religious interests in this way only to be suddenly overwhelmed by them when the occasion arises. This is well expressed, although in a rather dated form, by William James:

Let us hereafter, in speaking of the hot place in a man's consciousness, the group of ideas to which he devotes himself, and from which he works, call it *the habitual centre of his personal energy*. It makes a great difference to a man whether one set of his ideas, or another, be the centre of his energy; and it makes a great difference, as regards any set of ideas which he may possess, whether they become central or remain peripheral in him. To say that a man is 'converted' means, in these terms, that religious ideas, previously peripheral in his consciousness, now take a central place, and that religious aims form the habitual centre of his energy.

In more contemporary terms we can imagine the peripheral part of the personality as containing many sets of ideas which are often associated with primary or secondary social groups to which the individual has once belonged (as we shall see later, conversion is often associated with a change of social background or a changed attitude to a particular social group), and the energy of the nuclear personality as expressing itself predominantly through one of these sets of ideas with the potentiality of suddenly switching to another. Yet each of these possible 'personalities' is consistent with the nuclear one which remains relatively unchanged. James notes that when a man such as the President of the United States (he is presumably referring to 'Teddy' Roosevelt) goes out camping in the wilderness for a vacation he 'changes his system of ideas from top to bottom', and those who knew him only as the strenuous man of affairs would not know him for the same person. But, supposing he never went back to his duties, he would be for practical intents and purposes a permanently transformed being. Very often we suppose an individual to have a rigidly moulded personality because we habitually see him in the same social setting, whereas if we saw him in another milieu quite another aspect of his personality might become apparent; he would become a new man, to the superficial observer, although the skilled psychologist would soon trace the fundamental ways in which he had not changed.

Sex and the sense of guilt associated with it play a very large part in conversion and religious phenomena generally and it is significant that, as Starbuck demonstrates in *The Psychology of Religion*, the majority of conversions take place between the ages of twelve and twenty-five, a period when young people are going through the storm and stress associated with adolescence. Such conversions, however, tend to be impermanent and are grown out of as the stresses gradually resolve themselves. Similarly, psychiatrists might point out that the depressive states which occur at the change of life in men and women often have a considerable element of guilt and a conviction of sin which is associated with an absorption in religious matters. This, too, is a period of life when conversion is common. The religious sentiment thus has a waxing and waning which is concurrent with similar changes in the sexual life; for in both adolescence and middle life sexual desire tends to increase and subsequently decrease. Other observations too bring out the connexion between the two groups of phenomena. Thus the tendency of religions to suppress the natural expressions of the sexual drive would seem to indicate a subconscious awareness of the fact that, when normal outlets are allowed, sublimation into religious feeling is less likely to occur. One cannot help but notice the predominant role played by unmarried women in the Christian Church or the visible loss of enthusiasm for religious interests on the part of happily married women. Many have noticed the common use in devotional works of sexual symbolism and the tendency to express religious feeling in erotic imagery even to the extent of describing what, in another context, would be taken as an account of sexual orgasm. Lastly, one knows that in some religions of a highly emotional type excitement actually breaks down into overt sexual expression.

Intellectual conversions are probably rare in the pure form although intellectual difficulties often form a part of the struggle before conversion actually takes place. St Augustine, for example, describes his conflicting feelings over the problems of free-will and the existence of evil, but these did not bring about his conversion. On the other hand what we have in a very general sense described as social factors seem to play a disproportionately large part in religious conversion. This may be expressed by saying that rejection of one social group or rejection by such a group is often followed by acceptance of the *mores*, including the religious beliefs, of another. As mentioned earlier, it is impossible not to observe how often the acceptance of certain views is conditioned by one's basic filial attitude towards the family rather than by the intellectual considerations which are usually given as rationalizations. The number of parson's sons who have supported the Rationalist Association and become violent atheists must be legion and their 'conversion' has often been followed by a lifelong study of theology (although, of course, to different ends) which might well be the envy, so intensely is it indulged in, of any professional theologian. Conversely, how many sincere rationalists have produced children who later joined the Roman Catholic Church, the old enemy of their family! During the last war, while examining Arab volunteers for their psychiatric suitability to join the army, one could not help being struck by the fact that those who had become Christian converts had in many cases been social misfits in their own group before their conversion. (This did not, of course, apply to Arabs from those areas, such as the Lebanon, in which there were already large Christian communities.) The common belief amongst Europeans who had lived long in the Middle East that one should never trust a Christian Arab as a servant probably had some basis in fact since those who had been converted to an alien religion in predominantly Muslim areas were often maladjusted types.

We have already seen in connexion with political parties how often those who join minority groups (even if they happen to be right in the eyes of God) are the disaffected, the unstable, the outcasts, the misfits, and the ambitious who have failed to find a suitable niche in the more conventional parties. It is possible to have every sympathy with nuclear disarmament, pacifism, or vegetarianism yet at the same time observe that the true believers who join these movements are hardly typical of the population as a whole and, in fact, include many who are eccentric in other directions. None of this, it must be repeated, has anything to do with the rightness or wrongness of the views held any more than the demonstration of the sexual phenomena of religion shows that the religion is untrue or nothing but sex; what it does show is that conversion to particular views is frequently initiated by the social inability to fit into one's own group, and the constant searching for a 'true' philosophy often conceals the search for a social group into which one may fit and cease to be an outcast in one's own eyes. When such a group has been found, its beliefs and *mores* will be accepted no matter how absurd they may seem to the irreverent, and their removal will be resisted with all the strength of one who fears becoming an outcast once more.

We must now turn to the more dramatic phenomena of conversion which are more akin to 'brainwashing' in their use of such stimuli as fasting, physical discomfort and scourging, the induction of panic fear, regulation of breathing as in Yoga, drumming, dancing, singing, the use of incense or intoxicant drugs, and so on. It will be remembered that stirring up strong emotions of anxiety, guilt, or anger, causing mental conflicts, exhausting the individual mentally or physically, prolonging stress by leaving him in doubt for varying times without knowing what his fate is going to be, all bring about states of suggestibility in human beings just as they did in Pavlov's dogs. The fundamentalist Christian Evangelist employs three methods. Firstly, he never argues but inculcates beliefs by affirmation (Jesus is waiting for you!), by repetition (Hallelujah! Praise the Lord!), and by crowd contagion. Secondly, he utters terrible warnings of hellfire so that the possible non-existence of Hell never enters the listeners' minds; thus Jonathan Edwards, one of the leading figures of the New England revivals, tells his congregation:

The God that holds you over the pit of Hell, much as we hold a spider, or some loathsome insect over the fire, abhors you, and is dreadfully provoked. His wrath towards you burns like fire.

And the Rev. B. S. Taylor announces that

Hell has been running for six thousand years. It is filling up every day. Where is it? About eighteen miles from here. Which way is it? Straight down – not over eighteen miles down, in the bowels of the earth.

Even little children are not to be saved unless they are changed, for it must be realized, said Jonathan Edwards, that

...all are by nature the children of wrath and the heirs of Hell; and that everyone that has not been born again, whether he be young or old, is exposed, every moment, to eternal destruction, under the wrath of Almighty God. As innocent as children seem to us, if they are out of Christ, they are not so in God's sight, but are young vipers and are infinitely more hateful than vipers and are in a most miserable condition.

Thirdly, having induced fear and guilt in his audience, the evangelist tells them how they may be saved and as the agent of the divine holds out promises the fulfilment of which is never questioned. 'Repent and ye shall be saved.' The New England revivals, in which Edwards played the predominant part, were one of the earliest manifestations of the evangelical and largely fundamentalist campaigns of modern times. They began in the town of Northampton, New England, in the year 1734, following two tragic deaths in Edwards's parish which may not have been without their influence in conditioning the people to his message which, on that particular Sunday, was a sermon on justification by faith alone. To his own surprise 'scarcely a single person in the town, either young or old, was left unconscious of the great things of the eternal world', and, out of a population of eleven hundred, no fewer than three hundred made the orthodox Puritan public confession and were declared to be converted.

Public confession was a strange procedure which obviously bore a strong resemblance to what we know about 'brainwashing' techniques. The penitent would first make his confession before the assembled congregation, often in exaggerated language recalling that of the victims of the Russian purges of the nineteen-thirties: 'I appear to myself the most vile, abominable and loathsome of the human race. I can think of no person, however profligate and abandoned, who does not appear, in comparison with my own character, amiable and pious,' to quote one penitent. In this state the penitent would ask: 'What can I do to be saved?' To which he would be given the answer: 'Nothing!' There was just one slender chance and that was the grace of God which could not be won by any effort on his part, but only hoped for; and the alternative was an eternity of damnation. In the second stage the penitent would be brought to the point where he could say before the congregation that 'God may glorify Himself in my damnation' and if he refused to accept this belief all else was of no avail. Thus one man who declared that Christ had appeared to him and said that he was saved was told that this was not enough – he must be prepared to say that he would still love Christ if He decided to damn him forever. The penitent seemed to think not, whereupon he was told that he would have to assent to this if he were to be saved. During the height of the Great Revival the people were whipped into a frenzy of fear and it is reported of one penitent that 'when he was pricked at the heart and saw himself hanging over the pit of everlasting burnings, his distress was so great for the space of half an hour that he was obliged to cover his mouth with his hand to prevent screaming'. At the height of the Revival there arrived from England John Wesley's colleague the fanatical Whitefield, who made things even worse; there was collective weeping and wringing of hands, states of protracted coma, physical collapse, trembling, and the mass induction of hysterical symptoms. Finally the Revival was brought to an end by the discovery of a scandal which at first promised its further success: the young people of the town, it was alleged, were reading lewd books (which probably meant that they were reading ordinary secular literature). Edwards called a meeting and instructed the offenders to appear before their elders, but when it was found that the children of some of the most prominent figures in the town were involved, the parents quickly lost enthusiasm and the young openly defied Edwards, whose reputation soon declined.

Both John and Charles Wesley were converted within a few days of each other from the belief that the performance of good works could lead to salvation to a realization that faith alone could save and, significantly, the conversions took place following an attack of severe mental depression in both brothers. Formerly John had been a relatively ineffectual preacher, but now he discovered for himself the technique which had been so successful in New England. Thus, he would create high emotional tension amongst his audience by fear of everlasting Hell which, as Sargant points out, was as real to Wesley's own mind as the houses and fields in which he preached; and as in the case of Pavlov's dogs, anyone who became emotionally involved, whether positively or negatively, was equally open to conversion, since anger against the suggested ideas as well as fear can induce psychological disturbances which make a person highly suggestible, or apparently reverse his conditioned behaviour patterns, to employ Pavlovian terminology. Once this had been done, the way out of conversion was suggested powerfully – in Wesley's own words: 'After more and more persons are convinced of sin, we may mix more and more of the gospel, in order to beget faith, to raise into spiritual life those whom the law has slain' – the law being the certainty that hellfire awaited the unconverted sinner. One woman with a bad reputation came to mock and jeer and proceeded to shout and create a disturbance. Wesley remained calm and told the woman that God loved her, whereupon 'she was struck to the heart, and shame covered her face. From her I turned to the rest, who melted away like water, and were as men that had no strength.' Frequently Wesley, who was highly intuitive, would fix his eyes on a single man or woman in the crowd, making him or her his main target; this person was his immediate objective and if he could establish a sympathetic relation with such an individual the contagion would spread from thence to the crowd.

Some sunk down, and there remained no strength in them; others exceedingly trembled and quaked; some were torn with a kind of convulsive motion in every part of their bodies, and that so violently that often four or five persons could not hold one of them. I have seen many hysterical and many epileptic fits; but none of them were like these, in many respects.

A few weeks later another woman who had come to scoff remained to pray; she had been

remarkably zealous against those who had cried out and made noise, being sure that any of them might help it if they would. And the same opinion she was in still, till the moment she was struck through, as with a sword, and fell trembling to the ground. She then cried aloud, although not articulately, her words being swallowed up. In this pain she continued twelve or fourteen hours, and then her soul was set at liberty.

The Kentucky Revival of 1800 provided even more striking examples of mass hysteria, the evangelist in this case being the Calvinist fanatic the Rev. James McGready and his parishioners, largely horse-thieves, absconding debtors, bank robbers, murderers, and numerous criminals who had escaped from the more law-abiding States. The initial phase of the Revival closely resembled the Wesleyan one in its methods and results, until, in the summer of the year, it was decided to hold a great religious service in the open air. For months crowds had been descending on the state both on horseback and in covered wagons and the outdoor meeting was held because there existed no building large enough to hold them all. Trees were felled to provide seats and a rough pulpit was set up and within this clearing McGready and his assistants paced up and down exhorting the congregation to repent and so escape eternal damnation; from Friday to the following Tuesday the meeting went on continuously, being lit up at night by the light from bonfires. Under the constant barrage of preaching, praying, and singing, two women became hysterical whereupon hundreds of other men and women flung themselves to the ground, collapsed, and in many cases remained unconscious for hours, later regaining consciousness to declare themselves saved.

In the meeting which followed in 1801 twenty thousand men, women, and children assembled outdoors and listened to the doctrine of hellfire and eternal damnation for the unrepentant; almost immediately excitement broke out. Some ran about shrieking in agony or rolled on the ground for hours at a time, others rushed into the surrounding forest crying 'Lost! Lost!' at the full pitch of their voices. Convulsive jerking movements began amongst many and spread like a contagion throughout the congregation and elsewhere groups of men and women went through the process known as 'treeing the devil', where they crawled around on all fours barking and snarling at each other for long periods of time. Another phenomenon was the so-called 'frog-hopping', when both men and women occupied themselves by frenziedly leap-frogging over each other. As might be expected many in the final phases of the meeting went into trance or had visual hallucinations and ended up taking part in sexual excesses.

Not only conflicting emotions, fear, anger, anxiety, and mental or physical exhaustion but certain physiological stimuli such as rhythmic stimulation by percussion and bright light can induce stresses on the brain with consequent breakdown of former patterns of behaviour which are much emphasized by the Pavlovian school. Electrical recordings of the brain taken with an electroencephalograph show that certain rhythms of sound or flashes of light can create abnormalities of brain function leading to extreme tension and in some cases even to the induction of epileptiform fits. Dancing to the point of exhaustion especially when associated with the use of alcohol and drugs can lead to similar states of mental and physical breakdown. In the Voodoo cult of Haiti the *loa* or deities are believed to take possession of a person, usually while he or she is dancing to the drums, and those who are thus possessed behave in all respects as the deity according to tradition is supposed to behave. When they come to, an hour or so later, they allegedly have no recollection whatsoever of what they have done although to the observer their performance may have appeared to be an effective and intelligent one. J. F. Hecker in his *Epidemics of the Middle Ages* notes the same phenomenon amongst those who engaged in the Dancing Mania which followed the Black Death:

While dancing, they neither saw nor heard, being insensible to external impressions through the senses, but they were haunted by visions, their fancies conjuring up spirits whose names they shrieked out; and some of them afterwards asserted that they felt as if they had been immersed in a stream of blood, which obliged them to leap so high.

Other phenomena following the plague when the whole population of Europe was in a state of stunned terror were the groups of flagellants who marched from town to town flogging themselves (and often incidentally spreading the disease), and the tremendous outburst of anti-semitism which, beginning in Germany, spread later to all the surrounding countries. Wild dancing was also characteristic of the Shaker sect, founded in America by an ignorant English girl, Ann Lee, who died in 1784 and held that God was both male and female and that the original sin of Adam and Eve was the discovery of the pleasures of sexual intercourse which she therefore held to be the greatest of all sins. At their meetings they indulged in sacred dances in which the sexes danced separately, but in spite of, or more probably because of, this, they managed to reach crescendos of excitement which in this case were probably a manifestation of repressed sexuality. There is some evidence that dancing played an important part in early Christianity, and St Ambrose, one of the most celebrated early fathers of the Church, wrote:

For this reason the dance must in no wise be regarded as a mark of reverence for vanity and luxury, but as something which uplifts every living body instead of allowing the limbs to rest motionless on the floor or the slow feet to become numb. . . . But thou, when thou comest to the font, do thou lift up thy hands. Thou art exhorted to show swifter feet in order that thou mayest ascend to the everlasting life. This dance is an ally of faith and an honouring of grace.

The part played by repressed sexuality in epidemics of hysteria is shown by the frequency with which they occurred in convents. Aldous Huxley has given a detailed example in *The Devils of Loudun*, and other instances are the eighteenth-century case of a convent in France where one nun began to mew like a cat until presently the whole community was mewing day after day until stopped by the threats of the local militia; and the biting mania which spread through the convents of Germany, Holland, and Italy. In the latter case, powerful sexual excitement manifested itself not only in biting but in indecent exposure, tearing the hair out by the roots, and group howling and gnashing of teeth. In an appendix to *The Devils of Loudun*, Aldous Huxley notes the significance of these phenomena with special reference to the influence of dancing, chanting, and rhythmic song:

No man, however highly civilized, can listen for very long to African drumming, or Indian chanting, or Welsh hymn singing, and retain intact his critical and self-conscious personality. It would be interesting to take a group of the most eminent philosophers from the best universities, shut them up in a hot room with Moroccan dervishes or Haitian Voodooists and measure, with a stop-watch, the strength of their psychological resistance to the effects of rhythmic sound ... all we can safely predict is that, if exposed long enough to the tom-toms and the singing, every one of our philosophers would end by capering and howling with the savages.

Strong detestation of the process, so far from saving one from its influence, may well lead to the opposite effect, as we have seen in the case of some of Wesley's converts, and this result is probably best explained in terms of what the French psychologist Baudouin described as the Law of Reversed Effort, already mentioned, which was stated by him as follows:

When an idea imposes itself on the mind to such an extent as to give rise to a suggestion, all the conscious efforts which the subject makes in order to counteract this suggestion are not merely without the desired effect, but they actually run counter to the subject's conscious wishes and tend to intensify the suggestion.

This, of course, is apparent in everyday life to a mild degree when we make efforts to recall a fact and find that the more effort is made the more stubbornly does the fact remain beyond recall, whereas when we cease the effort it is likely to be remembered effortlessly. Thouless gives the example of the impossibility for most people of walking along a high plank with a sheer drop on either side, although the plank may be of such a width that it would be perfectly easy to walk along it if it were lying on the floor. Spontaneous attention is unavoidably caught by the idea of falling off, and there is a very powerful emotional accompaniment of fear or horror to this idea. If the person concerned could manage either not to think about falling off at all, or to think about it without any strong emotion, his danger of falling off would be less. As it is, his voluntary efforts to retain his balance are not only useless but tend to defeat their own end.* Hence those who were able to resist Wesley's suggestions were people like Horace Walpole who were cynical and emotionally detached.

It is obvious that conversion is likely to have been preceded by some sort of mental conflict since those who are satisfied with themselves are less likely to be converted. But it is striking to note how often it follows states of physical and mental exhaustion and how frequently mystical or semi-mystical states result from the experiences of being alone in a cell or in prison, especially when terror or fear are superimposed upon the strain. James describes the case of a drunkard who had pawned all his goods and sold everything he had in order to buy spirits:

I had not eaten for days, and for four nights preceding I had suffered with delirium tremens, or the horrors, from midnight till morning. I had often said, 'I will never be a tramp. I will never be cornered, for when the time comes, if ever it comes, I will find a home at the bottom of the river.' But the Lord so ordered it that when the time did come I was not able to walk one quarter of the way to the river. As I sat there thinking, I seemed to feel some great and mighty presence. I did not know then what it was. I did learn afterwards that it was Jesus, the sinner's friend. I walked up to the bar and pounded it with my fist till I made the glasses rattle. Those who stood by drinking looked on with scornful curiosity. I said I would never take another drink, if I died on the street, and really I felt as though that would happen before morning. Something said: 'If you want to keep this promise, go and have yourself locked up.' I went to the nearest station-house and had myself locked up.

* cf. the example of health propaganda on p. 80.

Later he went to a mission and experienced conversion. Another case quoted by James is of a man who

... being brought to an acute paroxysm of sin, ate nothing all day, locked himself in his room in complete despair, crying aloud, *How long, O Lord, how long*? 'After repeating this and similar language,' he says, 'several times, *I seemed to sink away into a state of insensibility*. When I came to myself again I was on my knees, praying not for myself but for others. I felt submission to the will of God, willing that he should do with me as should seem good in his sight. My concern seemed all lost in concern for others.'

Leuba, who made several studies of the phenomena of conversion, points out that the content of conversion need not be in relation to religion at all, giving examples of other drunkards' conversions to total abstention which were purely ethical, containing no theological beliefs whatever. Similarly, Arthur Koestler describes how, in a Spanish prison during the Civil War, and daily awaiting death, he felt that he was '. . . floating on my back in a river of peace under bridges of silence. It came from nowhere and flowed nowhere. Then there was no river and no I. The I had ceased to exist.' Subsequently, this experience

... occurred two or even three times a week, then the intervals became longer. It could never be voluntarily induced. After my liberation it recurred at even longer intervals, perhaps once or twice in a year. But by that time the groundwork for a change of personality was completed.

Tolstoy's conversion can hardly be described as one to orthodox Christianity, but, preceded by suicidal impulses, it brought him to embrace the life of the Russian peasants in which he remained relatively happy thereafter. Leuba also notes how often conversion is associated with a 'feeling of unwholeness, of moral imperfection, of sin, to use the technical word, accompanied by the yearning after the peace of unity', and he gives a large number of examples, in which the sin ranges from drunkenness to spiritual pride, to show that the sense of it 'may beset one and crave relief as urgently as does the anguish of the sickened flesh or any form of physical misery'. In psychological terms, the significance of this is that the 'sinner' feels cut off from reality either in the form of God or the lives of other human beings and feels a strong need to break down the barriers. This is important, especially when we come to consider political confessions in the next chapter; for we have to realize that there exists in most people a natural desire to share the mental and emotional experiences of others from which one is cut off by a sense of being different whether by reason of sin or the possession of beliefs which run counter to theirs.

The need to break down this feeling of separation by confession is a very real and pressing one, and psychoanalysts such as Otto Rank and Erich Fromm have pointed out the fact that to most of us, and particularly to the neurotic, the burden of individuality is hard to bear. There exists a 'fear of freedom', of self-hood, which makes people want to submerge themselves in the mass and confession is one of the obvious means by which they can do so, for thereby they lose those traits which cause them to feel separate. The other, of course, is to lose one's sense of personal identity by submerging it in the collective behaviour of a crowd since, as Hoffer puts it, when we renounce the self and become part of a compact whole, we not only renounce personal advantage but are also rid of personal responsibility. When we lose our personal freedom in the corporateness of a totalitarian movement, we find a new freedom to do as the mob does which may take such forms as 'treeing the devil' or going into a trance state or, on the other hand, the right to hate, bully, lie, torture, murder, and commit any crime without shame or remorse. It is no accident that public confession plays such an important part in totalitarian movements whether they be religious or political; for the totalitarian hates individualism equally in the saint or the sinner. The writer has known of several individuals who admitted that, in the Oxford Group days of the Moral Rearmament Movement, they either confessed to sins of which they were guiltless or grossly exaggerated the trivial peccadilloes of which they were guilty, because they did not want to feel 'different' when public confessions were being made.

As noted elsewhere, an important aspect of suggestibility is the fact that throughout life we have, on the whole, been rewarded for doing as others do and punished for failure to conform. This urge to imitate is potentiated by anxiety because, as Freud latterly pointed out, anxiety is the expression of the up-surge of anti-social impulses from the unconscious which might lead us to actions which are socially disapproved, and this can most readily be alleviated by shunning them and conforming still further. Erich Fromm describes this neurotic mechanism as 'automaton conformity' and Karen Horney calls the same process 'neurotic submissiveness'. The motive behind it may be expressed in the words: 'I am exactly like you, and shall be as you wish me to be, so that you will love and not hate me.' Other psychologists have shown that anxiety leads to a narrowing of the field of attention, the so-called 'tunnel vision', and when people are anxious they are unable to attend to the total situation as is necessary to enable them to act rationally, but impulsively do the first thing that comes into their heads which is usually determined by what others are doing at the same time. Hence the spread of panic in excited crowds, which is also conditioned by the fact that anxiety leads to a regression to more primitive forms of behaviour.

It is evident that proselytizing mass movements or even the God of the potential convert are jealous masters, and that the ideal prospective convert is the man or woman who stands alone and therefore needs a God or a collective body into which he can blend and lose himself to forget the pettiness, meaninglessness, and shabbiness of his existence as an isolated individual. Old ties, where they exist, must be severed, and John Bunyan writes:

I must first pass a sentence of death upon everything that can properly be called a thing of this life, even to reckon myself, my wife, my children, my health, my enjoyments, and all, as dead to me, and myself as dead to them. . . . The parting with my wife and my poor children hath often been to me as the pulling of my flesh from my bones, especially my poor blind child who lay nearer my heart than all I had besides. Poor child, thought I, what sorrow thou art like to have for thy portion in this world. Thou must be beaten, must beg, suffer hunger, cold, nakedness, and a thousand calamities, though I cannot now endure that the wind should blow upon thee. But yet I must venture you all with God, though it goeth to the quick to leave you.

When St Bernard preached it is said that his influence was such that mothers hid their sons from him and wives their husbands lest he should lure them away. In fact, he broke up so many homes that the abandoned wives had to form a nunnery, but after all it was Jesus who said in words which are sadly reminiscent of what has happened in our own time: '... the brother shall deliver up the brother to death, and the father the child: and the children shall rise up against their parents, and cause them to be put to death.' Brotherly love towards all, as Confucius pointed out, dissolves the family which is the mainstay against corporate movements whether political or religious.

Religious conversion, considered from the psychological point of view, may take the form of filling a vacuum which has caused dissatisfaction with the existing personality in which case it supplies, as it were, the missing piece of the puzzle; or it may take the form of substitution of one piece for another which may have been lying dormant for years, as happened in the case of Paul. Obviously, to the extent that it has been successful, it changes the individual's beliefs and actions, but it would not have 'taken' had the new beliefs not been in conformity with his basic personality. The individual convert, in fact, is the man or woman in search of the system of beliefs which will integrate him more closely with what he regards as reality. They are not forced upon him by anybody, and the teacher is the occasion rather than the cause of his conversion. As for the mass campaigns of the evangelist, these are for the most part exhibitions of crowd hysteria and, as Wesley realized, such effects are apt to be extremely impermanent unless followed up by later action to consolidate whatever gains have been made. What actions he took to do so are considered elsewhere. Wesley's campaigns were, at any rate, a sincerely religious movement with a coherent plan of action and, like the religion of the American Negro, helped to alleviate the discontent of the masses for whom it took the place of political action which might otherwise have replaced it. But, in general, this sort of campaign requires a simple audience of poor people and is increasingly rare under the conditions of the Welfare State where indifference to religion is the rule; for it was truly said that it is easier for a camel to get through the eye of a needle than for a rich man to enter into the Kingdom of God.

No attempt has been made in this chapter to underestimate the element of mass hysteria in the more primitive forms of religion. But, in conclusion, it is worth noting that the emotional and involuntary elements emphasized by Huxley in the case of Voodoo and made use of by Sargant in his *Battle for the Mind* to sustain the thesis that people are easily manipulated, are capable of being given quite another interpretation. There is good evidence from those more qualified in this particular field than either Huxley or Sargant that such performances are very much more stylized and deliberate than they may appear to the uninitiated observer. They are in fact 'acts' based on imitation and tradition. Thus Erving Goffman's book *The Presentation of Self in Everyday Life* (Doubleday Anchor Books, Doubleday & Company Inc., N.Y.), referring to the work on Voodooism of the leading authority Alfred Métraux, has this to say about the supposed spontaneity of the performers:

In reading of persons in the West Indies who become the 'horse' or the possessed one of a voodoo spirit, it is enlightening to learn that the person possessed will be able to provide a correct portrayal of the god that has entered him because, says Métraux, 'of the knowledge and memories accumulated in a life spent visiting congregations of the cult'; that the person possessed will be in just the right social relation to those who are watching; that possession occurs at just the right moment in the ceremonial undertakings, the possessed one carrying out his ritual obligations to the point of participating in a kind of skit with persons possessed at the same time with other spirits. But in learning this, it is important to see that this contextual structuring of the horse's role still allows participants in the cult to believe that possession is a real thing and that persons are possessed at random by gods whom they cannot select.

Thus these performances, and doubtless others of the same nature, are more contrived than Huxley suggests and cannot be used to support his argument that any group of philosophers exposed to the rhythmic sound of the tom-toms of 'Haitian Voodooists' would 'end up by capering and howling with the savages'. However, the influence of rhythm on the human mind must be discussed in greater detail later.

CHAPTER 10

CONFESSIONS AND INDOCTRINATION

By this stage we are beginning to see what manner of creature the ordinary man or woman really is, and this is important because, if we begin with wrong assumptions about what is vaguely described as 'human nature', we are going to be extremely puzzled by what in fact are perfectly commonplace phenomena and to look for complicated explanations where none are required. Most of us, in spite of all evidence to the contrary, still share the view of man which is a hangover from the individualism and rationalism of the eighteenth century and the hopes of the Renaissance and believe that the typical civilized human being is an isolated individual, unique in his 'I-ness', seeking out others for love or company but essentially independent of them, bartering relationships – so that he does something for his neighbour which is paid for by his neighbour doing something for him whilst both remain basically unchanged in the process – and above all a reasonable being apart from regrettable but brief lapses into impulsiveness. 'I am I' seems one of the most fundamental of truths. Even Freud, who more than any single scientist was able to demonstrate, not only that man is largely irrational, but that a large part of his personality remains for ever outside his knowledge, still adhered to the picture of man as a hard, circumscribed, social atom like the billiard-ball atoms of Dalton, battering each other about, and sometimes associating with other atoms, yet always remaining unchanged whilst doing so. The modern atom, however, is composed of many sub-particles, each of which is a whirlpool of energy rather than a material object in the accepted sense: each of these particles can reveal itself in various ways (by tracks in a cloud-chamber, for example), but when we try to locate it rigidly in space we are in the position of A. A. Milne's Pooh Bear searching for Piglet: the more we look, the more it isn't there. So with the modern picture of personality; it, too, is a centre of energy, 'the meeting-place of all relationships' as Carlo Levi has described it, and at its core is the part formed by early relationships within the family whilst surrounding this are the sub-group centres which have arisen in later life according to the other sets of relationships we have been, and still are, forming. According as one or other of these centres becomes more active than the rest, behaviour may change markedly (we are shy in one social situation, bold in another) whilst still remaining in important ways the same person, just as deuterium and tritium, the isotopes of hydrogen, have noticeably different properties from the basic form whilst still remaining the same substance. In short, people are much more variable than used to be supposed, the boundaries of the personality much more vaguely defined, and it may even happen that certain pathological processes such as organic disease of the brain or the dementia of chronic schizophrenia can cause almost total disintegration of the personality just as radium slowly turns into lead. Whether a process such as brainwashing can break down the personality and then create something which is in a significant sense new, whether it can really 'wash the slate clean' and then write something totally different on it, is open to question and, to say the least of it, dubious. What is certainly true is that, whilst it is impossible to turn lead back into radium, it is possible in some cases to bring a totally regressed and apparently demented patient back to his original state provided that no organic damage to the brain has occurred.

The consciousness of self arises from messages coming in from the material environment, the sensations within our own muscles which inform us of changes in space, the sound of our voice, and, above all, from the way other people react in relation to us; in a real sense the self is made up from the reflected appraisals of others and the roles it has to play in various social groups. We do not merely *have* experiences – we *are* our experiences. 'By constant comparison of them with other entities observed in other persons, an empirical self is woven and given abiding structure,' said Gardner Murphy in a statement already quoted, and this self 'represents a relative continuity from the cradle to the grave, is given a name, a social position and a sense of responsibility, and around it in time cluster the goals, values and norms and ideals which give meaningful purposive continuity to life.' But the continuity is relative and dependent to a greater or less degree on the persisting and consistent continuity of stimuli from our external and internal environment, and when these are changed, as when a gland begins to over- or underwork, or the social environment or even the physical one radically changes, the self may be shaken to the core. The disease of myxoedema in the thyroid gland may reduce one to a state of near imbecility, a soundproof room by cutting off the messages from the physical environment may induce hallucinations, and a change in the social surroundings causes quite a different facet of character to appear. For the clusters of goals, values, and ideals which in some sense belong to the self are not all consistent with one another, all our potential roles cannot be played together and in the interests of consistency there are systems which, created at some time during life, have been repressed yet can suddenly spring into new vitality with a change of circumstances. Our Walter Mitty selves may take over and long-forgotten daydreams become reality, Saul be transformed into Paul, and Gauguin the banker leave his respectable family life to become the artist and beachcomber of Tahiti. The nuclear self, with rare exceptions, persists, but it expresses itself through new channels and although a series of acts may seem inconsistent with our usual behaviour there will always be some sort of underlying organization. The change in circumstances which brings about these transformations need not always be in the external environment, but rather in the changed way in which a person perceives his environment and himself. This may happen spontaneously or be brought about by psychotherapy for, as Carl Rogers has noted, we find that in therapy as the perception of self alters, behaviour alters:

... we have observed that appropriate changes in behaviour occur when the individual acquires a different view of his world of experience, including himself, [and] that this changed perception does not need to be dependent upon a change in the 'reality' but may be a product of internal reorganization.

Personality is to a considerable degree a matter of role behaviour but even more is it a matter of role perception and of self-perception in the light of the role so that the long acting-out of a role, with its appropriate motives, will often induce a man or woman to become what at first they merely sought to appear. Thus a woman who spends a long time as a saleswoman may eventually find that large areas of her social life will be permeated and influenced by the characteristic points of view of her profession and, so far as the observer is concerned, it will be seen that the fact that we so often encounter people in certain specific situations tends to cause us eventually to judge them to a great extent from the way they act within these limited spheres. Such judgements are generally appropriate enough, because the spheres of action observed are relatively limited and the individuals are acting out their roles in relation to them, but it would be wrong to suppose that they have no other potentialities because their behaviour may only be consistent within these specific situations. It is often forgotten that the same person may show both honesty and dishonesty, shyness and boldness, aggressiveness and submissiveness, in rapid succession depending upon the particular role he is playing and the circumstances he is facing. The writer recalls a reserved, neurotic, and hypochondrial young man who, in a party on a mountaineering expedition, remained always on the edge of the group, seldom speaking to anyone in the base camp. Yet when during the descent a mist came down and the party was lost on the mountainside, the same youth took over complete control issuing confident and curt orders to the rest including the erstwhile leader who helplessly obeyed, remained utterly fearless throughout the most dangerous predicaments, and poured contempt on the hesitant, compelling them to do as they were told, until the whole party arrived back safely. Once the base had been reached, he burst into hysterical sobbing and subsequently reverted to his former self.

The fact is that, although most people think they know themselves pretty well, they have only experienced a limited number of situations and have really not the slightest idea how they or their best-known friends would behave under wholly different circumstances. How would we behave in a Communist prisoner of war camp, under the influence of Voodoo drumming, or at an uninhibited evangelical revival? Unless we have experienced them, we do not know. Nor, until they had the British and Turkish records for comparison, did the American army command have any conception of how their own soldiers could have been expected to behave in the Korean prisoner of war camps when submitted to political indoctrination by the Chinese, because the situation was a completely new one in the history of war. In previous wars the behaviour of the captors had on the whole been such as to draw their prisoners closer together, in spite of other factors which militated against good morale, but the thoroughgoing attempt to change the political views of prisoners *en masse*, if not wholly unknown in the past, had never been carried out quite so whole-heartedly or on such a scale. When we are dealing with people who have been subjected to unusual circumstances it is necessary to be careful before classifying their behaviour as 'normal' or 'abnormal' unless we have some scale for comparison.

It has been shown, too, that the idea that people can interact whilst remaining virtually unchanged in the process is untrue, that the boundaries of the self are much more vaguely defined than had previously been thought and become even more vague during mystical experiences, under the influence of drugs, or when the individual person becomes submerged in a crowd. Like an electron the 'real' self can be observed in action but is difficult to locate accurately. Suggestibility and imitation are present in varying degrees in all human beings, partly because we have from childhood onwards generally been rewarded for doing as others do and doing what we have been told, and partly because in the absence of strong internalized standards it is necessary to model our behaviour either by tradition or by copying the behaviour of others. But in most people the super-ego with its internalized standards has less validity than it used to have, because we are constantly being confronted in a rapidly changing society by totally unforeseen situations and living by traditional standards is no longer possible. Hence the suggestion that we become 'other-directed' in a mass society, as in all probability most human beings have been since the beginnings of history.

With the rise of the middle classes society took the form of units of diverse primary groups which led to a certain variety in behaviour and resistance to external pressures when these did not conform to the views of the group, while in the mass society behaviour is allegedly much more homogeneous. Although the thesis is dubious, it has been argued that this leads to even greater suggestibility to the views of the power élites and to a deliberate attempt on their part to get people to conform because in an increasingly homogeneous society those who do not conform become a nuisance. Certainly we can see how that individualism, so far as Europe and America are concerned, is characteristic of a certain historical epoch, not, as used to be supposed, the natural state of affairs. In most countries it has never existed to any significant degree and in Europe and America only in the few centuries since the Renaissance, but the question is whether it is being diminished now. Throughout history the mass of mankind has been afraid of traits or ideas that seemed likely to break the sense of communion with others and has found its self-hood a hard burden to bear. Hence it is unnecessary to be surprised at the number of techniques devised by various social groups to break down the individuality of their members or the willingness with which these have generally been accepted by those concerned. Somerset Maugham in *Don Fernando* says of the *Spiritual Exercises* written by Ignatius Loyola, founder of the order of Jesuits, that they are 'the most wonderful method that has ever been devised to gain control over that vagabond, unstable and wilful thing, the soul of man'; and we know that primitive tribes have their periodic group meetings where emotions are aroused by dancing and drumming in order to maintain religious beliefs and to consolidate previously implanted group attitudes. Confession is one of the methods whereby the individual removes the barriers caused by his own acts and secret thoughts when these have brought about a feeling of separateness from the group and, in view of the fear and anxiety resulting from the awareness of being cut off from society, it is not surprising that many people have an almost in-built need to confess. Anyone who does a fair amount of travelling cannot have avoided observing the frequency with which total strangers will enter into conversation with each other and admit to actions or thoughts which they would never care to confess to those with whom they are better acquainted and it has already been noted that in group confessions people will often vie with each other as to who has committed the most heinous sins, not infrequently telling untruths in the process.

There is therefore nothing astonishing about indoctrination or brainwashing either in the fact that it has become prominent at the present time (since we are living in an age of ideologies when in many parts of the world individualism has become the equivalent of heresy in the ages of belief), or in its methods, which have been practised for centuries. Nor is it true, as we shall soon see, that methods have been discovered which will cause anyone subjected to them to break down whether they will or not, but what has been said so far should make it evident that, although some of the procedures involve subjecting the victim to unnatural stresses, a great many of them are simply an exploitation of tendencies which are common to a great many people. The inquisitor is going along with human nature rather than against it. Even the discovery of new techniques has not, in itself, added greatly to the efficiency of methods designed to elicit *true* confessions and the 'truth drug', so far from being helpful in criminal practice, often has the opposite effect: it is useful in cases of neurosis where the individual is suffering from genuine amnesia resulting from unconscious repression but quite otherwise when the subject is deliberately suppressing the truth. Dr J. F. Kubis writes:

Those who confess in the drug interview would most likely confess under normal circumstances to a skilled interpreter. It is the criminal who stands to benefit from the technique: he may so contaminate the interview with conflicting information that the physician may become genuinely puzzled as to the validity of his story. And the creation of a doubt as to his guilt is all in favour of the guilty.

Regarding the lie-detector C. D. Lee in his book *Instrumental Detection of Deception* demonstrates conclusively that it is often a most unreliable instrument and its effects, such as they are, are in the main psychological. The subject is impressed by the array of pens swinging to every heart-beat and breath and may therefore be intimidated into confessing but the main factor is admitted by Lee to be the personality of examiner who must have

... confidence in himself and the method employed, his persuasiveness, perseverance, and a sympathetic attitude towards the suspect. By one means or another the examiner should impart to the subject the idea that he is certain of his guilt, as any indication of doubt on the examiner's part may defeat his purpose.

Those who are most susceptible to an appeal to the emotions are the easiest to induce to confess. Hence so-called accidental offenders such as the hit-and-run motorist, those who kill in the heat of passion, juveniles and first offenders, and sexual perverts, are most likely to admit to their crimes, whilst the career criminal who makes a profession of crime 'presents the only really difficult problem in the matter of obtaining confessions'. Interesting sidelights on Western police methods of interrogation are supplied in this book, which points out the value of playing on the self-justification that is usually in the mind of the prisoner for his misdeeds:

Suggest that there was a good reason for his having committed the deed, that he has too much intelligence to have done it without rhyme or reason. In the case of sex-crimes, explain that sex hunger is one of the strongest instincts motivating our lives. In case of theft, suggest that the subject may have been hungry, or deprived of the necessaries of life; or in homicide, that the victim had done him a great wrong and probably had it coming to him. Be friendly and sympathetic and encourage him to write out or relate the whole story – to clean up and start afresh.

A former Deputy Commissioner of the New York Police Department is quoted as follows:

My usual method is to take down the prisoner's statement when he is first brought in in just the form he is willing to make it. The next day, when we have gathered additional information, we question him again, pointing our questions from the light of this information. We then analyse the discrepancies between his first statement and the second one. Then we examine him the next day and again analyse the discrepancies and draw the net closer around him if the facts assembled point more surely to his guilt. We get him to talk again and again, day after day; and at last, if he is guilty or has a guilty knowledge of the crime, he is bound to break down and come out with the whole story.

There was never such a thing as the 'third degree'. You simply get a man into a mental corner, provided he is really guilty, and then he will wilt every time, that is, if you get a wedge in as a start. It's pretty hard to get a confession unless you have some little clue to start with on your line of questioning. But, having found that weak spot, the discrepancies in the man's story begin to widen until finally he becomes so confused and befuddled that he sees the game is up. All his defences have been beaten down. He's cornered, trapped. That's when he bursts into tears. *The torture comes from his own mind, not from outside.*

Dr Sargant comments on this statement:

The only thing to add is that in such a technique, it is known that truth and falsehood can get hopelessly confused in the minds of both the suspect and the examiner; and that if what he calls a 'weak spot' is not present, the police examiner determined to get a confession can create it by suggestion.

In brainwashing, however, such suggestion is not always necessary because it must be remembered that, although the subject may be guilty of no crime that is universally accepted as such, he is often or even usually guilty of *a* crime (if only in the sense of holding the 'wrong' beliefs) in the eyes of his examiner. It will be noted that in such cases the interviewer is trading on his subject's need for understanding and his desire to confess and, as every policeman is aware, an unreasoning sense of guilt is so common that hardly a major crime is committed without the police being bothered by those who voluntarily give themselves up and 'confess' to the offence when they are not, in fact, guilty. It is well known to psychoanalysts that even those who are fairly normal are often burdened by a sense of guilt that leads to their exaggerating and confessing to trivial faults and sometimes those of which they are not culpable because the real sin of thought or deed lies deeply buried in their unconscious and goes back to childhood days. In melancholia a common symptom is for the patient to tell everyone he meets that he has committed the 'unforgiveable sin', without being able to say specifically what that sin is. Thus, as we shall see, political indoctrination depends as much upon sympathy on the part of the inquisitor as upon threats, and physical torture plays little or no part in the process.

Before discussing political indoctrination and brainwashing any further it is necessary to distinguish between the two processes which are not at all the same, the difference being expressed by a leading psychiatrist in the American Army as follows:

The Army defines indoctrination as an effort to change a man's viewpoint while he is still a thinking individual by regulating his thoughts and actions. This falls far short of the effect (brainwashing) produced upon some defendants seen in Communist courts, defendants who had obviously been completely broken, and had ceased to be thinking individuals.

The term 'brainwashing' was first used by an American journalist, Edward Hunter, as a translation of the colloquialism *hsi nao* (literally, 'wash brain') which he quoted from Chinese informants who described its use after the Communist take-over. It need hardly be said that no scientific thinker could accept or use the concept of brainwashing; literally washing the physical brain could not remove memory traces in any way comparable to the demagnetizing of a recording tape; and, apart from this, the very concept of eliminating memories by 'washing the slate clean' and replacing them by new ones is ridiculous. As T. H. Pear has pointed out in *The Moulding of Modern Man*, the memories that cause our important beliefs usually result, not from a single source located at a particular point in time and space (or even on a particular point on the brain), but from condensations of experiences recorded at long time intervals, perhaps years, and it is unlikely that all of these could be wiped out. Except by physical damage to the brain there is no evidence that any memory of any significance can be wholly destroyed, although it can be repressed, as in hysterical amnesia or 'loss of memory', and there is plenty of evidence that even quite trivial memories or those we have never been aware of possessing remain permanently recorded in the brain. Thus few people know exactly how many steps lead up to the first floor of their house, but they can often be made to give the number when under hypnosis. In hysterical loss of memory the individual, to put it bluntly, forgets what it suits him to forget by the unconscious process of repression, but this too can be recovered by appropriate techniques (described elsewhere), and it will be remembered that St Paul's former anti-Christian complex kept recurring after his conversion in the form of hysterical fits. The amnesic patient often shows by his behaviour that a part of his mind is well aware of the material he has conveniently forgotten, for he will carry out actions which only make sense on the assumption that he in some sense still 'knows' the dissociated memories. Only severe damage to the brain can ever permanently wash the slate clean and then merely in certain areas. A man without memories is a contradiction in terms and such memories as he has must in some sense be integrated with the rest of his mind if he is not to be mentally ill.

The Communist becomes a Nazi, or vice versa, because the new part of the jigsaw fits in with the whole to a greater or less degree, that is to say both ideologies fit in equally well with his authoritarian temperament. This, of course, has little bearing upon the case of those poor shadows of their former selves who repeat parrot-wise false confessions at show trials, but it is extraordinary that nobody seems to have cared to admit that, so far as political indoctrination is concerned, at least some of the converts may have been perfectly genuinely convinced of the truth of what they were told by their instructors. After all, there is nothing inherently absurd about Communism and the forty or so British prisoners from Korea who came back convinced that Communism was the proper way of life were not an impressive haul (about 4 per cent), especially in view of the fact that some of these had gone out to Korea thinking just that before they ever met the Chinese. A straightforward political lecture on the subject at home in Britain might well have led to better results. The real reason why so many more American soldiers broke down, as the Army authorities freely admit, was not that the Chinese were so fiendishly clever but rather that American discipline and morale were so poor. Eugene Kinkead, in his book about the Korean War entitled *Why They Collaborated*, makes this quite clear:

All in all, sinister and regrettable things happened in the prison camps in North Korea. The public has been inclined to attribute them solely to the cruelty of the Communists, particularly to the mysterious technique known as 'brainwashing'. The officials involved, however – in the Defence Department – and especially in the Army, which, because of the nature of the operations in Korea, supplied more than 90 per cent of the American service men who fought there – could not accept an explanation as simple as that. For one thing, there was evidence that the high death rate (38 per cent of prisoners died in captivity) was not due primarily to Communist maltreatment – that it could be accounted for largely by the ignorance or the callousness of the prisoners themselves. For another, the prisoners, as far as Army psychiatrists have been able to discover, were not subjected to anything that could be properly called brainwashing. Indeed, the Communist treatment of prisoners, while it came nowhere near fulfilling the requirements of the Geneva Convention, rarely involved outright cruelty, being instead a highly novel blend of leniency and pressure.

The figures which disturbed the Defence Department were as follows: out of a total of 7,190 prisoners, 2,730 died in captivity for the reason given above – a higher death rate than in any previous war in which the U.S. had been engaged throughout its history; twenty-one Americans captured decided to remain with the enemy, again a unique event; and one out of every three American prisoners in Korea was guilty of some sort of collaboration with the enemy. The degree of collaboration varied from the writing of anti-American propaganda and informing on comrades to less serious offences such as broadcasting Christmas greetings home and thus putting the Communists in a favourable light. Some captives had behaved brutally to their fellow-prisoners or in a few cases had even been guilty of their murder and a certain number had been recruited as potential agents to engage in espionage for the enemy after their release. Of the latter group about seventy-five were discovered and these had codes and explicit instructions as to how to reach their future contacts, although this was not to be done until after a latent period to avoid arousing the suspicions of the authorities.

The first sign that something peculiar was happening was when, four days after the fighting had begun, an American officer who had been captured only forty-eight hours previously broadcast on the enemy's behalf over the Seoul radio. Amongst other things he said:

Dear friends, we, all prisoners, solidly appeal to you as follows: the armed intervention in Korean internal affairs is quite a barbaristic [*sic*] aggressive action to protect the benefit of the capitalist monopolists of the U.S.A. Let us fight for right against wrong, bravely opposing to be mobilized into such a war against Russia.

However, in addition to broadcasts, which continued for the duration of the war, the enemy soon began returning small groups of captives who had been subjected to indoctrination and brought with them propaganda leaflets which attempted to influence those in the front line to desert to Communism. Some of the families of the prisoners handed over to the Army letters which sounded totally unlike those who had written them, being basically concerned with a return to international peace, and shortly after the beginning of the war articles began to appear in the Communist-dominated press in India, North Africa, Indonesia, and elsewhere in which prisoners praised life under Communism.

The process of indoctrination began immediately after capture when, to their surprise, the Chinese would greet each prisoner with a smile, a cigarette, and a handshake. There was good grounds for this surprise since the North Koreans they had met earlier, having little food or amenities, often shot their prisoners in cold blood. After shaking hands, the captors would congratulate their captives on having escaped from capitalist bondage and kept repeating to them such simple slogans as 'Be a fighter for peace'. Anyone who showed hesitation was asked: 'Are you for peace? Of course you are. Every intelligent person is. Then, naturally you will fight for peace. Good! You are henceforth a true fighter in the cause of peace. Now you will have an opportunity to display the courage of your convictions and fight for peace.' The prisoner was then asked to sign a peace appeal, and if he resisted he would be told that by signing he would simply be reaffirming a universal desire of all thinking human beings. To many this seemed a plausible request and it was explained that the Communists wanted him to sign one such appeal only. These requests were so innocuous in appearance that many signed if only to escape the constant badgering, but they soon found that, having put their heads in the noose, it was difficult to escape. During this initial friendly period the Chinese tried to find out everything possible about the captives, but they were less concerned about military facts than those which revealed something about the individual's home background, thus giving them something to work on when indoctrination proper began. The prisoner was ordered to fill in a detailed questionnaire on a sheet of paper with a false heading of the International Red Cross, being told that the information was needed so that the Chinese Red Cross could inform his next of kin. The questions dealt with such matters as his father's occupation, the family's annual income, and his own educational background, so that some idea of the prisoner's socio-economic status could be obtained. Later other and more detailed questionnaires were issued, and the prisoners were asked to write autobiographies; some wrote three or even more. The actual process of indoctrination was apparently based on the more severe technique used by the Russians on their prisoners during the Second World War, when they had tried to bring about subversion by the formation of the 'German Liberation Committee'. Chinese interrogators had often been educated in the United States and all had a thorough knowledge of American affairs down to the smallest details of regional customs.

The permanent prison camps were established along the Manchurian border and all were administered by a military and a political section, both under the supervision of a camp commander who, however, was rarely seen. The prisoners had little to do with the non-English-speaking military who guarded them, the important people from their point of view being the English-speaking interrogators and the political instructors. Each instructor had the power, in addition to his work of bringing about subversion, of ordering or remitting punishments, of lightening a man's camp duties or making them more onerous. Prisoners were divided into companies of 60 to 350 men and there were anything from three to seven companies in a camp; each company was divided into three or four platoons, and these in turn into squads of six to fifteen prisoners. Ordinarily the prisoner's day began at seven in the morning and ended at seven in the evening and of these hours those from nine in the morning until noon and two in the afternoon until four were spent hearing lectures or attending discussions. Those who wanted more time to study, and had therefore shown their keenness, were permitted to remain until nine in the evening in the camp library which was well-stocked with reading matter in English. This included openly Communist literature such as books by the leading Marxist writers or the various Communist journals, and fiction by non-Communists such as Victor Hugo, Jack London, Tolstoy, John Steinbeck, Erskine Caldwell, Upton Sinclair, and others who tended to deal with the seamy side of capitalism. Lectures took place in a large hut, which at the end behind the instructor carried a huge flag showing a white dove of peace on a red background above which were printed the words 'Grand Rally in Support of World Peace'.

The first part of the programme was devoted to instilling hatred of America, and the prisoners were told that the South Koreans had treacherously attacked the peaceful North Koreans as the result of underhand dealings between President Truman and Syngman Rhee and that this, in turn, had been instigated by Wall Street capitalists who wished to start a Third World War in order to raise prices on the stock market; that the Chinese had come to the aid of the North Koreans in order to prevent the North being used as a base for the invasion of Manchuria; and that America was a country where race-hatred was indigenous, poverty widespread, and so on.

During the second part of the programme the teaching was more positive and aimed at showing the benefits of the 'new democracies' under Communism as contrasted with the 'old states of reaction' under Chiang Kai-shek and others. It is admitted by the American Army Authorities that this process of indoctrination was greatly helped by the ignorance of the captives most of whom knew little about the history of Communism and not very much about that of their own country.

Specific techniques employed by the instructors were the old ones of repetition, harassment, and humiliation. Repetition involved the memorizing of Communist pamphlets on which the prisoners would be examined day in and day out, asked questions on the subject, and allowed to read nothing else in the meantime. Many of those who came back could recite entire passages from memory and argue the principles of Lenin and Stalin with people much better educated than themselves. The slightest sign of inattention, lack of cooperation, or inability to answer correctly was dealt with by the harassing technique. Thus a man who failed to answer would be ordered to camp headquarters and given a long lecture on the necessity of paying attention and remembering what was said. The same evening he would be called for again, perhaps at midnight, and lectured once more, and on the following day he might be called for from the latrines to come immediately for the same discussion which was repeated possibly at two o'clock on the following morning, the prisoner being wakened from sleep for the purpose. The more a prisoner complied or showed 'progressive' tendencies, the more he was harassed to make him even more compliant; the different treatment meted out to 'progressives' and 'reactionaries' will be mentioned later. The third technique of humiliation was directed primarily at setting the prisoner's comrades against him. Thus during one indoctrination class a prisoner pointed out that if, as the instructor had said, South Korea had started the war it was odd that after the first day of fighting the North Koreans were already at the gates of Seoul, forty miles to the south. The instructor was furious and, calling him a stupid ignorant fool, said that everyone else in the class knew the answer so why should not he? The prisoner refused to retract and demanded an answer, whereupon the instructor ordered the whole class to stand, and remain standing, until this one man abandoned his objection. After some hours of standing, the other prisoners began to mutter against the objector who finally gave in under their moral pressure. The next day this prisoner had to write and then read to the class a long criticism of his own conduct with an apology to the class and the instructor and this had to be repeated and elaborated on for the next four or five days. His classmates were ordered to criticize him, which they did, and then he in turn was made to criticize his classmates. The step from criticizing classmates in this way to informing upon them was a small one, and incidents of this type led to chaos and favoured the establishment of an informer system. Men were turned against each other and felt they could trust nobody with the result that, in spite of the fact that it was their duty to do so, not a single man escaped from the permanent prison camps.

Interrogation was the other important technique for manipulating the prisoners; it was used both to obtain military information and to assist indoctrination, although mainly for the latter purpose. Those who accepted indoctrination slowly or who were wanted for some specific act of collaboration or informing were often subjected to interrogation for weeks, until they capitulated or the Communists finally gave up. Contrary to the Geneva Convention, which states that a man is bound to give only his surname, first names and rank, date of birth and army number, and that no physical violence or mental torture nor any other forms of coercion must be used in order to obtain information, Communist interrogation made frequent use of coercion to get as much information as possible. It was usual for the interrogator to remind the prisoner that he might be shot and physical torture was constantly threatened, although nobody was in fact shot or tortured for failing to cooperate. (The American Army authorities, perhaps somewhat naïvely, did not consider that being made to stand in water, being improperly clad, being kicked, slapped, or kept in confined quarters were torture in the ordinary sense since they led to stress of the same order as the combatant soldier might be expected to undergo in battle.)

The chief interrogator was a well-educated officer in each case and a fluent speaker of English who would begin by laying his pistol on the table. One of his assistants, who was often a woman, then brought in a large folder with the prisoner's name on it, some papers that were supposed to be reports marked 'Secret' and 'Top Secret', and a pile of United States Army Manuals. The prisoner was told that the folder contained considerable information about him, and it was claimed that the so-called secret reports had been sent from the United States by Communist sympathizers or Communists and held evidence that the American people did not want the war to continue and that the Truman administration had aggressive designs upon the rest of the world, especially Russia and China. Next the interrogator would reveal some of the facts he knew about the prisoner's own or other units and about the United States Army in general so that he was made to feel that it did not matter what he told and even that he himself was of no importance and had been summoned purely as a matter of routine. In the meantime, the prisoner's words were being recorded and his reactions watched through one-way vision mirrors.

The sessions lasted for indefinite periods of time, sometimes short, sometimes long, and it did not appear that the length of the session bore any necessary relationship to the amount of information the prisoner was willing to give, the obvious intention being to keep him in a state of stress and doubt. Sometimes prisoners were kept for a long time to instil anxiety into the others who were waiting, or they might be dismissed after only ten minutes to be recalled within the hour. Harsh talk served the same purpose of frightening the prisoner and impressing the others, to whom he told his experiences when he returned. The data mentioned by the interrogators were, of course, largely obtained from the questionnaires the prisoners and others had filled up on their capture, and the secret files were fakes. After each session, the investigator would often give the prisoner a personal history form and order him to fill it up in detail; the prisoner would then be left alone in the interrogation room, having been told to take as long as he liked and to put down everything, no matter how trivial, about his past life. Some would write as many as five hundred pages describing their lives, their families, their friends, and their experiences with the army, and these would be used as a guide for going deeper at the next interview.

Communications with home were another means of influencing the prisoners, and mail was never dealt with in the ordinary way. Since letters from home were likely to help morale, they were often withheld in order to make the men feel isolated and insecure by breaking their ties with relations and friends. Depressing letters were allowed through and those which did not suit the Communists' purposes were simply destroyed. If a prisoner complained, a 'friendly' Communist would offer to investigate and later hand him over a few letters thus causing him to feel grateful. Since no letters were censored in the usual way, the men were caused to suppose that no censorship existed and that lack of mail was due to U.S. bombing or neglect on the part of relatives, and therefore felt bitter towards both. Newspapers, magazines, books, and parcels were never received at all, since they might renew contacts with home. When men wished to communicate with their friends or home they were urged to do so by making broadcasts mentioning their desire for peace, or telegrams were allowed, but only when they contained propaganda messages.

These and other aspects of Communist techniques were highly successful in avoiding resentment against the Chinese, in marked contrast to the Japanese policy during the Second World War which, as in most other wars or even more so, not only turned prisoners against the enemy but banded them together solidly against him. The Chinese appeared to be lenient and used practical psychology to deal with the prisoners' resentment by turning it against other objects than themselves. Many prisoners on return to their homes said that the Chinese had treated them as well as they could, and even expressed sincere gratitude for the care they had received.

Psychologically, the prisoners fell into four categories: there were the outright collaborators, about 13 per cent of the total, who lacked the moral stamina to resist even slight pressure and gave up sometimes in as short a time as thirty-five minutes of not very intensive questioning; secondly, came the opportunists who yielded for strictly personal and selfish reasons and would inform, make broadcasts, or sign petitions for even slight benefits – freedom to walk outside the camp, cigarettes, or an extra egg; thirdly, and the largest group, which included three out of four of the total, were those who chose the path of least resistance, complying outwardly, making relatively harmless broadcasts, or signing petitions and cooperating with the indoctrination programmes in a passive way without doing anything obviously traitorous. This outward compliance was described by the men as 'playing it cool'. The fourth and last group, which was also the smallest, consisted of those who actually accepted Communism.

Most of these seemed to be men who had for various reasons been unable to form any strong attachments or loyalties in their past lives. They were the unsuccessful and the uncertain who felt that Communism had something to offer them that their own country had not. Those who did not collaborate, the so-called 'reactionaries', were about the same number as the frank collaborators, i.e. about 13 per cent. 'Reactionaries' were those men who never gave more than the information required under the Geneva Convention, and they fell into two groups: the first consisted of those who had a long history, even in their own country, of resisting any kind of authority. They had bad records in the American Army and in captivity merely persisted in their old pattern of rebelling against those in command. The second group consisted of those mature, well-integrated individuals with a strong sense of personal honour who often used the respect they got from other prisoners to sabotage the indoctrination programme. 'Reactionaries' were described by the Chinese as 'ignorant, stubborn, professional soldiers'. They were made to work hard but, once their nature had been discovered, were otherwise left alone. The Communist attitude is shown in the account of a soldier who was asked his opinion of General George Marshall and, on replying 'General Marshall is a great American soldier', was knocked down with a rifle-butt. A second time he was asked the same question and gave the same reply; but this time he remained unhurt, and was left alone during his three years in prison camp.

The behaviour of British soldiers was dealt with in an investigation held by the Ministry of Defence which published its results in the pamphlet *Treatment of British Prisoners of War in Korea* (1955). This revealed that out of a total of about 980 prisoners one had decided to remain behind but two-thirds of the men and lesser NCOs had done nothing that could be described as collaboration with the enemy. None of the officers or senior NCOs had yielded, and, as we have already mentioned, only 4 per cent came back convinced Communists, many of whom had already held these views before they left home. The Ministry noted that a feature of the Communist programme which had been absent in the case of American prisoners of war was the barrage of propaganda directed by Communist sympathizers in this country against the relatives of the prisoners. They were frequently offered information about their sons or husbands in exchange for attendance at anti-war rallies, to which their fares were paid.

The American record has to be contrasted with this and with the Turkish record which shows that, out of a total of 229 men, hardly a single one was guilty of even minor degrees of collaboration. Although almost half the men were wounded before capture, none died in captivity. In one temporary camp, where none of the 110 Turks died, the Americans lost 400–800 men out of a total of 1,500–1,800 men interned. The American explanation of these results was that the Turkish chain of command remained unbroken throughout and one Turkish officer gave the following account of the general attitude:

I told the Chinese commander of the camp that while we were a unit, I was in charge of the group. If he wanted anything done, he was to come to me, and I would see that it was done. When he removed me the responsibility would fall not on him, but on the man next below me, and after that on the man below him. And so on, down through the ranks, until there were only two privates left. Then the senior private would be in charge. They could kill us, I told him, but they couldn't make us do what we didn't want to do. Discipline was our salvation, and we all knew it. If a Turk had responded to an order from his superiors to share his food or lift a litter the way I understand some of your [i.e. the American] men did, he would literally have had his teeth knocked in. Not by his superior either, but by the Turk nearest to him.

The Turks were not spared indoctrination, and in fact became a special target for it, but, when a Chinese tried to explain Communism through an interpreter, both were heckled by the asking of ridiculous questions. The Chinese then imported a Turk who had resided in Russia, but his life was made so unpleasant that he suddenly left. He was followed by Monica Felton, the English leader of the National Assembly of Women, who after a few days was presented with an insulting document telling her (in effect) to go elsewhere with her left-wing doctrines. Two others, one an American prisoner who spoke both Greek and Turkish and was one of the men who remained in China, also failed and gave up their effort. As Colonel Perry, a senior American officer, pointed out:

There is no way of compelling a group, through methods of mass psychological pressure, to do something it says firmly it won't do. Mass resistance in that case always wins.

The conclusions to be drawn from this study may be summarized as follows:

1. In so far as the term has any meaning at all, none of the prisoners of war in Korea were subjected to 'brainwashing'.

2. They were, however, subjected to intensive political indoctrination, which caused some surprise, and even alarm, largely because nobody had ever tried out such a method before on such an elaborate scale.

3. In whatever results were obtained, the main factor was lack of morale amongst the prisoners themselves rather than any methods employed by the Chinese.

4. The methods employed, although borrowed from the Russians, had nothing to do with the deliberate use of Pavlov's techniques, although one may concede that in countries which know nothing about any other school of psychology what views a person has on the subject are likely to be coloured by Pavlovian theory.

5. So far from being 'brainwashed' prisoners behaved very much in character, the misfits becoming Communists, the well-integrated and intelligent remaining that way, and the resentful (or 'bloody-minded', to use the more expressive term) being as resentful towards their captors as they had previously been towards their own superior officers.

6. When prisoners said that the Chinese had treated them 'as well as they could', they meant just what they said, although they did not realize that the deliberate Chinese policy was to turn the prisoners' aggression against their own government and fellow-prisoners in order to sow dissension.

7. When it is said that many misfits tend to become Communists this must not be taken as meaning that all Communists are misfits; it is merely a statement based on the observed fact

that those who join minority groups are likely to be misfits within their own group, and this has no bearing on the 'rightness' or 'wrongness' of the views expressed. In a predominantly Communist country the majority of Communists are of course not misfits.

8. In any form of persuasion, from the mildest to the most severe, it is always the case that those who refuse to cooperate are in no danger while those who give the slightest indication of doing so are doomed.

9. The methods employed, although more thoroughgoing, were psychologically not dissimilar to those used by police forces in the West. For British police methods see Ludovic Kennedy's *Ten Rillington Place* (Pan Books), especially chapters 6–7.

CHAPTER II

BRAINWASHING

THE account given by Kinkead of political indoctrination in Korea has been criticized mainly on the grounds that it seems to accept without much question explanations offered by high officials in the U.S. Army and fails to show much sympathy or insight into the minds of the prisoners. This may be so, but from the practical point of view it shows clearly that political indoctrination is not a mysterious process, although certainly a peculiar one judged by experience of past wars, and that its success with the Americans and relative or complete failure with the British and Turks was due to the poor morale of the former and the better discipline of the latter. This is a salutary lesson because, shortly after its introduction by Edward Hunter, the term 'brainwashing' became so popular and sounded so terrifying that people really thought that something very odd and frightening was going on and the word was applied indiscriminately to the process of political indoctrination as carried out on prisoners of war in Korea, to the more severe type of indoctrination carried out by the Chinese on civilians, to Eastern European methods, and to those used by the Russians during, and presumably since, the purges of the 1930s. The many jokes made about brainwashing only served to show how uneasy people really felt. Rumours arose, some based on the myth that it was a 'mysterious oriental device' or the deliberate application of Pavlov's findings on dogs, others on the equally silly belief that no such process existed and that it was only an invention of American news correspondents. In fact, as we have seen, the term is psychologically and physiologically meaningless and the process, if real enough, is based on ancient methods carried out by the Chinese for many years and by the Russian secret police long before the Revolution. In November 1956 the American Group for the Advancement of

Psychiatry held a conference 'to clarify the differences between Orwell's fantastic account and the real processes actually used in authentic cases', during which Dr L. E. Hinkle suggested that the following conclusions can be accepted:

The methods of the Russian and satellite State Police are derived from age-old police methods, many of which were known to the Czarist Okhrana and to its sister organizations in other countries. Communist techniques, when their background is studied, remain police methods. They are not dependent on drugs, hypnotism, or any other special procedure designed by scientists. No scientist took part in their design, nor do scientists participate in their operation. The goal of the KGB – the present designation for the Russian State Police – is a satisfactory protocol on which a so-called 'trial' may be based. The Chinese have an additional goal; the production of long-lasting changes in the prisoner's basic attitudes and behaviour.

Of the Chinese Communist programme officially described as *szu-hsiang kai-tsao* (variously translated as 'ideological reform', 'ideological remoulding', or 'thought reform'), Dr Robert J. Lifton writes in *Thought Reform: A Psychiatric Study of 'Brainwashing' in China*:

Such a programme is by no means completely new: imposed dogmas, inquisitions, and mass conversion movements have existed in every country and during every historical epoch. But the Chinese Communists have brought to theirs a more organized, comprehensive, and deliberate – a more *total* character, as well as a unique blend of energetic and ingenious psychological techniques.

What is of particular interest is how the news of such techniques has been received by the public in America and elsewhere since it has exaggerated the latent feeling in the common man that he is being 'got at' by all sorts of wicked manipulators from the writers of advertisements to the heads of large business enterprises and the teachers in preparatory or public schools. A Sunday newspaper has only to print an article dealing with the procedure of 'subliminal perception' which has the alleged but very dubious power of causing people to make choices without being aware of doing so, to be bombarded by hundreds of indignant letters which reveal the paranoid fear of being manipulated by the élites that is so typical of modern mass society. Of course the public is often being manipulated, and the only surprising thing is that it has taken so long to find this out. What, after all, have priests being doing in their churches for centuries, if not trying to change people? What is the purpose of advertising if not the manipulation of the public within a limited sphere? And we may well ask whether the Communists have devised any method which is half as efficient in 'brainwashing' (or with results which are half as permanent) as the English public school. In an article in the *Spectator* (17 November 1961), the editor Brian Inglis wrote of his own experiences at public school and its efficiency in indoctrinating its scholars with its own peculiar code of behaviour:

> By the end of the first term the school code had been instilled: at the beginning of the second, I was ready to enforce it on the new boys, and looked forward to seeing them have their normal values talked, jeered, or beaten out of them, and replaced with the school's set. A very ugly set of values they were, in retrospect; elevating dishonesty into a virtue provided it was used against masters; stressing conformity as the prime need. . . . The craft of the brainwasher has never been a mystery to me, since.

It may be said, against all evidence, that these values are unreservedly good whereas those the Communists seek to instil are bad; but this is to ignore the fact that the Chinese Communists are perfectly sincere in their intentions and the values they attempt to instil are in their view good in comparison with the 'rotten capitalist' values of reactionary countries. Their 'thought reform' programme is aimed, not primarily at Westerners, but at the Chinese people themselves, and is vigorously applied in schools, universities, special 'revolutionary colleges', prisons, business and government offices, and labour and peasant organizations. For the most part social pressure, exhortation, and ethical appeal are employed and the methods used would seem quite in order to those acquainted with the official and unofficial means of bringing about conformity in our own army or public schools. Coercion to the point of breakdown is more in evidence in the prison and military programmes or in those directed against reactionaries, but, as in the public school, it often becomes extremely difficult to say where exhortation ends and coercion begins. As Lifton says:

Some people considered [thought reform] a relentless means of undermining the human personality; others saw it as a profoundly 'moral' – even religious – attempt to instil new ethics into the Chinese people. Both of these views was partly correct, and yet each, insofar as it ignored the other, was greatly misleading. For it was the combination of *external force or coercion* with an appeal to *inner enthusiasm through evangelistic exhortation* which gave thought reform its emotional scope and power.

Dr Lifton's book is concerned with the reform of Westerners and Chinese intellectuals regarded as 'reactionaries' who arrived in Hong Kong after their experiences in China rather than with the process as applied to the Chinese people themselves and it is the methods applied to the former who underwent what might be described as 'brainwashing' which we are now going to discuss. Before doing so, however, it is worth while mentioning Felix Greene's book *The Wall has Two Sides* which deals with the re-education of the people within China where, as he points out, the outstanding feature of life today is mass participation by means of meetings and group discussions. Mr Greene describes how even floor-boys and the crews of long-distance trains are accustomed to get together in informal meetings to talk over how they can be of better service to their guests or run the trains more efficiently.

I have come to believe [he says] that the Chinese derive their deepest satisfactions not from a sense of personal importance but from sharing in activities which have aims beyond the individual. The Government has been extremely skilful in giving nearly everyone a sense that his work fits in somewhere. A floor-boy in this hotel feels that he is participating in the rebirth of China every bit as much as a big shot in the Government. All of them, down to those who do the most menial jobs – pedicab drivers, say – are made to feel they are an essential part of the whole show.

It must be noted that this sense of participation, although regarded as of prime importance by industrial psychologists and others concerned with industry, is a feeling which the capitalist countries have on the whole been unsuccessful in arousing.

Unless we realize that the Chinese Communists are deeply in earnest about what they are doing, we shall not get very far in understanding their attitude to thought reform. Crime, including the holding of reactionary beliefs, is regarded as a hangover from the old days of capitalism and imperialism and the Chinese Communist Prison Regulations ordain:

In dealing with the criminals, there shall be regularly adopted measures of corrective study classes, individual interviews, study of assigned documents, and organized discussions, to educate them in the admission of guilt and obedience to the law, political and current events, labour production, and culture, so as to expose the nature of the crime committed, thoroughly wipe out criminal thoughts, and establish a new moral code.

This is the theoretical background to ideological remoulding.

The first of Lifton's subjects was a Dr Vincent who had conducted a lucrative practice in Shanghai until suddenly confronted in the street by five armed men who produced a warrant for his arrest and took him to the prison or 're-education centre' where he spent the next three and a half years. He was placed in a small (8 ft by 12 ft) cell which already contained eight other prisoners; these were a specially selected group, each 'advanced' in his personal reform and keen to reform others as a means of getting 'merits' towards his own release. All were Chinese and the 'cell chief' immediately ordered Vincent, addressing him by his prison number, to sit down in the centre of the cell whilst the others sat in a circle around him taking it in turn to denounce him as an 'imperialist' and 'spy' and demanding that he recognize his crimes and confess everything to the government. Vincent protested quite sincerely that he was a doctor, not a spy, and had worked in China for twenty years; but they accused him all the more saying in effect 'the government has all the proof, they never make a mistake, and you have not been arrested for nothing'. They then questioned him about the activities in which he engaged to cover up his spy identity. This process was known as a 'struggle' carried on for the purpose of 'helping' a prisoner to confess and Vincent had to undergo it frequently during the early months of his imprisonment.

After several hours of this unnerving treatment, Vincent was called for his first interrogation. He was taken to a small room with three people in it: the interrogator, an interpreter, and a secretary. The interrogator or 'judge' began with a vague accusation concluding: 'You have committed crimes against the people, and you must now confess everything.' The prisoner's protestations of innocence brought the reply: 'The government never arrests an innocent man.' This was followed by a series of questions relating to Vincent's activities, professional contacts, friends, and acquaintances, during the whole twenty years of his life in China. The judge kept repeating: 'The government knows all about your crimes. That is why we arrested you. It is now up to you to confess everything to us, and in this way your case can be quickly solved and you will soon be released.'

After several hours of this questioning, the subjects discussed began to centre more and more upon alleged connexions with several groups – with his own (the French) embassy, American government officials, and Nationalist Chinese, Japanese, and Catholic agencies. Following ten consecutive hours of interrogation, although he had given much information, Vincent still maintained that he was innocent and did not know why he had been arrested. The judge became angry and ordered the prisoner's hands to be fixed behind his back with handcuffs, dismissed him from the room, and told him to go and think over his crimes. Ten minutes later he was called back and, still protesting his innocence, had chains placed on his ankles and was sent back to his cell. There the cell-mates began the 'struggle' once more and this went on all day after his sleepless night with the judge.

You are obliged to stand with chains on your ankles and holding your hands behind your back. They don't assist you because you are too reactionary. You eat as a dog does with your mouth and teeth. You arrange the cup and bowl with your nose to try and absorb broth twice a day. If you have to make water they open your trousers and you make water in a little tin in the corner. . . . In the w.c. someone opens your trousers and after you are finished they clean you. You are never out of the chains. Nobody pays any attention to your hygiene. Nobody washes you. In the room they say you are in chains only because you are a reactionary. They continuously tell you that, if you confess all, you will be treated better.

Towards the end of the second day, Vincent began to be obsessed with the idea 'I must be rid of the chains' and that night he gave a wild description of spy activities which he knew to be false. But, when he was asked for details, inconsistencies appeared and his confession was rejected by the judge, whereupon the round of interrogation and 'struggle' continued.

On the third night, Vincent changed his methods and began to reconstruct and confess every detail of all the conversations with associates that he could remember from the whole of his life in China. Whilst he was thus talking freely, the judge began to make use of his advantages: increasingly demanding interrogations took up the greater part of each night, and were interrupted only to take the prisoner for a walk in his chains every two or three hours which increased his physical discomfort and kept him awake. In the daytime he was made to dictate to another prisoner everything he had said during the night, adding other details as he thought of them. When he was not doing this the 'struggle' went on and everything in the cell seemed to centre upon him and his confession. Everything he did or said, even his slightest expression, was written down by the others and passed on to the authorities. For eight days and nights this went on without sleep and under constant pressure from the others: 'You want the chains! You want to be shot! Otherwise you would be more sincere and the chains would not be necessary.' Finally, overwhelmed by fatigue, confusion, and a sense of helplessness, he gave up resisting:

From that moment, the judge is the real master of you. When he asks how many 'intelligences' you gave to that person, you just put out a number in order to satisfy him. If he says, 'Only those?', you say, 'No, there are more.' If he says, 'One hundred', you say, 'One hundred' . . . You do whatever they want. You don't pay any more attention to your life or to your handcuffed arms. You can't distinguish right from left. You just wonder when you will be shot – and begin to hope for the end of all this.

A confession began to make its appearance which, although still full of inconsistencies, was nevertheless closely related to real events and people in the prisoner's life, and within three weeks he was required to report on others and complied once more with a mixture of truths, half-truths, and lies. Within two weeks, under the pressure of judge and cell-mates, these descriptions became denunciations and with the continuing demands of 'Confess all! Show your faith in the government! Come clean!' associates and friends were drawn into the web.

About two months after the date of his arrest Vincent was thought to be ready for the 'recognition' of his 'crimes' and was expected to look at himself from the 'people's standpoint' based on the principle that 'the people's standpoint makes no distinction between news, information, and intelligence'. Thus he admitted that at the time of the 'liberation', when he had seen the horse-drawn artillery of the Communist army, he had mentioned this to an American friend. 'The judge shouted that this American was a spy who was collecting espionage material for his spy organization, and that I was guilty of supplying him with military intelligence.' At first Vincent did not accept this, but soon he had to add it to his 'confession'.

Once he had adopted the 'people's standpoint', he was surprised to find that his circumstances were much improved: his chains were removed, he was allowed to sit comfortably when talking to the judge, and the latter spoke to him in a friendly tone. He was told that the government was sorry he had had such a difficult time and really wanted to be lenient with him; he would soon be released if he would make a complete confession and work hard to reform himself. He was offered friendly guidance in rewriting his confession, including denunciations and descriptions of other people; but on a few occasions when he claimed 'This I didn't do' he was put back in chains for two or three days. But, on the whole, from this time onwards he was allowed eight hours sleep, relatively quiet interrogations, and was free from the harassment of his cell-mates. Nevertheless, he was still addressed by his number, was given poor food, and had to run head down twice a day along with the others for the permitted forty-five seconds at the two toilets, being sharply criticized if he took longer than this.

Three weeks after the beginning of 'leniency' he had to take part in the cell's 're-education' programme which took up ten to sixteen hours a day. The general procedure was for the cell chief to read out a piece from a Communist newspaper, pamphlet, or book, and each member was supposed to discuss this and criticize the views of others. Each had to learn to express himself from the 'people's standpoint' and was severely taken to task for lack of cooperation. Initially, the discussions were concerned with past Western insults to China and the message was conveyed to Vincent that 'under the cloak of medicine' he had been nothing other than a life-long spy, an agent of the imperialists, and so on. When his views were found to be 'erroneous' he was requested to 'examine himself' and seek the causes of his 'reactionary' tendencies. Thus each discussion, beginning at an intellectual level, soon became concerned with personal analysis and criticism. The Communist, of course, unlike other people who consider many problems to be matters of opinion only, has a metaphysic which holds that certain beliefs are correct in some sort of objective sense whilst others are objectively wrong. For Vincent, everything was a 'problem' which had to be 'solved' according to the 'facts', which naturally were those which fitted in with the 'people's viewpoint'. At first, he simply gave lip service to what was regarded as the 'correct' attitude, but within some weeks or months he began to accept these views inwardly and to apply them to himself:

In the cell, twelve hours a day, you talk and talk – you have to take part – you must discuss yourself, criticize, inspect yourself, denounce your thought. Little by little you start to admit something, and look to yourself, only using the 'people's judgement'.

At this stage, prisoners were referred to as 'schoolmates' and prison officials as 'instructors', and it would be emphasized that the ignorant should only be taught by 'discussion' and 'persuasion'. The prisoners were told about Russia and the 'people's democracies', about the victory against imperialism in the Korean War, and the Chinese three- and five-year plans in order to arrive at a socialist society: 'They solve every problem through discussion – the Korean War, the Indo-Chinese War. . . . They never use force; every question is solved through conference.' When Vincent was not talkative enough he was criticized for not being sincere, and when his views showed the slightest trace of heresy in relation to Communist orthodoxy he was told that he was 'too subjective', 'individualistic', and other crimes in Communist eyes. Some part of the day was devoted to 'daily-life' criticisms where such subjects were discussed as general conduct, eating and sleeping habits, feelings towards others, and willingness to do one's share of work in the cell. This was very closely similar to what we have already seen of the process of group psychotherapy except that interpretations, instead of being given in Freudian terminology, were couched in that of Marx. Vincent suffered from 'imperialist' or 'bourgeois' greed and exploitation; if he dropped a plate he was 'wasting the people's money', if he drank too much water he was 'draining the blood of the people', and if he took up too much space in sleeping this was 'imperialist expansion'.

After a year of this 're-education' Vincent was again subjected to a series of interrogations to improve his confession and this time the judge focused upon a few special points related to actual events. So 'from a wild confession, you go on to a more concrete confession' and this time eight 'crimes' emerged, including membership of a right-wing French political organization, espionage, 'intelligence' in association with American, Catholic, and other reactionary groups, other anti-Communist activities, and 'slanderous insults to the Chinese people'. This confession seemed to him to be more real than before:

Not all the time – but moments – you think they are right. 'I did this, I am a criminal.' If you doubt, you keep it to yourself. Because if you admit the doubt you will be 'struggled' and lose the progress you have made.

Then there was another fourteen months of full-time re-education and, during his third year of imprisonment, another revision of his confession. Vincent came to believe a great deal of what he was saying although not in the simple manner that those who accept the thesis of brainwashing as 'washing the slate clean' might suppose:

You begin to believe all this, *but it is a special kind of belief.* You are not absolutely convinced, but you accept it – in order to avoid trouble – because every time you don't agree, trouble starts again.

He was told that his attitude had greatly improved, and was transferred to another part of the prison where he lived in harmony with his captors, and was given an hour of outdoor recreation a day and additional recreation periods in the cell. Soon he was called for a formal signing of his confession in French and Chinese whilst photographers and cinema camera men took pictures and he also read it aloud for sound-recording. Later he was called before the judge and sentenced to three years of imprisonment (which he was considered already to have served) for espionage and crimes against the people. The account was widely disseminated throughout China and the outside world as propaganda and, being expelled immediately, Vincent was within two days on a British ship heading for Hong Kong.

Unlike the study of Allied soldiers in Korea by Kinkead, Dr Lifton's account is a painstaking piece of psychiatric research and the prisoners were not only examined when they regained freedom but were followed up thereafter. From his account, it might appear that Dr Vincent was an extremely successful product of Communist re-education; but psychiatric examination immediately following his release revealed quite another picture – a man who was confused and afraid, with the feeling that he was being constantly watched and manipulated: 'I have a certain idea that someone is spying on me because I came from the Communist world.' And, thinking aloud about Dr Lifton: 'I have a feeling he is not just a doctor. He is connected with some imperialist organization which will bring me danger. . . . I think maybe someone else is telling you the questions to ask me.' Vincent even missed some aspects of prison life ('It is not that I miss it, but I find that it was more easy'), and had thoughts of contacting Communists when he got home:

When I left China I had this strange feeling: Now I am going to the imperialist world. No one will take care of me. I'll be unemployed and lost – everyone will look on me as a criminal. Still, I thought, there is a Communist Party in my country. I am coming out of a Communist world; they must know I have had reform training. Perhaps they will be interested in keeping me.

Such feelings are, of course, common amongst those who have left hospital or prison after a long period; they are glad to be outside, but miss the security of the routine and the feeling of being looked after without having to make decisions of their own. Indeed, in many respects the process of being hospitalized bears similarities to brainwashing, in that the patient, in this case by reason of his illness, is reduced to a state of near infantile dependency and subsequently begins to accept in varying degrees the hospital atmosphere as his own. In severe instances of long hospitalization he may even develop an 'Institutional neurosis' which unfits him for life in the outside world. Like the hospital, the thought-reforming establishment is a severely controlled environment and, as Dr Lifton says:

The penetration of the psychological forces of the environment into the inner emotions of the individual person is perhaps the outstanding psychiatric fact of thought reform.

Brainwashing first takes deliberate and active steps to strip the individual of his self-hood, and then strives to build up something new on the foundations that remain; long hospitalization with inadequate nursing staff and hence loss of social contacts strips the patient of his self-hood no less effectively, and we now know that many cases of dementia following schizophrenia or what appear to be the degenerative changes of old age are really instances of unwitting brainwashing. Institutional neurosis is a real entity caused not by the disease process but by the doctors themselves when they are forced to herd 'hopeless' cases together, with inadequate staff to provide the social stimuli which are necessary in most people in order to maintain their personality. It is brought about by the unresponsiveness of the environment, whereas brainwashing in its first stage makes use of the unyieldingness of the environment; the prisoner is faced by circumstances which relentlessly insist 'You have committed a crime, the government is never wrong', and, since he can make no impression on his environment, it ends by penetrating him.

It will be remembered that John Wesley, in his insistence on salvation through faith rather than works, put his listeners in a similar spiritual predicament which said in effect that nothing they could *do* would make any difference and only *believing* could save. In the words of Toplady's hymn:

Could my soul no respite know,
Could my tears for ever flow,
All for sin would not atone;
Thou canst save and Thou alone.

However, the sufferer from institutional neurosis, no matter
how apparently demented and unresponsive, will begin to
return to his old modes of behaviour when he is removed to a
socially responsive environment and those who have undergone brainwashing, although not wholly unchanged, are
likely to behave similarly. After a few weeks in Hong Kong,
Dr Vincent was saying: 'I have the feeling that if I meet a
Communist in my country, my first reaction toward him will
be violent.'

The case of Dr Vincent has been chosen as typical in the
methods employed and fairly typical as regards their results.
Dr Lifton analyses the various steps in the brainwashing procedure beginning with the first and most obvious: *the assault
upon identity*. Vincent is told that he is not a doctor and that all of
what he considered himself to be was really a cloak covering
up what he really is. He is addressed, not by his name, but by his
prison number. Other prisoners were told the same sort of thing
in relation to what they thought most precious – in the case of
priests, their religion. This was followed by the pain, fear, and
humiliation of his early experiences, from the unremitting
'struggles' to the chains and the inability to attend to his own
excretory needs. Soon he had entirely lost his bearings as to who
and what he was and where he stood in relation to his fellows.
Like the long-hospitalized patient he was reduced to a state of
infantile dependency. He was further weakened by loss of sleep
and poor food, and the constant interrogations at irregular intervals caused him to become disorientated not only to matters of
personal identity but also as to time. Finally, to use Dr Lifton's
significant phrase, he 'dies to the world', a state which the
evangelist sees as a prerequisite to salvation.

The second stage begins with the *establishment of guilt* which
is both factual (you *are* guilty) and psychologically demanding
(you must learn to *feel* guilty). The prisoner becomes so permeated by the atmosphere of guilt that external criminal accusa-

tions become merged with subjective feelings of sinfulness. It will be recalled that in Chapter 2 attention was drawn to the psychoanalyst's belief that in every individual there exists from the early months of life a reservoir of vague guilt-feelings which are only waiting to be tapped, and soon the prisoner becomes aware of a pervasive sense of guilt which says: 'It is my sinfulness, and not their injustice, which causes me to suffer – although I do not yet know the full measure of my guilt.'

Then comes the *self-betrayal* with the denunciations of friends and colleagues, which not only leads to a vicious circle of more and more genuine guilt and the need to confess further but to an additional renunciation of the people, organizations, and standards of behaviour which had formed the core of the prisoner's former life. In betraying others he is betraying himself, and now he is left with no loyalties to the past behind him and the non-acceptance by his captors before. He is totally isolated and in much the same position as a man taken from his ordinary surroundings and put in a hospital for the criminally insane where he is accused of some vague but terrible crime which he does not know about but is expected to recognize and confess; each protestation of innocence is looked on by those in charge as a symptom of his disease and all the other inmates are dedicated to forcing him into confession and 'cure'.

This situation, reminiscent of Kafka's *The Trial*, brings about the stage of *total conflict and basic fear* when the prisoner is experiencing one of the most primitive and terrifying emotions possible to man – the fear of total annihilation as a person. This is the point where physical and psychological integration break down and the prisoner seems to be left with the three prospects of physical illness, insanity, or death. Some of the other prisoners responded with suicidal preoccupations, many with delusions and hallucinations:

I heard investigations taking place below, and one day I heard my name called. I listened while Chinese were indoctrinated to testify how I had been gathering information on troop movements. . . . The next day I recognized the voice of my Chinese accountant, who was told that I had confessed everything and therefore his confession had better agree with mine. . . . Once I heard the guards saying in a social conversation with a German that they would soften me up by locking me in a cage.

As soon as this state has been reached the official attitude becomes one of *leniency and opportunity* and the prisoner grasps at the first sign of kindliness on the part of his interrogator with heart-felt gratitude. A priest reported of this experience:

It was Christmas Day. I was brought to see the judge. For the first time I found the room full of sunlight. There was no guard and there were no secretaries. There were only the kind faces of the judges offering me cigarettes and tea. It was a conversation more than a questioning. My mother could not have been much more good and kind than the judge was. He said to me, 'The treatment you have received here is really too bad. Maybe you are unable to stand it. As a foreigner and a priest, you must be used to good food and better hygienic standards. So just make a confession. But make it really good, so we can be satisfied. Then we will close your trial and finish your case.'

The *compulsion to confess* thus comes from a realization that only those who confess can survive. The early confessions are preliminary to the *total* purging of the soul which, as we have seen, is not only an aspect of this particular situation but a deep-seated need in most people. Once confession has begun it gathers momentum and brings about an increasing feeling of submission as in a description by another priest:

After a while one wants to talk, they press you so you feel you must say something. Once you start you are deceived: you are at the top of the tree and you go down. . . . If you say the first word, there is always something more. '*Lao shih* – No, no, be a good boy! Say the truth! "*t'an pai*" – Confess!' are constantly repeated every two minutes. I felt myself wanting to say more to make him shut his mouth, he was so insisting. . . . It made me weak: it made me want to give in.

Dr Lifton makes the important point that, although these fantasies of the prisoner's confession are carefully selected and moulded by the officials and cell-mates, *they are never entirely divorced from the man who produces them.* 'His compulsion to confess dedicates him to the task of continuously carving out and refilling his own inner void – under the active supervision and broad moral guidance of his captors.'

The next stage is the *channelling of guilt* when the prisoner's non-specific guilt feelings are directed into a paranoid pseudo-logical system. By accepting 'the people's standpoint' the prisoner joins in condemning himself not so much for what he has *done* as for what he has *been* – a Westerner and an 'imperialist'.

The stage of re-education which is *logical dishonouring* ensues when he learns to criticize and condemn every aspect of his being in Marxist terminology, and this in turn is followed by the stage of *progress and harmony* leading up to the *final confession and summing-up*.

Not all of Dr Lifton's cases reacted in the same way: there were the obviously confused, the apparent converts, and the apparent resisters. Although all of these reacted broadly in the ways described above, there were equally significant dissimilarities, and during and after his reform each subject showed his own particular pattern of emotion and belief, strength and weakness, which were largely dependent upon his own basic character traits. The obviously confused were unable to trust themselves in relation to either the Communist or non-Communist worlds and some were near to psychosis, facing both outer chaos and inner confusion. The apparent resisters were those who seemed at first to have been little affected by their ordeal beyond a certain amount of physical and mental strain and ideologically they were bitterly anti-Communist. Yet as Lifton probed more deeply he found that their inner resistance was not nearly so complete as their external expression suggested; for, paradoxically, those who outwardly had been least influenced by thought reform unconsciously felt themselves to be most in danger of being overwhelmed by its influence.

Typical of these was Bishop Barker, who held fundamentalist Catholic principles, his own version of totalism, and after his release even advocated a preventive war against Communism now. Yet it soon became obvious that many of the Bishop's protestations were, in effect, a kind of 'whistling in the dark' and in demanding war he was really saying: 'If we can destroy all of the demons in the world, it will eliminate those within me without my having to recognize that they have been there.' Totalism calls to totalism, and Bishop Barker was deeply impressed by the Communists whose main fault was that their totalism was not his:

> The Communists have tremendous enthusiasm in their outright devotion to their doctrine. . . . What they believe they do. . . . We are divided between doctrine and practice. . . . There is a discrepancy between religious life and doctrine. Therefore we are weak.

All his life he had dealt with problems by the psychological mechanisms of denial and repression in order to keep from himself the recognition of undue weakness, but this weakness showed in his constant need for defiance in face of something that basically appealed to him. But the apparent resisters showed a strong sense of personal identity in contrast to the apparent converts who tended to show identity confusion, although they too had long shown tendencies to totalism or authoritarianism. Bishop Barker had to keep on asserting his opposition to Communism because he secretly admired it, whereas the converts in the same situation were unable to resist it. Thus, of a Jesuit priest and the daughter of a liberal missionary who were both apparent converts, Dr Lifton notes that, although both were in many ways strikingly different, there were striking similarities in their emotional reactions. Both responded strongly to the opportunity to merge with the Chinese people, both experienced a particularly strong sense of guilt and a strong need to be absolutely sincere with their captors; both eventually achieved a greater harmony with their prison atmosphere than with any they had previously known, and were unwilling to give it up for the 'fear of freedom'.

> The authoritarian priest shared with the liberal missionary's daughter psychological traits characteristic for the apparent convert: strong susceptibility to guilt, confusion of identity, and, most important of all, a longstanding pattern of totalism.

Four years later, most of the subjects had succeeded in neutralizing the ideological effects of their experience but, as might be expected, nobody who has once been through the process of thought reform ever wholly throws off the new light in which he has seen himself. There were two striking non-ideological results, the one bad, the other, strangely enough, beneficial. The bad one was the persistence of fear and guilt, the fear being related to the basic fear of total annihilation as a person, already mentioned. It is an unconscious memory which some equate with the experience of having felt totally controlled and dangerously threatened by a powerful parent, but, whatever its associations, everyone dreaded the return of the situation through being brought again under total control. On the other hand, some felt a deeply repressed desire for the return of just such a situation as a means of getting rid of the pervasive sense of guilt which had been awakened by thought reform. It is interesting in this connexion to note once more that the sadness at leaving China frequently expressed by many who had recently been freed was perfectly genuine, and years later a few still missed the special intimacy of the thought reform group – the delight in total exposure and sharing which, as Professor T. H. Pear observes, is one of the special pleasures of the Moral Rearmament Movement. Guilt is something that separates us from others, and confession and 'sharing' are the means of assuaging it.

Amongst the good results noted by those who had undergone thought reform was a sense of having become more sensitive to their own and other people's inner feelings and more flexible and confident in human relationships. Unlike most of us, who (as already remarked) really do not know our limitations because our experience has been so limited, these people had had the experience of testing their emotional limits. They had undergone the ultimate in physical and psychological pain and yet had survived; they had been forced to analyse themselves and yet had come out of it with some degree of self-respect. In the experience of thought reform these men and women gained an insight into parts of their minds which they had previously never known to exist. Indeed, the late Professor Alexander Kennedy in a lecture to the Royal Institution on 'Scientific Lessons of Brain Washing' (*Proceedings of the Royal Institution*, April 1960) explained how the exploitation of personal relations in men who had been 'softened up' by isolation from human contacts and by deliberately induced disorientation in space and time could be beneficially used to restore to lonely old people self-respect and a sense of the nature of their personalities and it seems quite likely that the lessons learned in brainwashing will be further applied therapeutically.

The technique used, or formerly used, in the Soviet Union and the East European Communist countries in order to produce 'evidence' for show trials is sufficiently well-known from such books as A. Weissberg's *Conspiracy of Silence*, F. Beck and W. Godin's *Russian Purge and the Extraction of Confessions*, and Z. Stypulkowski's *Invitation to Moscow*. Khrushchev (if his word may be accepted in the circumstances) has already admitted the use of physical torture although, as suggested elsewhere, it may well be the case that some of the accused in the Stalin purge required little pressure to make them confess to crimes of which they were already guilty in thought if not in deed. Confession or self-criticism is part of the ideology of Communism, and convinced Communists may be more ready to confess to deviations than other people in the same situation, especially when they already know that they have little choice in the matter. It need hardly be said that only a very credulous person would accept the details of some of the confessions; but whether these were willingly added after a mental struggle on the part of the accused to make their confessions sound more factual or forced upon them under torture we have no means of knowing.

People have been drawn by the fantastic nature of the admissions at these trials to suppose that the human mind is at the mercy of new and cunning methods which nobody can withstand; and some, like Aldous Huxley, have made our flesh creep with the statement that 'new and previously undreamed-of devices' have been invented against which nothing can avail. This, as will be shown in more detail later, is simply not true. There has never been a time since history began when it was not possible, given complete power and lack of scruples, to induce the majority of people to confess to anything, profess or denounce any creed we might wish, and that by the simplest and crudest of methods; nor has there been, or is ever likely to be, a time when a stalwart minority will not prefer to resist to the end. The Russian purge trials had their exact parallels in the witch-craft trials of the fifteenth and sixteenth centuries and those of the Spanish Inquisition; and even if in the former case many of those tried were, in their own estimation, 'witches' as Dr Margaret Murray believes, whilst others were undoubtedly innocent, both groups confessed to offences they could not possibly have committed just as some pathetic creatures in the Soviet Union admitted to killing the novelist Maxim Gorki by injecting tuberculosis germs – an excessively improbable and inefficient means of causing death. Broadly speaking, very similar methods were employed and the same results obtained at all these trials and there is very little of psychological interest in observations which confirm what we already know: that most people under the appropriate circumstances will confess to anything.

It need hardly be said that the use of torture of one sort or another is not limited to the Communist half of the world, for there is plenty of evidence that the French 'paras' in Algeria have used torture to extract information from the Algerians and their suspected sympathizers; here, however, it would appear that, in place of the somewhat long drawn-out process of mental breakdown, they have substituted the use of painful electric shocks, choking, and suffocation by water, which also have the advantage that, if carefully used, they leave no trace on the body. But there is no reason to suppose that electricity is any more effective than the red-hot irons of former days, so this can hardly be described as a 'new and previously undreamed-of' device.

The basic method employed by the Russians for extorting confessions is the more severe prototype of Chinese 'ideological reform' and the 'political indoctrination' carried out in Korea. In its simplest form it involves the three stages described in Dr Anthony Storr's article 'Torture Without Violence' in the *New Statesman* (12 March 1960): (1) *Disorientation and Disillusion*; (2) *The Interrogation*; (3) *Rationalization and Exploitation*. The aim of the first stage is to break the prisoner's resistances down; he is completely isolated in a cell, severed from all contacts with the outer world, alone with his fears, and totally at the mercy of his captors. Since, as we have seen, his sense of personal identity depends upon communication with others, he ceases to be 'himself'. Other sensory messages are cut off and he is deliberately subjected to confusing stimuli, e.g. all regularity of feeding, sleeping, and visiting is stopped (hence the intentional irregularity of interrogations which happen without rhyme or reason); this disorientates him in time and space. Other refinements are directed towards causing fatigue and physical debility and further loss of the sense of personal identity: he may be prevented from sleeping, offered little and poor-quality food, and given old and ill-fitting clothes which (on the excuse of removing the opportunity of suicide) may have no buttons or means of support such as belt or braces. One recalls the pictures of those accused of attempting to take Hitler's life: former generals and other eminent people were reduced to clutching their trousers to keep them from falling down; clothes are an important aspect of one's personal identity. The prisoner is addressed by his cell number, but has to give the prison authorities their full title when he has to speak to them. Loss of sleep is perhaps one of the most potent factors in breaking a man down. Thus Sargant quotes the case of a West Berlin journalist captured and made to confess in an East German prison in the following manner:

The torture consisted of treatment which prevented him from sleeping for ten days. Sleep was forbidden during the day. At night, lying under a bright electric light in his cell, he was awakened every fifteen minutes. Fifteen minutes after 'lights out' he would be awakened by pounding on his cell door, fifteen minutes later there would be shrill whistling, and next the electric light would be connected to an automatic device alternating a dim red light with a fierce white light from a powerful bulb. . . . This was repeated night after night for ten nights until (he) collapsed with shivering fits and hallucinations.

After about four weeks of complete isolation, or less if they have been prevented from sleeping and if the other refinements have been applied, most prisoners become severely depressed, cease all spontaneous activity, and allow themselves to become dirty and dishevelled. They may sit all day, muttering to themselves, like chronic schizophrenics who, by reason of the same withdrawal of social contacts, have developed 'institutional neurosis' and become demented.

The stage of interrogation is often welcomed by the prisoner and he may be so overwhelmed by the opportunity of talking to another human being that he may burst into tears and feel deep gratitude towards his inquisitor. How the latter responds will depend upon his estimate of the particular case; he may try kindness, where the prisoner is already on the verge of admitting to anything, or he may feign complete indifference to whatever the prisoner says. The disorientated victim is by now uncertain of the dividing line between his own thoughts and the interrogator's and wide open to suggestion. If he is still in a position to resist, he may be subjected, like Weissberg, to what was called the 'conveyor' system, an 'endless moving band' in which the accused is kept under continuous interrogation day and night until he breaks down: 'as the examiners were regularly relieved it could go on indefinitely ... some prisoners had even held out under torture, but I only knew one man who managed to resist the "Conveyor".' Or, as with the West Berlin journalist already mentioned, other subtleties may be introduced:

After this softening-up process he was considered fit for interrogation, which took place almost nightly for six to seven hours at a time over a period of three months and another period of two months. Interrogation was endlessly prolonged because the interrogator deliberately put down the opposite of what the prisoner said and then laboriously started a new and corrected deposition.

Weissberg was confronted by an interrogator who was capable of bawling exactly the same question for hours on end without the slightest variation and without showing any signs of fatigue. By these means, or variations upon them, the prisoner sooner or later comes to believe that the contents of his thoughts, which by now he may not be able to distinguish from the interrogator's, are known to the interrogator. He may be confronted by the real or pretended confession of an associate charged with the same crime and told in effect: 'It's all up now, you'd better come clean.' By systematic conditioning, anxiety is produced which, at a later stage, is attached to artificially synthesized conflicts based on circumstances carefully chosen from the subject's life-history. At some stage, when it is adjudged appropriate, the interrogator will switch over suddenly to kindness, usually when some sort of 'confession' has been obtained and the line of retreat has been cut off. A token act of treachery to his former beliefs such as denouncing a former friend seals the bargain. It will be remembered from the Chinese examples that these confessions are in many cases rooted in some real event, as when Vincent admitted telling an American friend that he had seen the Communist horse-drawn artillery; this perfectly innocuous act was defined by the Chinese Communists as 'espionage', and therefore, since it was they who made the laws, Vincent was in that sense guilty. Similarly, there can be no doubt that there existed an opposition to Stalin, and many of those charged must have talked with each other to that effect and, knowing this to be treasonable, must have already felt guilty; equally, of course, there can be no doubt that most were not guilty of the specific acts to which they confessed.

The stage of kindness may begin with the interrogator apologizing for what has gone before and pointing out that he only wants to help the prisoner to purge himself of his faults. Vincent's Chinese interrogator apologized for the discomfort to which Vincent had been put, and Stypulkowski's Russian interrogator told him: 'I am sorry for you. I see how tired you are. I am happy to inform you, on behalf of the authorities, that the Soviet Government has no wish you should lose your life, or spend thirty years rotting in some labour camp in Siberia. On the contrary, the Soviet Government wants you to live and work as a free man.' This sudden exhibition of 'friendship' takes the prisoner off balance and he pours out his emotions, freely admitting to whatever is suggested to him and giving whatever information is required of him. When this stage is reached, he is treated as a 'convalescent' which indeed is necessary if traces of his ordeal are not to be too evident to the public at the time of his trial, and the last period is devoted to rationalization and ordering of all the various elements of his confession. He is likely to be placed in a cell under improved conditions with a group of the already converted and his re-education and training carried out by these, and possibly by special instructors. The converted group freely confess to each other and inform the authorities on each other's behaviour and admissions. As already noted, nothing is left out of these discussions, which are a parody of group psychotherapy with a Marxist terminology replacing the Freudian one: everything from the subject's feelings about others to his smoking habits and most personal thoughts and fears are discussed publicly and openly. Soon, if the method has been successful, the 'new man' has been grafted more or less securely and has attached itself to the fundamental traits of the subject's basic personality and temperament. The slate has not been 'wiped clean', but a new role has been implanted which, if it turns out to be more satisfactory than the old ones, may persist, as in the case of the apparent converts. More commonly, it is gradually replaced by the earlier one when the subject of brainwashing is once more returned to 'reactionary capitalist society'.

In the sense that nobody can undergo such an overwhelming experience without being influenced, brainwashing undoubtedly produces some results upon all who have been submitted to it; but these results are not always or even frequently those intended by the inquisitor whose aim is permanently to change minds to a particular form of orthodoxy. In fact, as we have seen, those who are converted permanently or semi-permanently are people who in any case possessed the sort of totalist authoritarian type of personality to which orthodoxy would naturally appeal. They are the 'true believers' who spend their lives seeking what Dr Robert Oppenheimer has described as a 'self-sealing system' – that is, one which has a way of almost automatically discounting evidence which might bear adversely on the doctrine. The convinced Roman Catholic finds that his opponents are suffering from 'invincible ignorance', the Communist that non-Communists have submitted to a 'rotten bourgeois ideology', the orthodox psychoanalyst that those critical of the pure Freudian doctrine are 'rationalizing' their unconscious hostility to what they do not really want to believe. No argument is permitted (or, at any rate, it is only permitted up to a fixed point), for in the ultimate analysis one must have the sort of faith enjoined by John Wesley upon his followers, the faith which believes because it is impossible. To all such, the orthodoxy of the group becomes in time more important than the ostensible ends for which it was founded, and as Rhadakrishnan has said of organized religion:

... it is not God that is worshipped but the group or the authority that claims to speak in His name. Sin becomes disobedience to authority and not violation of integrity.

Despite their great doctrinal differences, all forms of totalism are brothers under the skin and appeal to the same type of person, and those 'converted' by brainwashing in any final sense are converted not in spite of, but because of, themselves. They have always wanted to be of the elect, and as for the damned they shall be cast into hell-fire or as the Communist Mao Tse-tung puts it:

... to the hostile classes the state apparatus is the instrument of oppression. It is violent and not 'benevolent'. Our benevolence applies only to the people, and not to the reactionary acts of the reactionaries and reactionary classes outside the people.

The whole fallacy about brainwashing (if by this one means that an ideology can be implanted in a person's mind permanently and regardless of his original beliefs or external circumstances) is the peculiar notion implied in Sargant's book *Battle for the Mind* that an idea is a 'thing' located in the brain which can be planted there or dug up at will. In fact, of course, although undoubtedly represented in the brain, an idea is the result of interaction between the organism and its environment both past and present. Now if Sargant's thesis be correct, there is no reason why *any* idea should not be implanted and retained regardless of circumstances. For example, it should be possible to brainwash an individual into believing that the earth is flat or that the moon is made of green cheese.

Let us suppose that this is indeed possible, and that subsequently all the other people who believe that one or other of these ideas is true should die tomorrow, or that the society into which the prisoner is released contains no people who share them. What would happen to the brainwashed individual then? Is it seriously maintained that he would continue to believe the material with which he had been indoctrinated? Or we might implant the notion that the individual concerned was Napoleon in which case we should have succeeded in making a presumably normal person psychotic. This may happen in the plays of Strindberg, but it is hardly likely to happen in real life. In short, neither Aldous Huxley nor Sargant seems to realize that, although the individual may modify his experiences to coincide with his basic personality, the only type of person who holds ideas wholly unrelated to his social environment is a lunatic. This is the sort of absurdity into which those who share a basically mechanistic materialist and neurological approach can be led because this attitude makes them suppose that mind and brain are synonymous, whereas the truth is that mind is inseparable from the environment. It may be located in the brain, but it is not created in the brain in isolation; for mind is a social product.

Lastly, ideas and ideologies are *functional* – that is to say, even psychotic delusions play some part in the economy of the mind. It is therefore impossible to conceive of free-floating ideas, unrelated either to the past history of the individual or his present social environment, being made to take root by any technique whatever. The individual accepts his beliefs, not merely because they are 'true' or 'untrue', but because they are *useful* in adjusting him to himself or to his social surroundings. The deluded schizophrenic interpreting his 'voices' as coming from without rather than from his own unconscious is no more failing to make some sort of adjustment (although an inadequate one) to his version of reality than is the anti-semite whose belief enables him to explain away his failures or the over-enthusiastic conservative whose beliefs are used to justify his fear of social change. The man who is a convinced Communist in an anti-Communist society is, perhaps, using his political belief to explain to himself and others his anti-authority (i.e. anti *any* authority) bias, whereas the man who is a moderate party member in a Communist society is using his politics, amongst other motives, to relate himself to his society. (This, of course, is why the original 'old guard' in any revolution is ultimately rejected, since you cannot continue your basic 'agin the government' pattern when the party you helped into power becomes, in turn, the hated orthodox authority.)

What we have seen is that the individual will accept a substitute belief *either* because it is capable of performing the same function as the old one – for example, in satisfying the need for a totalist creed which provides certainty and controls his 'bad' impulses – *or* because the belief has become orthodox and it is 'natural' to conform, unless he is prepared to become a social outcast. Thus, in a Communist community brainwashing is likely to work but is hardly necessary, since in the long run people tend to conform merely because they are social; but when applied to non-totalist individuals who are returning to a non-Communist society, it will not work at all. Like ordinary physical torture, it may cause the victim to make true or untrue admissions; but, also like ordinary torture, it will not change his thoughts. The sole exception to this rule is, as mentioned above, when the new belief is a perfect substitute for the old ones. Aside from these situations, brainwashing, we must conclude, is largely eyewash.

CHAPTER 12

CONCLUSIONS

ONE of the most significant findings of psychiatrists and social psychologists in recent years is that, provided they are not grossly abnormal, it is often easier to change the attitudes of small groups of people than those of a single individual. Thrasher, the American social psychologist, in his study of delinquent gangs was able to show that such gangs give the adolescent important social contacts and a certain status which he is reluctant to relinquish. Thus the best way to deal with them was not to treat each individual member separately, but rather to seek out the gang leaders and turn their attention to more socially-acceptable means of satisfying the same needs. When the leaders changed, everybody changed with them. The reason for this, and for many other examples of attitude-change already studied, is that a person's attitudes are not always something locked up within himself or built-in attributes of his personality, but rather a function of his role within a particular group or series of groups. Since one of the functions of the mind is to enable the organism to adjust to a changing environment, we need not be surprised that it is precisely the statistically most 'normal' people who are not only the most prone to absorb the attitudes current in their social milieu but are equally prone to relinquish them for others when the milieu changes.

This concept of normality as total adjustability to almost any circumstances (although basically on one's own terms) has become a much-criticized aspect of present-day American thought, which is attacked in some of its more obvious forms by such writers as David Reisman and W. H. Whyte. The latter notes in his book *The Organization Man* that '. . . the view is now coming to be accepted that the individual himself has no meaning except as a member of a group'; and in this country D. W.

Harding points out that 'we too easily sanction the view that "social adjustment" is only a matter of the individual's adjustment to his group', whereas '. . . a necessary quality for the attainment of individuality is the ability to tolerate some degree of loneliness in the sense of independent adherence to values that those around you will not support'. This is well said, yet it should not blind us to the fact that throughout most periods of history the majority of people have not cherished individuality but have rather allowed themselves to be guided by tradition or, as in the present period of rapid technical change when the world is being transformed before their eyes almost from one day to the next, by observing the behaviour of others and doing likewise. The 'inner-directed' man has always been the exception rather than the rule.

Those who wish to criticize the modern mass society seize upon the 'other-directedness' of its citizens and allege that, in general, it demands an ever-increasing uniformity in matters of taste or ideology and regards individualism as an undesirable luxury. But even if this view were wholly correct (and good reasons will be given later for believing that it is far from being the whole truth), it would be foolish to deny that a great many people are, and always have been, conformist in all things, and the great majority are so in most things where these do not conflict with their own deep-rooted set of values.

In the more philosophical sense, 'normality' must include the ability to adjust to the demands of the basic personality as well as to the needs of society. The psychotic person is characterized by the fact that he adjusts as well as he can to his inner conflicts but little if at all to his social milieu, the neurotic by the fact that his methods of adjustment are rigid, stereotyped, or limited in range, and the 'normal' person by the fact that his adjustments, whilst adequate, are not such as to do violence to his real self, whether he has any depth of personality or not. A person is not therefore abnormal simply because, having no great depth of character, he chooses in the main to conform. The abnormal conformer is the one who conforms for neurotic reasons such as the 'moral masochism' or 'automaton conformity' described by Fromm, both based on the unconscious tendency to feel 'I am exactly like you, and shall be as you wish me to be'. Sociability is not necessarily opposed to individualism, since, for example, the individualism of eighteenth-century bourgeois Europe was based, not upon the lonely isolated man, but rather upon the man who was a member of many small groups with widely differing opinions. He was a unique individual precisely because he was a social one and subjected to so many different climates of opinion. Mass man, so it is said, is more uniform in his views because many of these primary face-to-face groups have been destroyed and others, such as the family, are under attack. Thus it is generally assumed that he is at the mercy of the mass media which bring the same messages to all. We have seen, however, that all the evidence points in the opposite direction; for the 'two-step hypothesis' makes it clear that the content of the media, so far from being accepted directly, tends to reach the individual either at second-hand or in an atmosphere of discussion with groups of friends, neighbours, or within the family.

Just as the economic conditions of nineteenth-century England drew Darwin's attention to the perfectly correct thesis of 'the survival of the fittest' in the sphere of biology, so the social conditions of our own time have brought us to a realization of the importance of social and cultural factors in the moulding of man. The coming of the Industrial Revolution had caused philosophers and psychologists to think of man as almost a prefabricated structure coming ready-made from the womb, and totally to underestimate his social nature. They thought of him as a kind of biological island, because the 'self-made man' was a myth suited to that period. It was a false one; for many people, as well as our own inherited nature, have been consciously or unconsciously responsible for building our personality. The fact is that we are both more rigid and more malleable than has hitherto been supposed, rigid in our basic personality pattern and malleable (within certain limits determined by the basic pattern) in our peripheral personality, whose various roles alter as we move from one group to another. This is becoming evident even to psychoanalysts, who have tended in the past to overemphasize the isolated individual and his built-in traits which they have concentrated on to the exclusion of social factors. On the one hand, they are discovering that the basic self is more resistant to change than was formerly supposed, and Helene Deutsch, for example, admits that '. . . we do not eliminate the original sources of neurosis; we only help to achieve better ability to change neurotic frustrations into valid compensations'. On the other hand, it is becoming increasingly evident that neurosis is a group malady in which the whole family, and beyond that, society, is involved. S. H. Foulkes, in a paper entitled 'Psychotherapy 1961' (*Brit. J. Med. Psychol.*, 1961, 34, 91) says:

> The original neurotic manifestation in the childhood situation is but a symptom of a total constellation, a family neurosis so to speak. The acute neurotic breakdown in the adult is a product of interactional processes in which a number of people are actively engaged. This insight – apart from its profound theoretical significance – is of very considerable practical importance for psychotherapy.

Foulkes quotes E. Lindemann of Harvard and others to show that often, if not always, improvement in the patient provokes active, if largely unconscious, opposition on the part of others involved, and in some cases improvement in one patient leads to the falling ill of other members of his family. 'The pathological process concentrates on another member or members of this network and becomes manifest in them.' He concludes:

> The basic limitations of psychotherapy are seen by Freud as being due to biological factors, deemed to be unalterable. Modern research shows that much of what appeared to be biological inheritance is in fact cultural inheritance transmitted socially. The equilibrium of the individual, i.e. mental health, would therefore be dependent on his interaction with other members of the social network.

These observations suggest, as we have shown elsewhere, that attitudes are difficult to change (*a*) when they are a part of the individual's basic personality structure, and (*b*) when they are a function of the group situation or environment within which he is virtually trapped. Thus the suspicious worker may be paranoid because he has been that way since childhood, or, on the other hand, because he is a member of a group which is confronting a paranoid situation in which suspiciousness is a natural response to the circumstances. The former case would be difficult to treat by any means; the latter will change when the individual is moved to a different environment. But since we cannot always change our social contacts or circumstances at will, he will remain the same so long as the situation remains unaltered. The normal person is adaptable within the bounds of his personality structure as he moves from one group to another, and, within these limits, adaptability is a sign of normality. The experiences of political indoctrination in Korea showed that, so long as the morale of the group remained intact, other pressures were powerless to influence its members, and therefore one of the main efforts on the part of the Chinese was to break down this group solidarity by setting one member against another. Group morale is a kind of armour protecting the individual against external pressures, including those of the mass media, and it was often found during the Second World War that neurotic men who would otherwise have broken down remained useful members of the group when it was one with good morale, only to collapse when moved to another unit where morale was poor.

Of course, an individual has a kind of personal morale even when he is by himself, and this derives both from his acute sense of personal identity and the social and environmental contacts which preserve this identity and in large measure create it. Therefore the first object of any brainwashing technique is to remove both by such methods as social isolation and humiliation. Even so, the normal person, although naturally not unchanged by his experiences, soon picked up the threads again when returned to his old surroundings. The most striking thing about brainwashing or political indoctrination is its relative *ideological* ineffectiveness once the atmosphere within which it has been conducted is left behind. There is no reason to doubt its efficacy with those who remain in a Communist society, because there, where it is least needed, its lessons are constantly being reinforced and conformity is natural – at any rate amongst the young. Where this is not the case, the results are very different. Nor is it otherwise with the converts to any political or religious creed; for, unless the creed fits in with other dominant personality trends, it is soon neglected in the absence of constant contact with the evangelist and his enthusiastic supporters or permanent

membership of the group itself. In this connexion, it is interesting to study the methods used by John Wesley to hold his converts, which, although directed to a very different end, have a
curious similarity to those employed by modern totalitarian
political movements. Although originally a High Churchman
and for most of his life a member of the Church of England, the
system upon which Wesley organized the 'people called Methodists' was to arrange them in a number of societies, these societies being united into 'circuits' under a superintendent
minister, the circuits into 'districts', and all into a single body
under a conference of ministers. The ministers were itinerant,
and to prevent their freshness being lost were changed from one
circuit to another every year. The unit of the organization was
the class-meeting, at which, under a chosen 'leader', members
were expected to tell their 'experiences' and were often subjected
to a close examination about the most personal matters, similar
to those already described in other connexions. Confession
obviously has a binding effect upon a group of people because
each feels tied to the other, not only from the experience of
'sharing', but also because each has something 'on' his neighbour by reason of his admissions. No matter with what assumed
dignity or conceit a man or woman may tend to act outside the
group, he is aware that members know him for what he really is.
At the end of the quarter each person received a ticket of
membership which entitled him to be present at monthly
Sacramental services and Wesley was extremely strict in insisting on regular attendance at these meetings. Lists of attendance
were kept and no one was counted as a member whose name was
not on these lists, even three or four absences being calculated to
disqualify; for Wesley cared nothing for numbers, and did not
regard the 'penny a week and a shilling a quarter' which was the
price of a ticket as being worth having from anyone who was not
enthusiastically devoted to the cause. Great attention was paid
towards capturing the youth and children at an early age, and
Wesley, being deeply impressed by Robert Raikes's Sunday-
school schemes, saw to it that practically every Methodist chapel
had its Sunday school. He also revived the 'Agapae' or 'love-
feasts' of the early Church which were fellowship-meetings for

telling 'experiences' and deepening the sense of brotherhood amongst the members of the Society. The class leader was expected to visit weekly each one out of his group of twelve, ostensibly to collect their contributions but actually to decide whether their conversion was sincere or not: those who were not sincerely repentant were immediately expelled from both the class and the Society. As Wesley wrote:

I called together all the leaders of the classes (so we used to term them and their companies), and desired, that each would make a particular enquiry into the behaviour of those whom we saw weekly. They did so. Many disorderly walkers were detected. Some turned from the evil of their ways. Some were put away from us. Many saw it with fear, and rejoiced unto God with reverence. As soon as possible, the same method was used in London and all other places. Evil men were detected and reproved. They were borne with for a season. If they forsook their sins, we received them gladly; if they obstinately persisted therein, it was openly declared that they were not of us. The rest mourned and prayed for them, and yet rejoiced, that, as far as in us lay, the scandal was rolled away from the society.

Sargant, looking at the matter from the point of view of Pavlov's Behaviourism, notes the different methods needed for converting persons of different temperamental types. Normal extroverts, for example, seem to be 'got at' more easily, and their new patterns to be maintained, by quite crude and non-specific group excitatory methods, provided that they result in a strong, continued, and often repeated emotional arousal. The obsessional person, or the introvert, 'may be more unresponsive to such an approach; physical debilitation, an individual approach, and very strong individual pressure is then perhaps needed to change his behaviour and, in the follow-up period, repeated reinforcement and meticulous explanation of doctrine.' From the more Freudian viewpoint we have adopted here, there is no reason why these observations should not be accepted, since the extrovert is notoriously a good subject for the hypnotist, whilst the obsessional person is difficult to influence by any method: he is on the whole resistant to drugs, is often made worse rather than better by electric shock therapy, and provides a difficult problem for the psychoanalyst in spite of the fact that one would expect the generally intellectual obsessional to respond more satisfactorily.

What Lifton found, and this is basic to an understanding of the process of brainwashing, was that the brainwashed individual remained very much the same kind of person as before; he might, for the time being, have a new set of beliefs, but they were quickly rejected if they did not fit in with his previous character. The authoritarian totalist, with his all-or-nothing tendencies, either more or less willingly accepted the new form of totalism, or after a time reverted to his old form; the anti-authoritarian resisted indoctrination and showed the same hostility towards the new authority as he had towards the old; and in the absence of continued reinforcement the ordinary extrovert returned to his original pattern of adapting to whatever environment he encountered. The significant point is that neither political indoctrination nor brainwashing showed any permanent results of the type intended, except in those cases who might have been expected to accept the beliefs engendered even if they had been offered them under normal circumstances. Under political indoctrination people collaborated for all sorts of reasons, such as taking the line of least resistance, fear, or greed, but only in a tiny minority of cases were the reasons ideological and, so far as this was concerned, the total results of the intensive Chinese programme were, in the final analysis, no more effective than one might expect from an enthusiastic political rally. The Communists in many instances obtained collaboration from the American soldiers, but they produced few genuine converts. Brainwashing has its uses in extorting or manufacturing evidence for show trials, but it is doubtful whether as a method it is any more satisfactory in this respect than ordinary physical torture as allegedly used by the French in Algeria. For producing permanent converts it is useless.

We must now examine in more detail the two statements by Aldous Huxley: (a) that a group of the most eminent philosophers subjected to the rhythmic sounds of 'African drumming, or Indian chanting, or Welsh hymn singing' would end up 'by capering and howling with the savages', and (b) that 'new and previously undreamed-of devices for exciting mobs have been invented'. This second statement is elaborated as follows:

There is the radio, which has enormously extended the range of the demagogue's raucous yelling. There is the loud-speaker, amplifying and indefinitely reduplicating the heady music of class hatred and militant nationalism. There is the camera (of which it was once naïvely said that 'it cannot lie') and its offspring, the movies and television. . . . Assemble a mob of men and women previously conditioned by a daily reading of newspapers; treat them to amplified band music, bright lights, and the oratory of a demagogue who (as demagogues always are) is simultaneously the exploiter and the victim of herd intoxication, and in next to no time you can reduce them to a state of almost mindless subhumanity. Never before have so few been in a position to make fools, maniacs, or criminals of so many. (*The Devils of Loudun.*)

The first statement is concerned with the effects of rhythm upon the human brain, of which Sargant has this to say:

It should be more widely known that electrical recordings of the human brain show that it is particularly sensitive to rhythmic stimulation by percussion and bright light among other things and certain rates of rhythm can build up recordable abnormalities of brain function and explosive states of tension sufficient even to produce convulsive fits in predisposed subjects. Some people can be persuaded to dance in time with such rhythms until they collapse in exhaustion. Furthermore, it is easier to disorganize the normal function of the brain by attacking it simultaneously with several strong rhythms played in different tempos. This leads on to protective inhibition, either rapidly in the weak inhibitory temperament or after a prolonged period of excitement in the strong excitatory one.

The discovery that the brain has natural rhythms of its own which can be measured by the instrument known as an electro-encephalograph was due to Berger, who first noted them in 1928, and the method employed is simple in theory if not in practice: electrodes are firmly held to the scalp where they pick up the minute voltages due to the electrical fluctuations in the brain and these are greatly amplified by the instrument which then actuates a series of pens which inscribe the waves on paper on a revolving drum. Amongst the most prominent are the alpha waves with a frequency of 8 to 10 cycles per second, the theta waves with a frequency of 4 to 7 cycles per second, and the abnormal delta waves with a much lower frequency which are associated with such conditions as epilepsy, some cases of psychopathic personality, and brain tumours. In 1946 Dr Grey Walter, Head of the Burden Neurological Institute at Bristol, to whom many of these other discoveries are due, found that the information contained in electroencephalogram (or EEG) records could be greatly increased by subjecting the brain to rhythmic stimulation, particularly by the flickering of a power-light before the eyes, whether they were open or closed – since light easily penetrates the translucent eye-lids. Originally the experiments were done by shining a light through a rotating wheel with wide spokes, but later an electronic stroboscope was used with a very short brilliant flash which could be regulated in frequency. It was soon found that at certain frequencies the rhythmic series of flashes appeared to be breaking down some of the physiological barriers between different regions of the brain. This meant that the stimulus of the flicker received in the visual area at the back of the brain was breaking bounds and overflowing into other areas. Since this is what is presumed to occur when an epileptic has a fit, it suggested the use of the flicker device as a diagnostic aid in epilepsy where it was actually found to lead to seizures when an appropriate frequency was reached. But it was not only cases of clinical epilepsy which responded in this way, for after studying the effects of flicker upon several hundred control subjects, it was discovered that three or four per cent of these when subjected to carefully adjusted flicker produced responses indistinguishable from those previously regarded as diagnostic of epilepsy. Although these cases were not allowed to go on to the stage of having a major seizure, they did note 'strange feelings', faintness or swimming in the head, and some became unconscious for a few seconds or began to jerk their limbs in rhythm with the flashes of light.

In fact, much the same thing may happen under ordinary circumstances outside the laboratory; for example, when driving along a lane with trees set at regular intervals through which the sun is shining directly into the face. One of Grey Walter's subjects had several times 'passed out' for an instant whilst thus cycling home on fine evenings down an avenue of trees. In this case, the failure of control induced by the flicker stopped his pedalling and so lowered the flicker frequency and terminated the experience. In another case a man found that when he went to the cinema he would suddenly feel an irresistible impulse to strangle the person next to him; he never actually harmed anyone but came to himself with his hands round his neighbour's throat. This man, when subjected to artificial flicker, developed violent jerking of the limbs when the rate was about fifty per second – that is, about the flicker rate of the cinema projector – but he could prevent this jerking by voluntarily tensing his limbs.

These effects were found to be more pronounced when the flicker was synchronous with the alpha rhythm of the brain. This synchronization was later achieved by a feedback system of automatic control, the flash being fired by the brain rhythms themselves, and, under these circumstances, the effects of flicker were even more pronounced, more than fifty per cent of normal young adult subjects showing paroxysmal discharges of the type seen in epileptics. But this early response soon died away with continuous exposure, suggesting that the brain 'learned' not to respond in an abnormal way. An additional peculiar effect was the production of a vivid illusion of moving patterns whenever the eyes were closed; this was most marked when the flicker was between eight and twenty-five flashes per second and took a variety of forms. Usually it was a 'sort of pulsating check or mosaic, often in bright colours. At certain frequencies – around ten per second – some subjects saw whirling spirals, whirlpools, explosions, catherine wheels.' Simple sensations other than visual ones are experienced:

Some describe feelings of swaying, or jumping, even of spinning, and dizziness. A few subjects yielded epileptic patterns, as already described. Auditory experiences are rare; but there may be organized hallucinations, that is, complete scenes, as in dreams, involving more than one sense. All sorts of emotion are experienced: fatigue, confusion, fear, disgust, anger, pleasure. Sometimes the sense of time is lost or disturbed. One subject said that he had been 'pushed sideways in time' – yesterday was at one side, instead of behind, and tomorrow was off the port bow.

However, from our present standpoint, the most significant fact is that such experiences can be controlled at will:

The will of the subject can also be brought into play; he can, for instance, consciously and with effect resist or give way to the emotions or hallucinations engendered by the flicker, a matter of no little social interest as well as enlightenment on the question of self-discipline.

If such effects produced by the most delicate equipment so far known can be resisted by ordinary individuals, it is obviously more than likely that the rhythms of primitive drumming or singing can be similarly withstood by those who choose to do so. Of course, everyday experience shows that this is so; for in these days of widespread foreign travel there are plenty of people who have been exposed to just these stimuli with no other result than boredom, mild curiosity, or emotional excitement of a quite moderate degree. People are deeply excited by drumming and chanting, not by the mechanical effect alone but because they believe in the particular creed that they signify and permit themselves to pass into a state of frenzy. That, indeed, is generally their object in attending the meeting. The unbeliever may well feel excited and moved but he does not lose control of himself and we have seen that even the believer is more controlled and the performance more contrived than Huxley seems to suppose. None of the stimuli we have been discussing can induce belief save in those already converted or about to be converted. Rather is it the case that belief plus exposure to these stimuli leads to the observed results. The discovery of the effect of rhythmic stimuli upon the brain is of the greatest importance to neurophysiology, but it has added nothing that we did not already know to our knowledge of the effects of rhythm on human behaviour *en masse*.

We must now turn to Huxley's second statement which, of course, refers to the mass media and here again we have only to look at the evidence to see that considerable reservations are necessary before we can accept the statement as true. Hitler, who must be quoted again as the greatest demagogue of modern times, had complete control over the media and, in addition, was confronted by millions of people who were already on the verge of revolution. He was able to tilt the balance in favour of Fascism rather than Communism largely because he offered people what they wanted. Apart from the already predisposed Germans he had almost no influence at all upon other countries with the exception of their German minorities. When we think of mob hysteria as being a characteristic of the mass society of today, we are forgetting our history; for nothing in recent centuries could even approach the hysterical social manifestations of the Middle Ages, from the Crusades and the Childrens' Crusades to the dancing and flogging manias already mentioned. Without benefit of radio, bands, amplifiers, or loudspeakers, Peter the Hermit riding on a mule, clad in a coarse woollen shirt and hermit's mantle, created an unbelievable wave of hysteria which swept over most of Europe. With the collaboration of the Pope, Urban II, he preached war on the Infidel, and everywhere the populace flocked to hear him.

The pretence of debtors was admitted, that the calls of heaven were of greater obligation than any claims of man. Murderers, adulterers, robbers, and pirates, quitted their iniquitous pursuits and declared that they would wash away their sins in the blood of the Infidel. In short, thousands and millions of armed saints and sinners ranged themselves to fight the battles of the Lord

writes Charles Mills, the historian of the Crusades. The pilgrims pillaged lustily as they went and, right along the basin of the Danube, through Hungary, to the coast they left a trail of loot and rapine. 'Slay all; the Lord will know his own!' the Pope is alleged to have said. When Peter continued his great march, forty thousand men, women, and children followed him, and although it was called the Peasant Army, it was never an army at all in any significant sense of the word:

A few men of gentle blood rode in the throng with their servants, and some scores of men at arms trudged afoot. Beribboned women of the Paris streets sat on the baggage-wagons; ragged ribalds trotted beside them – masterless and penniless alley folk. In the rabble bands came mock-monks and weepers, halegrins and fit-throwers, hymn-chanters and cut-purses.

Marvellous signs and portents were seen, stars fell flaming from the night sky and a great sword shone in the heavens, pointing towards the Holy City. There was news of a great plague of locusts on the vineyards of the Infidel Turks and, in Malleville, seven thousand Hungarians were slain or taken prisoner:

[The Crusaders] abandoned themselves to every species of grossness and libertinism. Neither public treasures nor private possessions were spared. Virgin modesty was no protection, conjugal virtue no safeguard; and in the midst of their savage excesses they vowed that in such a way as that they would requite Turkish atrocities.

The Children's Crusade of 1212 was started by a French shepherd-boy named Étienne who had a vision of Christ, who appointed him his ambassador to make a pilgrimage to the Holy Land and recover the Holy Sepulchre from the Infidel. Marching through France, he was joined by thousands of boys and girls, some bearing arms and all carrying emblems of the Cross. As the madness swept through the country, parents were unable to control their children, who howled until they were permitted to go or made off secretly at night on the road to Marseille where they expected the sea to roll back at Étienne's command. Since this did not occur, they embarked on seven ships, two of which were sunk with the loss of all aboard, whilst the others steered for the slave-markets of Bougia and Alexandria where the remaining children were sold into slavery. A later Children's Crusade began in Erfurt in 1237, and a last one in France took place as late as 1458.

Of course, it could be argued that all wars are a form of mass hysteria, but this would be to talk figuratively for a war would be of little point unless it were carried out with a great deal of cold, calculating planning: even Hitler's excesses were strictly under rational control. The cases we have been discussing were cases of mob hysteria, yet they, too, had their economic and political background; for at this distance of time, it is clear that the Crusades were a phase in the political and economic expansion of Western Europe, the medieval chapter in the history of Imperialism. Now there is every reason to believe that mass hysteria has become increasingly rare in the more technically advanced countries and that a leading characteristic of modern mass society, in spite of the powerful media under its control, is a kind of deadening of feeling accompanied by a rather sterile tendency to rationalize all experience. Our trouble, if trouble it be, is not that people come together too often in collectivities but that, even when they do, they are essentially the 'lonely crowd' described by Riesman. Where are those people who make fools, maniacs, or criminals of so many?

We are, in fact, so hard up for mobs that even the Fascists and Communists have to rely on carefully staged 'demonstrations' composed of compulsory 'volunteers', and for the first time since advertising began we are becoming increasingly critical of its claims (witness the formation in Britain of Consumers' Associations and the Moloney Committee of 1962). Dr Billy Graham's evangelical campaigns or the Wembley Cup Final may arouse some collective emotions, but they are poor stuff compared with the campaigns of Wesley, and to find examples of genuine mob behaviour in this country we would have to go back to the Chartist physical-force men of the middle of last century, and, for a really good example, as far back as the Gordon Riots of the eighteenth century. The general effect of Huxley's 'new and previously undreamed-of devices' has been to bring about, not mass excitement, but (if we must speak in Behaviourist terms) a state of cerebral inhibition similar to that found in Pavlov's over-stimulated dogs. It is to the over-romanticized 'organic' societies of the under-developed countries, where such devices are as yet hardly available, that we must look for factual instances of mob hysteria.

The point to be observed here is not that nobody is trying to manipulate us, since it is evident that in certain fields, such as politics and advertising, strenuous attempts are being made to do so. It is rather that, if manipulation is taking place, it is certainly not through herd intoxication induced by powerful élites. Some degree of conformity and standardization are necessary characteristics of an egalitarian society; for just as the economic state of the eighteenth century with its freely-competing entrepreneurs was paralleled by free competition in the intellectual sphere, so a society based on mass production and large economic units tends, within limits, to standardize taste if not opinions. This fact was used by those who foresaw, and feared, the advent of the century of the common man, to suggest that the inevitable result of popular democracy would be a tyranny of the majority. De Tocqueville made this prophecy of the United States, and, in Britain, John Stuart Mill's essay 'On Liberty' expressed his anxiety that in such a society there would 'cease to be any social support for nonconformity, any substantive power in society which is interested in taking under its protection opinions and tendencies at variance with those of the public'. According to Ortega y Gasset, the problem arises in part from the assumed right of every individual in a mass society to have a view of his own without reference to any fixed standards; for, whereas in earlier times the man in the street was silent and either accepted the views of his 'betters' or demonstrated against them by outbursts of mob violence, today '. . . there is no question concerning public life in which he does not intervene, blind and deaf as he is, imposing his "opinions"'. We may disagree with the ethical standpoint taken by Ortega, but there can be little doubt that his description of what has happened or was about to happen is much closer to the truth than the picture of the masses subjected to the manipulation of designing, sinister élites.

The real question, of course, is where the man or woman in the street gets these opinions which, according to Ortega, he is so ready to impose on his 'betters', and to this question there are many who would reply without further analysis that they come from the mass media. That this is true of the totalitarian countries, where there exists a genuine élite which not only controls the media but also holds the much more important power to shut out by censorship any conflicting opinions, nobody can reasonably doubt, although even in these cases we have seen how the masses are hungry for external information and how trends in fashion or peculiar cults manage somehow to slip through the barriers. But it would appear that the main lesson to be drawn from our present study of propaganda is how very resistant people are to messages that fail to fit into their own picture of the world and their own objective circumstances, how they deliberately (if unconsciously) seek out only those views which agree with their own. Thus, in spite of the concentration of power in the British press already noted, and the vast numbers (one out of every three people) who read Lord Beaverbrook's *Daily Express*, it would hardly be claimed that even a large minority of individuals have been willing to accept the idiosyncratic views which, from time to time, Beaverbrook has put forward with all the force at his command. The majority of people in this country are still Socialists, in spite of the lack of Socialist organs for expressing their opinions and even in spite of the fact that relatively few read such Socialist publications as do exist. In other words the great majority of Socialists prefer to read the right-wing capitalist press whilst retaining their own political views; they vote in terms of their group affiliations and objective circumstances as reflected in such matters as wages, housing, and so on, no matter what they are told by their political opponents. Almost since its inception the BBC (with the best of intentions) has been expressing a predominantly middle-class view of life presented in a 'cultured' accent, but public-opinion polls have shown that the working class still regard the BBC as representing 'them' (i.e. the Establishment), the accent has not spread, and although it is true that the Britain of today has become more middle-class in such matters as buying and spending, the basic working-class attitudes to all that pertains to work, livelihood, and social and cultural values have remained little altered. On the other hand, many working-class influences have begun to penetrate literature, the stage, radio, and television, and a great many of the best-known novelists and playwrights are proletarian in origin in spite of the fact that the mass media have remained predominantly in the hands of the upper and middle classes.

The fundamental issue of the mass media in the Western democracies lies in quite another direction from the generally accepted one: it is not that they are a means whereby the foreign ideals and beliefs of a small élite are being imposed upon the masses, but rather that, so far, there has existed a vicious circle, whereby – through a kind of feedback system – what the masses get is but the reflection of their own vociferous needs and demands. In the sphere of opinions and attitudes the élites are not the controllers of the people but their victims. That is the meaning of opinion surveys, Gallup polls, motivational research, and all the other methods of finding out what the masses 'really' think. They are designed to find out what the people want so that both the élites and their productions may be modelled into their likeness. The would-be brainwashers of the Western democracies are being brainwashed, whereas it might well be argued that it is only in the Communist 'people's democracies' that they are performing their proper function. The picture presented by some members of the Pilkington Committee and by such writers as Raymond Williams or F. R. Leavis and Denys Thompson of a once sturdy and self-reliant peasantry living in an 'organic' society with their genuine folk-arts, or of industrial workers who at a later period had a warm and cosy working-class culture worthy of preservation, both now perverted by a mean, money-grubbing, and ignorant élite which has 'brainwashed' them into accepting Western films when what they 'really' want is Shakespeare and John Bunyan, is ludicrous when translated into the terms of modern realities. It is not that there may not be a tiny nucleus of truth in this picture of bygone days, but that the picture is a highly idealized one and the changes which have occurred in popular culture were the result of inevitable technological developments, not a plot designed by a malignant minority trying to pervert the taste of decent people. In fact, as we have seen elsewhere, although it would be as foolish to idealize the motives of those who control our radio and television as it is to idealize the 'organic society' of the past with its ignorance, prejudice, and superstitions, there is every reason to believe that what the people get in the way of culture is usually a good deal better than what they demand. Even Himmelweit falls into the trap of supposing that it is meaningful to speak of what people 'really' want when the only means of finding this out is by observing what they ask for and noting the most popular programmes. It has been pointed out (a) that in a social democracy the people who try to influence popular taste can only be a few steps ahead of their audiences, and (b) that, as a matter of objective fact, the belief that choice of programme subjects is limited is the merest nonsense. Nobody but themselves stops the mass audience from listening to Shakespeare, Ibsen, and Strindberg rather than to Westerns and thrillers since all these programmes, even on the much-maligned commercial channels, are equally available.

The conclusions reached by some of these authorities rest upon a number of fallacies, of which only a few need be mentioned here. In the first place, they are frequently based on the assumption, not that élites as such are bad, but that those concerned know of a better élite more qualified to tell us what we ought to like than the vulgar commercial and other interests who, limited only by the laws relating to libel and obscenity, give people what they ask for. It is not too much to say that only the most simple-minded will be ready to accept this belief; for, bad as we may suppose the existing controllers of the press, radio, television, and the cinema to be, there is no guarantee that other controllers would be any better. It has often been suggested that our affairs would be better run by scientists in spite of the obvious fact that science has produced as rich a crop of bigots and sheer lunatics as any other body whenever its experts step outside their own limited speciality. (We have only to think of the extremely odd theological views of Newton and the naïve credulity of the great Sir William Crookes in relation to spiritualism to realize that those who relied on their intuitions in any other field than physics and chemistry would have been foolish indeed.) Others, including unfortunately some psychologists, have supposed that people with a high intelligence as revealed by modern tests might be able to help in solving some of our problems, although, again, high intelligence does not exclude psychopaths and the insane or criminal. But most dangerous of all is the idea that those connected with the arts – writers, producers, and critics – should have a say in the cultural consumption of the nation when the slightest acquaintance with art or literary criticism would show that these are the people who are often the least qualified to judge the works of their own generation. Where would the works of Richardson, Scott, Dickens, Trollope, or Hardy have been had we been dependent on the intellectuals rather than upon the public which seized them to its bosom? Richardson and Hardy succeeded only in moving the critics to a consideration of whether their works were a danger to public morality, whilst the rest were despised as 'common' because they appealed to the average reader and 'commercially minded' because they made no secret of the fact that they wrote for money. Or, to take another example, it is not the man in the street who condemns the works of Picasso, Stanley Spencer, and other modern artists, but highly-respected members of the Royal

Academy who specialize in painting horses or life-like portraits and in the Soviet Union would doubtless be highly regarded as exponents of 'realism'. Yet, if we understand him correctly, one of the suggestions put forward by Raymond Williams in his book on communications is that '. . . it is the duty of society to hold [the means of communication] in trust for the actual contributors, who for all practical purposes will control their use'. But in matters of taste there are no experts; we can only know what people like or dislike.

A second fallacy is the usually unspoken assumption that any production which does not improve or instruct an audience and has no serious cultural value is therefore to be condemned, in the words of the Pilkington Committee, as 'vapid, puerile, and cheaply sensational'. Yet there is surely a place for entertainment which merely amuses, relaxes, or passes the time. There are highly-cultured people who waste their time in playing bridge or chess, watching cricket and tennis, or reading detective stories under the pretence that they are using their brains to solve an intellectual puzzle – although, curiously enough, very few detective stories are written around any other crime than murder when it might be supposed that, on the purely intellectual level, burglary could be just as interesting. What right have such people to complain that radio and television programmes are sometimes 'repetitive, sordid, and unsavoury'? There is a real need in the life of a majority of individuals for mere psychological doodling (crosswords, bridge, and chess), and even, in an ordinarily dull existence, for sensationalism, violence, and sex at second-hand. But one of the most important implications of this study is the suggestion that the effects of a production are determined, not by those who produce it or even by its objective content, but rather by the psychological traits of the observer or listener himself. Those who allow themselves to be narcotized into insensibility by the mass media are the victims not of the producers but of a dull job, and the children who are morbidly attracted by horror films, plays, or books, are not the normal ones but the already frustrated and neurotic. There may be plenty of good reasons for changing the existing policies and organization of the mass media and for holding the belief that they are far from satisfactory. It is even possible to argue that, if there are many children who are likely to be adversely affected by certain programmes or publications, then these should be withdrawn.* But this ought not to be allowed to conceal the fact that, in the long run, it is ourselves, the audiences, who most need changing. There is something far wrong with a group in which some members are so bored with their jobs that they use the media solely as a stupefying drug, and those who are in this state of mind are just as likely to be narcotized by Beethoven and the news as by 'pop' music and thrillers. Similarly, those children who are drawn into delinquency are the result of an unsatisfactory home life and an environment within which delinquency is a possible and even socially-accepted way out for frustrated youth. The supposition that they are perverted by the mass media alone is a gross oversimplification of a serious and complex problem. There are, or have been, horror comics and films which should not be shown to children, but to suggest that children have been turned into delinquents in this way is to put the cart before the horse, since it is those who continue to be attracted by such books and films who are showing the symptoms of potential delinquency. Horror stories are, indeed, a natural component of growing up, but few modern tales could be as horrific, offensive (e.g. in their anti-semitism), or terrifying as those of the Grimm brothers on which many of us were reared, and we have tried to show that similar horrific fantasies occur in all children whether or not they are exposed to stories, films, or plays about them. One suspects that when matters of taste are being discussed the question of class prejudice is not entirely excluded. It is 'right' for the middle or upper classes to engage in such time-wasting (and, as some might think, foolish) activities as watching cricket and tennis, playing bridge and chess, or reading detective stories and thrillers, but when the working-class man watches league football in the middle of the week he is 'loafing', while his family, occupying themselves with bingo, darts, or watching quiz programmes on the 'telly', are being perverted by 'vapid

---

* It is, of course, impossible to conceive of *anything* which might not stimulate someone sexually or aggressively. For example, the Bible or Shakespeare have this effect on many and, to the fetishist, a pair of shoes may be sexually exciting.

and puerile activities'. The fact is that frequently those who profess most concern and admiration for the ordinary man are, at heart, the people who most despise him.

But perhaps the most dangerous delusion is the failure to see that the mass audience itself is changing and that with it the content of the media must also automatically change. Many of the British people whose low standards of taste so shock the intellectuals are only sixty years removed from the days when the novelist Jack London had to bribe a cab-driver to take him as far as the fringes of the East End of London, where no respectable person would dare set foot; they are little more than twenty years removed from the beginning of the Second World War, when those who accepted evacuees from the slums were shocked to find the children dirty, covered with lice or fleas, and badly toilet-trained. America, whose cultural standards have come under the same sort of criticism so that it might even be supposed that she was engaged in a plot to pervert the taste of the rest of the world, has performed the stupendous task of absorbing no less than thirty-five million Europeans of every conceivable nationality, religion, and race right up to the period of the restrictive legislation of the 1920s. The greatest wave of immigrants, in 1907, brought in one and a quarter million people, not only from Britain, Germany, Ireland, and Scandinavia as before, but also from Italy, Poland, Austria, Russia, Greece, and the Balkans, together with many more from Africa, Asia Minor, and the Far East. Yet, apparently, the children and grandchildren of these generations in Britain and America are expected not only to have solved their major social problems but to be the possessors of impeccable good taste. It is as dangerous to idealize the public as to feel contempt for it, but in this country it is necessary to realize that, in the words of Sir David Eccles the former Minister of Education, '. . . the parents whose children are now beginning to reach our schools are those who were the first in their families to have secondary education. They know what education is, and what it can do for their children. They will ask for it for their children – *and they will know what to ask for.*' This is an indication of a trend which is clearly going to continue with revolutionary effects on public taste. It is not by government control or censorship that the media are going to be changed but by the demands of new audiences, more sophisticated, more cultured, and more critical – a process which is already well under way.*

The judgements of the Pilkington Committee, as we have seen, were not based upon the Committee's own analysis of programmes, but upon the 'disquiet' and 'dissatisfaction' voiced by such various bodies as the Association of Municipal Corporations, the Trades Union Congress, and the Ulster Society of Teachers of English. What the Committee learned from this so-called evidence, as Barbara Wootton has pointed out, was nothing more impressive than the fact that the people who are active in these organizations do not like what they see (or what other people have told them is to be seen) on independent television. Another leading sociologist, Edward Shils, has noted the odd convergence of both Conservatives and left-wingers in their attacks on mass culture. The radicals, such as Hoggart and Williams, have taken over quite uncritically the view of the aristocrat that the past was dominated by a high culture that is now being debauched. In fact, the lives of most people in the idealized organic society were brutalized by long hours of work which gave them little time or inclination for education while the modern mass society has resulted in the extension of culture – of art, music, and literature – to a degree hitherto undreamed of. Nor is individualism endangered in the mass society; for, apart from the standardization of goods and services inseparable from new methods of production which have raised the general standard of living throughout the world to a higher level in the last fifty years than in the previous fifty centuries, it is doubtful whether men and women have been more individually diverse since the Italian Renaissance. In clothing, it was the Victorians, not the youth of today, who were conformist; in the clash of ideas and variety of opinions we vie with the eighteenth century; in criticism of the views of the élites and in unconventionality

* 'In a mere four years, from 1956 to 1960, the number of pupils aged between fifteen and seventeen in all types of secondary schools went up by 50 per cent, and that was before the effect of the exceptionally high birth rate of 1946–8 was felt. In the ten years since G.C.E. was introduced, the number of passes at 'O' level has nearly doubled and at 'A' level more than doubled.' (*Spectator*, 27 July 1962: 'The 1965 Education Act' by Henry Fairlie.)

of behaviour, whether in the campaign for nuclear disarmament, the satirical political review, modern art or literature, or even sport (how many working-class men and women went mountain climbing, skiing, cave exploring, or hitch-hiking across the world in the nineteenth century?), youth has never been more active. In London, there are queues for Van Gogh and Picasso exhibitions and in many American cities it is more difficult to get a ticket for a symphony concert than a baseball game. There is not much sign of Aldous Huxley's gloomy prognostications here. Reviewing E. Neville Williams's fascinating if often horrifying book *Life in Georgian England*, the historian J. H. Plumb wrote that he would have this book, which reveals what life was really like in the times so lovingly romanticized by a certain school of thought, chained to the bedside of Mr Hoggart and read aloud to Dr Leavis. It should be, he said, required reading for all craft-obsessed socialists, all feudal-minded Tories, and all those who denigrate the triumphs of industrial society: '"What's My Line?", "Coronation Street", horror comics and glossies, bingo and the pools, are infinitely to be preferred to the mindless, drink-sodden, blood-splashed pastimes of our eighteenth-century forefathers, just as a suburb is better than a slum, health better than disease, a full belly better than an empty one . . . and the greatest revolution in social living that has ever happened to man has not only given us bingo and the bomb but also brought to millions of men an appreciation of art, music, literature and science that would never have been theirs. The pity is that men will not sacrifice more of their nature and their habits to the government of their minds.' So far from debauching the high social standards of the past, we are only now beginning to recover from the damage they have done.

In themselves, the mass media are neither good nor bad but simply a tool for communication to be used towards ends which are ultimately determined by the audiences themselves rather than by the producers, who merely reflect the audiences' changing tastes. It is admittedly true that a society based on methods of mass production has limited the freedom of choice of a few, but the accompanying economic and educational revolutions have resulted in greater freedom of choice for more people than ever before in the history of mankind. The poor and illiterate of impoverished communities rather than the citizens of prosperous societies are the real conformists, and it is in those lands where men work to exhaustion for the very right to survive and women are worn-out by constant childbearing that all talk of freedom of choice, whether of goods or ideas, is a mockery. The mass media have played their part in bringing about this freedom and will have an even greater part to play in the future. In the words of Archibald MacLeish:

The development of the instruments of mass communication make it possible for the first time in human history to reach great numbers directly and peacefully and vividly and humanly with an expression of the lives and manners and customs and the arts of people of other nations. Our technology, wiser than we, has given us the unforeseen and unforeseeable means of worldwide understanding at the moment when worldwide understanding is the only possible means to lasting peace.

BIBLIOGRAPHY

COMMUNICATIONS AND THE MASS MEDIA

Wright Mills, C., *The Power Élite*, Oxford University Press.

Williams, Raymond, *Britain in the Sixties: Communications*, Penguin Books.

Wright, C. R., *Mass Communications: a Sociological Perspective*, Random House, New York.

British Association Granada Lectures 1959, *Communication in the Modern World*, Granada TV.

Himmelweit, Hilde, Oppenheim, A. N., and Vance, Pamela, *Television and the Child*, Oxford University Press.

Jacobs, Norman (ed.), *Culture for the Millions: the Mass Media in Modern Society*, C. Van Nostrand Co. Ltd.

Doob, Leonard, *Public Opinions and Propaganda*, Cresset Press.

Pickard, P. M., *I Could a Tale Unfold: Violence, Horror, and Sensationalism in Stories for Children*, Tavistock Publications.

Hovland, Carl, Janis, I., and Kelley, H., *Communications and Persuasion*, Yale University Press.

POLITICAL PROPAGANDA IN PEACE AND WAR

Lasswell, Harold D., *Politics: Who Gets What, When, How*, McGraw-Hill Book Co.

Milosz, C., *The Captive Mind*, Mercury Books.

Becker, Howard, *German Youth: Bond or Free*, Kegan Paul.

Ortega y Gasset, José, *The Revolt of the Masses*, Mentor Books.

Kulski, W. W., *The Soviet Regime: Communism in Practice*, Washington Square Press, Inc., New York.

Rolph, C. H., *All Those in Favour ? The ETU Trial Presented*, André Deutsch.

Ponsonby, Arthur, *Falsehood in Wartime*, Allen and Unwin.

Money-Kyrle, R. E., *Psychoanalysis and Politics*, Duckworth.

Carew Hunt, R. N., *A Guide to Communist Jargon*, Geoffrey Bles.

Fraser, Lindley, *Propaganda*, Oxford University Press.

Taylor, A. J. P., *The Origins of the Second World War*, Hamish Hamilton.

BIBLIOGRAPHY

Lasswell, H. D., *Psychopathology and Politics*, Compass Books, University of Chicago Press.

ADVERTISING AND BUSINESS

Dichter, Ernest, *The Strategy of Desire*, Boardman.

Gundrey, Elizabeth, *Your Money's Worth*, Penguin Books.

Mayer, Martin, *Madison Avenue U.S.A.*, Penguin Books.

Turner, E. S., *The Shocking History of Advertising*, Michael Joseph.

Packard, Vance, *The Hidden Persuaders*, Penguin. *The Status Seekers*, Longmans.

Lucas, D. B., and Britt, S. H., *Advertising Psychology and Research*, McGraw-Hill Book Co.

Thompson, Denys, and Leavis, F. R., *Culture and Environment*, Chatto and Windus.

Thompson, Denys, *Voice of Civilization*, Muller.

Whyte, W. H., *The Organization Man*, Penguin Books.

RELIGION

Huxley, Aldous, *The Devils of Loudun*, Chatto and Windus.

Godwin, George, *The Great Revivalists*, Watts.

Leuba, H., *The Psychology of Religious Mysticism*, Kegan Paul.

Thouless, Robert H., *The Psychology of Religion*, Cambridge University Press.

James, William, *The Varieties of Religious Experience*, Fontana.

POLITICAL INDOCTRINATION AND BRAINWASHING

Kinkead, Eugene, *Why They Collaborated*, Longmans.

Lifton, Robert J., *Thought Reform and the Psychology of Totalism*, Gollancz.

Sargant, William, *Battle for the Mind*, Pan Books.

Hunter, E., *Brainwashing in Red China*, Vanguard Press, New York.

Meerloo, J. A. M., *Mental Seduction and Menticide: the Psychology of Thought Control and Brainwashing*, Cape.

Bone, Edith, *Seven Years Hard*, Pan Books.

Reik, Theodor, *The Compulsion to Confession: on the Psychoanalysis of Crime and of Punishment*, Evergreen Books, Grove Press, New York.

GENERAL

Allport, G. W., *The Nature of Prejudice*, Anchor.

Hoffer, Eric, *The True Believer*, Secker and Warburg.

BIBLIOGRAPHY

Young, Kimball, *Handbook of Social Psychology*, Routledge.

Hoggart, Richard, *The Uses of Literacy*, Penguin Books.

Walter, E. Grey, *The Living Brain*, Penguin Books.

Freud, Sigmund (ed. Rickman, John), *Civilization, War, and Death*, Hogarth.

Richards, I. A., *Practical Criticism*, Kegan Paul.

Fyvel, T. R., *The Insecure Offenders*, Penguin Books.

Marcuse, F. L., *Hypnosis, Fact and Fiction*, Penguin Books.

INDEX

THE INTEGRITY OF THE PERSONALITY

Anthony Storr

'Self-realization is not an anti-social principle; it is firmly based on the fact that men need each other in order to be themselves.'

With this axiom of psychology Anthony Storr, at the outset of an excellent and simple study of human personality, counters the fear expressed by Bertrand Russell and others that analytical psycho-therapy may tend to produce an anarchical race of Byrons or Hitlers.

Tolerant and impartial in tone, his book stands securely on the ground that is common to Freudian, Jungian, and other schools of psychology. Maintaining that many roads lead to self-realization, he discusses in successive chapters the mental mazes of identification, introjection, projection, and dissociation, through which the individual, sooner or later, must find his way on the path to maturity.

'The book is well written, concise and clear, and is cordially recommended' – *Mental Health*

'He deals frankly, in comprehensible terms, with the hypotheses the therapist uses in treatment' – *British Medical Journal*

'His emphasis on the beliefs shared rather than the areas of controversy is right for a book intended for the lay public' – *Lancet*

PSYCHOLOGY IN PELICANS

Pelican Books have achieved an enviable reputation for publishing first-class books on psychology for the general reader. Among the titles available are:

CHILDHOOD AND ADOLESCENCE
J. A. Hadfield

KNOW YOUR OWN I.Q.
H. J. Eysenck

THE NORMAL CHILD
AND SOME OF HIS ABNORMALITIES
C. W. Valentine

INTRODUCTION TO JUNG'S PSYCHOLOGY
Frieda Fordham

SENSE AND NONSENSE IN PSYCHOLOGY
H. J. Eysenck

USES AND ABUSES OF PSYCHOLOGY
H. J. Eysenck

IDEOLOGY AND INSANITY:
ESSAYS ON THE PSYCHIATRIC DEHUMANIZATION
OF MAN
Thomas Szasz

Also available:

A DICTIONARY OF PSYCHOLOGY
James Drever

MORE PSYCHOLOGY IN PELICANS

Among the other books on psychology published in Pelicans are:

PSYCHOLOGY OF STUDY

C. A. Mace

Of its kind this little book is a classic. For this Pelican edition the author, a Professor of Psychology, has entirely re-written several sections and revised the remainder.

Briefly *Psychology of Study* explains the mental processes by which we 'read, mark, learn, and inwardly digest' information of all kinds. It deals with perception, memorization, original thinking, concentration, and preparation for examinations.

In its earlier editions this is a book which has proved particularly useful to students who have found difficulty in adapting themselves to the more self-reliant conditions of study at college. But the advice it contains is addressed to all learners – boys and girls at school, students at colleges, and even amateurs who support local literary, historical, or scientific societies.

At heart we all wish to learn. Professor Mace suggests ways in which we can free the channels of this desire, so that it can act as a positive driving-force in our studies.

THE PSYCHOLOGY OF PERCEPTION

M. D. Vernon

When we look at the world with our eyes, do we see it *as it really is*? In this authoritative study the Professor of Psychology at the University of Reading shows how, behind the retina of the eye, many more fallible mental processes cause errors and inconsistencies to creep into our perceptions. We are seldom aware of these.

Here then is a non-technical outline of the psychological processes which have been shown to be involved in our visual perceptions of things around us. These perceptions of shape, colour, movement, and space develop gradually from infancy upwards. Special processes also emerge to enable us to deal with symbolic material such as printed words and diagrams, for the purpose, in particular, of reading. Finally this book, which is based on over thirty years of psychological research at Cambridge and elsewhere, shows how the perceptions of different people are not always alike: they vary with attention, interest, and individual personality factors.

FUNDAMENTALS OF PSYCHOLOGY

C. J. Adcock

As publishers we recommend this new addition to the Pelican psychology series as a simple, logical, authoritative, and fair-minded introduction to psychology for all kinds of readers.

The author, who is a senior lecturer in New Zealand, has studied psychology both in England and in the United States. He approaches the study of human behaviour from the starting-point of our most primitive responses, the reflexes, which he explains simply in neurological terms. Illustrating his statements with concrete examples, and with many instances from the most recent study of animal behaviour, he goes on to discuss our basic drives and needs, such as hunger, thirst, and the need for air, sleep, and security. His particular gift for advancing the reader's knowledge in easy stages allows him to explain the more complex workings of the automatic nervous system and the processes of fear and anger, of learning, perception, and thinking, and of the patterning of personality, in chapters which are as simple to comprehend as they are to read.

'Has succeeded in that most difficult task, the production of a good introductory text in psychology' – *The Times Educational Supplement*

THE SOCIAL PSYCHOLOGY
OF INDUSTRY

J. A. C. Brown

In recent years it has become increasingly apparent that the classical approach to industrial psychology is inadequate. This approach regarded the worker primarily as a machine to be studied by the techniques of physiological psychology and as an isolated individual whose aptitudes caused him to be suited or unsuited for a given job. The results obtained by such an approach are not necessarily wrong, but, as Elton Mayo demonstrated conclusively more than twenty years ago, they are bound to be incomplete because the 'isolated' human being is a fiction. Since each individual is a member of society and each worker a member of a working group, the attitudes of these groups are bound to play a large part in influencing his behaviour both as citizen and worker.

This book makes no attempt to replace other text-books on industrial psychology; it should rather be regarded as an attempt to supply the reader with an understanding of the social background of industry. Believing that if we begin with the wrong assumptions no amount of accurate research can produce the correct answers, the author has tried to discuss such fundamental questions as: what is human nature? what causes men to work? what is morale? and what influence has the nature of industrial work upon the mental health of the individual worker and his community?

FREUD AND THE POST-FREUDIANS

J. A. C. Brown

Freud and the Post-Freudians explains the main concepts of Freudian psychology and goes on to review the theories of Adler, Jung, Rank, and Stekel. Later developments in the orthodox Freudian school are also discussed, as are those of the American Neo-Freudians and Post-Freudians in England.

This is the first book published in Britain to bring together all these psychological and sociological schools and criticize them, both from the Freudian standpoint and that of the scientific psychologists.